DARK VALLEY

...and Beyond

Rae Churchill

A Story of Recovery from Traumatic Grief

J. B. LaMann

XULON PRESS

Unless otherwise indicated, Bible quotations are taken
from the Amplified Bible (AB). Copyright by
Zondervan Publishing House or the King James Version (KJV)
I am most grateful for these translations of Scripture.

Scripture quotations are given in italics within quotation marks.
At times portions have been underlined to focus attention
on thoughts drawn from them.

Besides quotations from various Scripture translations,
from time to time brief reference is made to words of other authors,
with acknowledgement of the sources. Other than such instances,
the work is directly from the heart of the author—original.

Lyrics to *Jesus Whispers Peace* by Della M. Warren
and *Only a Touch* by Ida L. Reid / B.D. Ackley are used by permission
of Word Music, LLC., 20 Music Square East, Nashville, TN 37203

Authorship of poetry and short quotations from other works
by the author is indicated by "–jbl"

Cover picture was taken by the author from the entrance to
Sundance Canyon, west of Banff, Alberta

www.xulonpress.com

TABLE OF CONTENTS

DEDICATION

This story of my journey through

Dark Valley ...and Beyond

is dedicated to every broken heart who travels

that path through shadows in

the vale of tears.

God grant that as you read this Journal,

you may find something that will encourage you, too,

to hope, to persevere, to keep reaching—

until you find consolation

for your hurting heart.

- ~ ~ ~ -

"Yea, though I walk through the valley of the shadow of death,
I will fear no evil,
for Thou art with me."
Psalm 23: 4

DARK VALLEY ...and Beyond

ACKNOWLEDGEMENTS

Above all, my heart overflows with thanksgiving to the GOD OF ALL COMFORT, Who has not allowed the anguish of grief to destroy me. When I could not even see His face for tears He stayed with me, never allowing the fires to consume or the floods to destroy.

At my point of deepest need, He placed in my life a friend, mentor and counselor who stood by me unfailingly through a long and painful journey. There are no words in any language, or enough of them, to begin to express my heartfelt gratitude to God for the caring, gentle ministry of that one whom He, Himself, placed in my life when I was so utterly broken. Often through that minister of His, sometimes directly by His Spirit, He taught me. Always, He held me.

Thank you, Lord!

This book would never have been written had it not been for the urging, encouragement and counsel of DR. T. E. LOEWEN. It was he who recognized the depth of my grief-struggle after my husband died and undertook to counsel and guide me through that time of profound inner pain. It was he who asked searching questions and opened topics for deep thought and heart-searching which helped me to work through hindrances to recovery. Knowing that our faithful God would see me through, he suggested writing, both to help in working through the grief and to provide a record for others who would surely follow, who might find encouragement for their dark hour in seeing God's faithfulness to me.

Above all, he prayed.

So much, so very much of the understanding and insight which led to peace have come through him that, in truth, his name should appear as co-author of the work. That might, however, seem to implicate him as sharing the weaknesses, doubts and inevitable errors that are mine alone...

For your genuine concern, your wisdom, your understanding, and your long-suffering patience, Doctor Loewen, may the God of Heaven Himself pour into your life His most precious blessings, in God-measure.

Thank you!

Personal thanks are also due to:

<u>Rev. Norm MacLaren</u> of Crossroads *100 Huntley Street* for supportive correspondence.

<u>Rev. Alex Parachin</u> of 700 Club for the key understanding: "It is not 'theological explanation' that is wanting in your heart, but a meeting of His Spirit that somehow transcends the very questions themselves."

<u>My Children</u> for on-going love and support.

<u>Fellow-Believers</u> who prayed and stood by me, even without understanding.

<u>Irene Stiller</u> for on-going encouragement.

<u>Rev. Bruce Brand</u> for editing, counsel and encouragement while shaping this writing for publication.

<u>Others</u> who have given encouragement and advice regarding the writing.

FOREWORD

This Journal is the record of a step-by-stumble journey over uncharted territory through the dark shadows of traumatic grief. Trauma over-rides reason, clouds perception, and, at its peak, even challenges faith. When the beloved Father-God hides His face for a time His child may panic, feel dreadfully lost, and be distraught with fear. Though unseen, the Father's hand tempers the storm, guides the footsteps, and sustains the spirit, leading to a point known only to Him where the spirit finds its home within His arms and peace is spoken to the deep recesses of the soul. He is always there. He never leaves, however dark the way may be.

Parts of this Journal will be highly disturbing to some people. How dare anyone express the fears with which I was assailed? How dare I take issue with so many commonly revered doubts? Why go over and over the "ups and downs" of the path through the valley? Why be so open about the whole inner journey? At the time of writing, it was a matter of searching my own heart; in the desperate search for Truth I must be honest.

Why share it? My experience is not unique. Since "there is no testing... which is not common to man," it may help others in pain face their questions before God and, in so doing, find Him.

This writing is simply an honest account of one person's tortuous passage through a very dark night of the soul. It is a record of each faltering step, each anguished cry of a heart in pain as it journeyed through the shadows of the Valley of Death. The story of my search for healing is presented here with the hope—the prayer—that others passing this way may also persevere, take heart, and find God in the shadows.

I urge the reader to keep reading; read past the pain, the tears, the stumbling, to the simple, precious touch of God near journey's end.

J. B. LaMann

DARK VALLEY *...and Beyond*

PROLOGUE

Anyone traveling though the Rocky Mountains is familiar with the sense of awe invoked by majestic snow-capped ranges rising thousands of feet into the heavens. On a clear day those peaks are gilded with the first golden rays of morning sun, and as hours pass, constantly shifting light and shadow play upon the contours of spires, rock walls and canyons until at day's end, as shadows deepen in valleys between them, snow-capped crests flame fiery red and soft mauve with the setting sun. Then, silvered by moonlight, their bulk bodes mystery and strength, still pointing to the sky. They are inspiring, glorious!

There are valleys among those peaks. Often they are lush and green, blessed with rivers coursing along their winding depths. Sometimes they are rough and rock-strewn, with deep gouges cut into their slopes where avalanche or rock-slide has roared downward from the heights denuding its course of all growing things.

Always, valleys lie far below the peaks, often in shadow, frequently enshrouded in fog.

Mountain-tops may be visited. Valleys may be dwelled in—or traveled through.

On the inner journey of the soul, too, there are mountain-tops; wondrous moments of triumph and of joy when the heart leaps within and the song flows free and clear into the vault of heaven.

There are also valleys. Some are sunlit; fragrant, lush, and filled with peace. Others, torn with rock-slides of broken dreams and smothered with avalanches of disillusion, are often wrapped in the deep fog of pain and confusion, and beset with storms that set their slopes awash with tears. Such are fearsome places!

Most dread of all is the Valley of the Shadow of Death.

Dread as it may be, all will travel it—some sooner, some later. The following pages recount my own journey through this dark valley, and beyond.

This work is not an easy read. It is, at best, an attempt to express the inexpressible. Language fails in the effort; analogy often seems the only way to try to convey the intensity of the trauma. Hence the name of the Journal, DARK VALLEY ...and Beyond, for the process is much like a tortuous journey. Yet even that analogy cannot portray the horrendous turmoil and confusion that rage unseen within—particularly in those early stages when shock and numbness begin to lift, opening the soul to the full onslaught of the anguish of bereavement. It is there that the Valley opens upon a rugged coastline...

Grief comes larger than life-size. It more than overwhelms. It comes in huge waves one upon another, with incredible intensity—towering, rushing in, hammering, receding briefly only to sweep in again—and yet again. No two waves are exactly alike, but they come, and come, and come again, with devastating force and unbelievable fury. They dredge up debris long buried in the sands of time and slam it upon the beach of mind and heart. For the soul to survive, the wreckage must be dealt with—the beach cleared—piece by piece. Waves come in and recede; some of the same water returns again and again in succeeding waves. Some aspects of grief are like that; being most profound, they recur with such regularity that, in truth, they never quite seem to leave.

There is tremendous confusion in the experience of deep grief. Everything once taken for granted is shaken. No, more than shaken—battered! There is a terrifying sense of lost-ness. There is neither map nor compass, for this journey takes the griever through uncharted territory. There is profound *alone*-ness, for each one's journey through grief will be unique to that individual. There are deep shadows in the soul.

Yet, in retrospect, the griever will see that the Master, though unseen, was always near—tempering waves, controlling winds, sending help, always, when it was most needed. Whether or not we sense His presence, always, He is there. And He has a way of bringing something beautiful out of the storm.

He has a plan!

What I have experienced of those shadows thus far in my life I have set down here in an attempt to gain understanding of the way I have come, hoping also to leave for fellow-travelers some comfort by way of understanding—and hope—that there *is* something beyond the pain. If, in the writing, these goals can be reached in some measure, in that same measure the effort will have been worthwhile.

I have not yet traveled the valley's full length in my own walk to the other side; that will come in due course. The "other side" of that final journey is a wondrous attraction. To see the face of that One Who redeemed me, to be welcomed into His presence forever—that will be joy beyond compare. There, too, I shall meet again those "whom I have loved and lost a while," never to be parted, evermore. So, though the valley itself be "the valley of the shadow," the path through it leads to the Light of eternal day.

We do not travel its length alone.

BROKEN. . .

It's broken, Lord—

This little alabaster heart of mine.

Hot tears that rush from depths within

I never knew existed

Now flood my world with sorrows

Overwhelming—so profound, immeasurable—

That I am lost within their dark

And heaving tides.

I kneel before You, Lord,

And only ask that, as they flow, my tears

Shall fall upon Your feet,

Nail-pierced for me.

I bring to You my pain. Poor offering!

Yet, may the simple coming to Your heart

Be something 'kin to spikenard

Which You accept—and bless.

– jbl

DARK VALLEY *...and Beyond*

1

WALK WITH GRIEF

For me, the first close encounters with the fact of human mortality were the deaths of my parents, twenty-four years apart. Memories of those events are indelibly impressed upon my mind. Many years later, sensing some apprehension on the part of my own children, I wrote as follows:

We mothers spend our lives trying to shield our children from things that would cause them pain, yet through all this recent whirl of emergency surgery I know I've caused you worry, and I regret that. I have the sense that the unexpectedness of it all, on top of the obvious fact that years are slowly but surely piling on, have caused the nagging awareness of mortality to surface a little more strongly than before. I'm still here; yet I hurt for the concern I caused you, remembering my own anguish years ago as realization slowly dawned that one day my parents were bound to leave me, should Jesus tarry.

You have opened your heart and said some very wonderful things, things that many mothers never get to hear in a whole lifetime. I thank you for those expressions of love. My heart has been profoundly moved by your tender words, and they will be treasured in my heart as long as I live. But, as I have mentioned, they also brought back memories of my own early dread; first, of losing my father.

He had angina for years while we were still small, and there was the ever-present knowledge tucked in the back of our minds that he could leave us at any time. I wish I could hug that same kind of hurt away from you. The fleeting nature of life on this side is a haunting enemy, which will one day be destroyed, thank God.

For now, God kept me here, and has kept your father as well. We will all take that as from Him, and enjoy each other a day at a time. But let me tell you, from experience, that when God does take His own Home He gives wonderful, sustaining peace to those who stay behind. He's that kind of Father. He doesn't give it ahead of time, for it is not needed then; but He is there in a most gracious way when difficult times come. It is good to relish each day as He gives it, and to know that He is with us now and is already in our future.

Darling, would you slip your hand in mine like you used to when you were small, go back in time and walk with me through the memories of my own times of grief—and God's sustaining presence in them? It is not an easy journey, but a true one. The solid evidence of His hand in those vicarious experiences might do much to lift the dread you are experiencing.

You never knew your Grandpa. You would have loved him. Are there words to describe him? So gentle, quiet, intelligent. So clever with his hands. Such a logical thinker. A man with a delightful sense of humor. Always, an encourager. We shared a special, special bond. I used to help him in the hardware store, and later on, very unobtrusively, here and there, he prepared me for taking over. Once, his words were more direct; it was startling to hear him explain why one of the show-tables was on blocks—because it provided more airflow to the floor furnace and kept the display table from getting hot. Was he thinking that one day, *on my own,* I might remove the blocks?

The Sunday that he died, I think he knew something was amiss. He was flushed, and mentioned that the doctor had told him that would not be a good sign. But he went upstairs to lie down. The Sunday evening service had already started when he came in and sat down beside my brother, who was fifteen at the time. He sang part of the hymn that was in progress, and another, then the pastor started to read Scripture. Part-way through the reading I sensed a bit of disturbance behind me and looked down from the piano toward the back of the church; Dad had slumped over against my brother, and my husband was standing behind him, steadying his shoulders. And Dad's face was—empty! Mother's nurse-friend shortly confirmed it: "He's gone."

What a shock!

I remember realizing after a few minutes that my young brother was standing, quite lost and alone at the back of the church. I went over to hug him and confirm what had happened. Sometime in that first while I searched back over those last moments of Father's life and realized through all the shock and pain that God Himself had prearranged my unassuming father's home-going.

As he came in we had been singing the old hymn, "Nor Silver Nor Gold":

> Nor silver nor gold hath obtained my redemption,
> No riches of earth could have saved my poor soul;
> The blood of the cross is my only foundation,
> The death of my Savior now maketh me whole.

I am redeemed, but not with silver
I am bought, but not with gold
Bought with a price—the blood of Jesus,
Precious price of love untold.
— James M. Gray

And the last words he ever sang were the chorus of the next hymn, "Is My Name Written There?"

"Yes, my name's written there
On that page white and fair
In the book of Thy kingdom,
Yes, my name's written there."
— Frank M. Davis

The Scripture reading? 1 Thessalonians 4:16-17

"For the Lord Himself shall descend from heaven with a shout, with the voice of the archangel, and with the trump of God: and the dead in Christ shall rise first: Then we which are alive and remain shall be caught up together with them in the clouds, and so shall we ever be with the Lord. Wherefore comfort one another with these words."

The Pastor never quite finished the reading, for just about the time he read the words I underlined, my dear father went Home.

Pre-planned! Three small but significant incidents had been arranged to remind us—of Calvary-redemption, Father's personal acceptance of it, and the blessed hope that he would rise again. That He would so tenderly give that assurance prior to receiving Father into His arms was treasured evidence of our Savior's love.

Yes, I'm crying again as I write this. But God's planning was so gently evident that we could only accept it as His time. For weeks afterwards it seemed that the gates of Heaven never quite closed behind him. Our dear one was in the presence of Jesus; Jesus was there with us.

Easter followed two weeks after his home-going. Let me tell you, the eternal wonder of what Jesus did on Calvary was overwhelming to me that year; because of it, I knew my father was safe. I knew where he was. I would see him again. My father could have left me no more treasured legacy than that certainty.

Yes, I felt a strip had been ripped right off my heart. When I went back to the store I remember wearing a black velvet blouse with a grey skirt; the deep black of the velvet suited a heart black with grief in a world turned grey with loss...

17

I remember the well-meaning but shallow remark of one person who came in and asked me if I'd got over the loss of my father yet. ! It was like a blow to the pit of my stomach. I wonder if you *ever* really "get over" such things, though acceptance, adjustment, and the passage of time gradually ease the pain of it, especially for a Christian. You know, thirty-three years later, while the sun streamed in through the high east windows of an office where I worked, out of the blue there came a sweeping loneliness for my Dad. Just for a few moments. But part of who he was and his input in my life remain—a constant enrichment.

Can you stand another little trip? You do remember your Gram. She and my sister were much alike. Perhaps my Mom never did quite catch on to why I was different from her. But she was a tender, intelligent, loving Mom, who spent quality time with us. I treasure yet some of those heart-to-heart talks we had when she instilled into my thinking strong values and her good understanding of life. When Dad died she was left alone for twenty-four years. She was a real part of our immediate family—a great blessing to all of us. As her health gradually worsened, roles increasingly reversed; I became her part-time caregiver. That creates a whole new type of bond.

When she became ill that final time and I went with her in the ambulance to Saskatoon, we all realized that it was different this time. It was difficult for her to be so sick, and she would often say, "Why does He leave me here like this?" Each night the Lord would give me a short phrase of Scripture to give her the next day. Always, it fed her spirit. The last day the little phrase was, "I will fear no evil, for Thou art with me." You know the words that come before that phrase...

After another family member came I went home just overnight because one of you children wasn't well, then came back in the morning to find that Mother had slipped into a coma. "Heart failure brought on by kidney failure," the doctor said. I hope she realized I was back. She would know when she slipped out of her mortal frame, anyway; I have read many near-death reports telling that people saw everything going on around them as they left their bodies.

When the final moments came, as her breathing became labored and uneven and the reading on the heart-monitor became erratic, there came the most profound sense of the literal presence of the Lord standing just by her right shoulder. I was nearest to her, then the others, all of us holding hands. The sweetest touch of the Spirit rested down. I gave her back to Jesus, and for a few moments I felt my whole soul go wide open to His presence in a way I had never experienced before. When I looked down again, the ragged breathing had stopped and the lines on the monitor had gone flat, but though the pupils were relaxed, her eyes, which had been dull from coma, were wide open and bright. From her first glimpse of Him as he reached out for her? There was such light in those beautiful eyes!

When we left the hospital and went back to where I was staying, I slipped down to the little bed on the floor where I'd been spending those long nights and for some time just let the grief wash over me. It had been a very stressful few weeks from the morning I had found her so ill in her home and took her to the little hospital in the next village until she left us for the next world. And those good-byes seem so final.

Sure, I'm blubbering again. Maybe you are, too. But the presence of Jesus is a very real factor, most especially in grief. Always, always He is there. Grief is one of the hard things no one wants to experience, but He comes so close at such times; and always, He is enough. He is called "a man of sorrows, and acquainted with grief"; He knows how to comfort those who are hurting.

While waiting to get to this letter, I remembered a quotation from a book by Lester Sumrall:

> "No one departs this life without leaving something behind. The things said and done become living memorials. It is more than a memory. Left behind are the dynamics of that life."

"The dynamics of that life." When you think about it, you carry with you still an essence of your Gram, don't you? Part of her love for you, her sense of humor, her personhood, still grace your life. That is just how it is. Influence is a lasting thing. The Lord Himself spoke of that often. It is why parents were to teach their children well; He knew that, while evil would affect generations to come, righteousness would affect many times more generations.

Every once in a while your father and I reminisce about our parents. In spite of their very humanness, or maybe even partly because of it, something of their spirit, the warp and woof of who they were—all they came to stand for—have been far more valuable through the years of our lives than we realized when we were younger. Something remains with us; we still benefit from who they were. And it is so wonderful to begin to recognize it. Perhaps the added years give better perspective.

I guess that what I am trying to say is this: If Jesus doesn't come again before we leave this world for the next, He will be more than enough to see you through any change, and as time goes on you will become aware that something of our privileged association here will never leave you. Besides, because of our Jesus, we can one day be together again, forever. Meanwhile, live in the "todays." The way world events are shaping up, Jesus could return at any time, and you may never have to walk your own vale of tears.

I have spent four or five hours re-living all of this; you will have read it in perhaps as many minutes. But I pray that this sharing will minister peace to you. In my heart I am holding you close, loving you.

Your Mom

2

HIS PRESENCE IN THE VALLEY OF THE SHADOW
Some reflections

My father was a very unassuming person: quiet, gentle, soft-spoken, unobtrusive in manner, yet a man of high intelligence and deep sincerity. When he left this world for the eternal home, God gave a heightened understanding of the way He sees people. Hidden behind a veil of ordinariness, God sees the prince—the glory of one reflecting the beauty of His Son. That awareness came again when a dear Pastor left us; there was a vivid realization that the person we had loved while he lived here veiled in his house of clay was more intrinsically beautiful in the eyes of his Lord than we had known.

Twenty-four years after the death of my father, I stood by the hospital bed of my mother as she approached her death. I remember stroking her forehead, reaching back to hold the hand of one next to me, and seeing the others join their hands as well.

I said, "It's OK, Mom. It's OK. 'I will fear no evil, for Thou art with me.' " As her breathing became labored, I closed my eyes and said, "Yes, Jesus. Yes, Jesus! She's Yours." Then, as my whole soul opened up to him (you hold nothing back at a time like that) there flowed from my lips for several minutes a most fluent, intricate and beautiful unknown language. (Could it have been "the tongues of angels" of 1 Corinthians 13:1?) And it seemed—no, it was more than seeming—Jesus Himself was there, standing beside Mother's bed just at her right shoulder. I have never felt Him so close and real. I opened my eyes then, to see that her eyes, which had been dull during the coma, were fully open and bright (from her first glimpse of her Savior?), and her labored breath eased as she left her earthly house to join her beloved Lord. Their presence lingered for a time. I am sure she saw us all, and loved us, as she left the hospital for Heaven.

"Precious in the sight of the Lord is the death of His saints." Psalm 116:15

21

When Uncle Paul told us he had responded to the account Jesus gave of the publican's plea, "God, be merciful to me, a sinner" and His assurance that the man went home justified before God, there was a very powerful sense of some of that heavenly "knowing." It rang through my soul and spirit like the very song of Heaven. My husband, Jim, felt it, too, though he had not heard what had been said and had not even been looking at the time. It was a surge of ecstatic joy, like the echoes of angel-song. My mind leapt to question what it meant—if it were *real*—because it was not like anything on earth; but into my heart came the joyful words of the Redeemer: "Believe it, Beth. This is the language you will be using in Heaven!"

If these things are a foretaste, what will the reality be?

3

That was <u>*Phase One*</u> *of the Grief Walk.*

Phase Two:

When Jim died, there was no glow. No sense of God's presence, will or purpose, none whatever; just raw grief more profound that I could ever have imagined possible. I was not only filled with it, but engulfed by it—swallowed up by a tormenting tide of infinite proportions: dark, suffocating, immeasurable. As I later wrote,

> "There is no way to plumb the depths
> Of grief, or find its shores, or flee its pain..."

As I stood by his open grave, it felt as if not only my Jim, but my God, too, had been torn from me. Yet, there was a stand of evergreens along the south side of the cemetery; *Someone must have made those trees...*

The numbness, the total blackness of spirit remained beyond peak level for many, many months. This was mitigated a little when my daughter told me that she did sense God at her father's Home-going. After some time, there came a momentary, familiar lift of worship toward that One I have loved so long. It surprised me, but I welcomed it. Those moments still come, and I am glad for them.

There is still a huge area of confusion within, though I have, uncharacteristically, sought help from many sources. Perhaps the most outstanding evidence of God's love through this time is the tender caring of one of His servants; may God, Who works through him, bless him more than he can ask or think.

There *must* be some purpose in the heart of God for all of this. May I find it—soon!

4

WHY WAS "PHASE TWO" SO *DIFFICULT?*

The most obvious answer, and a perfectly correct one, is that it ended a very close and uniquely beautiful relationship.

We first met when we were sixteen and seventeen, as students at a Bible college. That should give one indication as to why what we shared was most special; we both sincerely loved God. We loved Him even more than we came to love each other. We wanted nothing in life more than to please that One we loved. It stayed that way. Much as we came to love each other, our love for our God remained, always, the greatest love and highest motivation of our lives.

Although we never dated until two weeks before graduation at the end of our third year, we had got to know each other quite well. That was important. I was a very shy, quiet person, but I had observed Jim's sincere love for the Lord, his practical approach to life, his good humor, and his confident, direct dealings with other people. Those are excellent traits.

Even after we became friends, then more than friends, we held to the standards set out by the One we loved most. To do otherwise would have been unthinkable. That was one key to the joy and success of our relationship; after all, Who better to establish a code of conduct than the One Who invented the whole thing? That instinctive perception was far more important than we realized at the time. The foundation of our relationship was kept strong, clean, and free of regrets because of the simple understanding that it was God's deep love for His creation which moved Him to establish those guidelines.

We were not in a rush to get married. Having seen the heartache in unhappy marriages, I knew it was not a step to be taken lightly. We both understood that God alone knew the depths of both of our hearts, and that, since only He knew the future, He alone knew the best route to take. We chose to commit our lives to His direction. We knew that when He gave each of us life He did so with a plan in mind, and that in His plan for each of us lay the greatest fulfillment for our lives.

How would we be really sure of His will? I had no idea; but I did know that He was well able to make us sure, one way or the other. We did not want just His permission; we wanted His *com*mission. So we waited—until we both knew beyond doubt, deep in our hearts, that it was His best plan for us to be married; then it was pure joy to proceed.

That certainty was a strong and wonderful foundation for our relationship through the rest of our lives together. We went through some severe storms during our shared sojourn—the kind of storms which have destroyed relationships down through the years. But our love remained constant and our relationship most treasured through all of the tough times that came. Our joys were shared joys; our griefs, also shared, were bearable because of our love. Our challenges were faced *together,* and the bond only grew stronger and more precious for the testing. Through it all, our love for our God only grew greater; He was always the supreme Love of our lives.

No, we were not a couple of perfect beings. But we followed One Who is. The beautiful miracle of an indwelling Savior is that He brings His perfection with Him—as much as we allow. He continually works in the hearts of those who love Him to change them, to plant His image there. We each had our share of weaknesses and downright faults; but He forgives rather than condemns, so we did, too. He delights in those He loves, so we did, too. He always supports, builds up, strengthens; we did, too. We each delighted in the good qualities of the other, choosing to overlook inadequacies. We rejoiced to serve each other; our greatest joy was bringing joy to the one we loved. We turned toward each other, not away. We were faithful, because we *loved.* Looking back now, I marvel at how God Himself guided us in our love-walk. How wise He is! His way is truly wonderful.

We became one—truly one. And we treasured that one-ness as a gift from God. For fifty-one and a half years...

When the great tearing came, grief was a tidal wave. There are no words to really describe the beautiful one-ness—or the unfathomable devastation when death ravaged it.

Other factors compounded the grief to titanic proportions. One of the most drastic of these was the trial of my faith. My other Love—the greatest—was thrown into such desperate confusion that at times I despaired of life itself.

Underlying both the depth of my grief and the severe testing of my faith was something I had not recognized until well into this desperate journey. In my youth and later in life there were deep wounds to my spirit which not only altered my persona and severely curtailed its ⹁ development, but also impaired my ability to cope.

The overwhelming tide of anguish, confusion and pain sent me on a desperate search for answers, for understanding, for relief. Hence, the Journal that follows.

5

ENTRANCE TO THE VALLEY

What a year this has been! How long had trouble been brewing? What started it?

Sometime in 1995, Jim began to experience some health problems. One doctor, suspecting prostate abnormality, wanted him to undergo testing; he did not want to face the possibility of serious illness, and did not. A year or so later the problem could no longer be ignored, and when testing was done it was confirmed that he had advanced, virulent malignancy of that gland. That was a jolt to both of us.

If we had asked for a diagnosis sooner...?

That first brush with the big C he did eventually face, and seemed to master. What encouraged him to go ahead with treatment were words from Psalm 1: "*whatsoever he doeth shall prosper.*"

What a blessing it was to be living in a city where excellent help was available! We went almost daily to the local cancer hospital for his radiation treatments—thirty-six in all. As I sat in the adjacent waiting room through each of those treatments, I prayed with all my heart while the red light over the treatment room door was on, asking our Lord to make the radiation effective in destroying every cancer cell. The treatments themselves were not difficult, but radiation damages normal cells while destroying malignant ones, so that there was a rather long period of discomfort after their conclusion while the resultant burn to normal tissues healed. However, periodic testing after the series of treatments eventually indicated that he was cancer-free. The original PSA (Prostate-Specific Antigen) reading had been 15; it had dropped to below 1 after the radiation.

Though he was given an all-clear from the Cancer Institute on that issue, he never really felt well again. It was thought that hormonal changes resulting from the radiation were the cause of that malaise. Was it only that, or was other trouble already building up? Was it a combination of both? Did all of that radiation give rise to the deadly form of cancer that followed, or had it, also, been brewing for some time? Was the prostate cancer a metastasis of something more sinister already at work—or was it the reverse?

The first small hint of more serious trouble was a diagnosis of anemia, but we didn't follow up on that; perhaps, again, there was reluctance to face cruel possibilities.

Later, while trying to repair a washing machine in the apartment building, he cracked a rib. Not long after, he cracked another. Then came the day when he lost his balance and fell backward to the rug-covered concrete floor. He was treated for dizziness, but the pain in his rib-cage became most troublesome...

I took him to a clinic for a bone scan. Watching the screen as the scan progressed, I saw one hot spot on his right foot, and more than twenty in his rib-cage.

The diagnosis by the radiologist? Osteoporosis...

His health continued to decline. As time passed, it became increasingly uncomfortable for him to lie down. He found the high, straight-backed glider rocker the best place to rest. A sleeping bag folded in three made it a little more comfortable for him, with a couple of small pillows pinned in place for his head. He never went to bed again until he was later admitted to hospital.

Jim's pain must have been unimaginable. Home-Care began sending help to stay through the night. When he needed to move from the chair, the assistant would help him up. The only problem was that when they left, Jim still preferred that help. Apparently I did not know how to do it properly; on one try, something gave out in my lower back. The pain continued to worsen until by the first of January it became intolerable; I called my doctor, who ordered an ambulance to take me to a local hospital where I was kept for twenty-five days. What a lot of wasted time!

A retired nurse for whom I had done a lot of clerical work came to stay with Jim that first night, and our dear daughter flew in from Arizona the next day to be with her Dad for a week or ten days. That meant the world to Jim. He loved to hear her play hymns on the piano; he would join in and sing the familiar words he loved.

When she had to return, one of Jim's sisters came to stay with him. During the following days, a friend from church took Jim for a bone marrow biopsy. While I was still in hospital I called our doctor, who gave me the dreadful news that the report from the biopsy had come back indicating that my precious Jim had multiple myeloma. The news was like a dagger through my heart! I think something in me began to die right then. I was assured that it was treatable... I kept remembering, and clinging to the knowledge that "with God, all things are possible." I know, and am still convinced from Scripture that one Word, one touch from Jesus would have been more than enough to have restored full health to my dear one...

Meanwhile, a friend of another of Jim's sisters sent word (supposedly from the Lord) that it was not cancer, but osteoporosis, and that he would be all right. I think Jim and the sister staying with him let that "word" (which later proved to be so terribly wrong) delay requesting the biopsy report, thus foregoing earlier treatment of the cancer. When I finally returned home, I'm afraid I had to push past resistance on the part of some by insisting that we know the truth and begin to deal with it.

February fourteenth was the last day we had at home together. St. Valentine's Day, but such a day of suffering—for both of us. On the fifteenth I took him to the local Cancer Institute. He needed a wheelchair to get to the volunteer driver's car, and another to take him into the Hospital.

There, when the doctor finally came to the bed on which Jim was lying, he showed me the results of the biopsy: "fifty-one per cent plasma cells." Whatever that meant, I knew from the way he said it that it was not good. His next words knocked the breath out of me. "It *will kill* him (!) but we should be able to give him two or three relatively good years."

The appointment which had originally been scheduled as an out-patient visit ended with his admission to the hospital. The plan was to use radiation to reduce the pain in his bones, after which they could begin to treat the cancer itself more aggressively. How thankful I was that they provided a little cot so that I could stay near the one I loved.

There followed many days that were a different kind of agony for each of us. Each time they tried a different pain medication, Jim had to go with practically no pain relief for twenty-four hours so that one medication could get out of his system before the next one was tried. Some of them affected his sense of reality. That was agonizing for me. Finally they found that oxycodone worked fairly well and left his mind clear. He had one radiation treatment to relieve the pain in his bones, and had begun to feel just a little relief in a week's time. They followed that treatment with one more.

So many things transpired while there: a urinary tract infection, the time he broke the IV tubing (the nurse marveled that he had the strength to do that), the discomfort during hospital routines, the steady stream of noisy visitors to the patient in the other bed...

Worst of all was the time an x-ray technician with a terrible chest cold coughed all over him repeatedly without covering her mouth or even turning her head. It was then that, naturally speaking, the end came rushing upon us; he developed pneumonia. I noticed a change in his breathing sooner than the nurses did, but they brushed off my concern.

Very soon the outcome was apparently clear to the staff; they had us transferred by ambulance to another hospital—Palliative Care wing. I tried not to allow myself to think of what that usually meant; after all, I was still being told that Jim would be returned to the Cancer Institute for treatment when they got his pain under control.

There were some good things, too, that happened during his time in hospital. When they wanted him to show them what strength he had in his arms and legs he astounded them, much to his satisfaction. It was a joy to find that some of the people on staff were true Christians; God has a way of tucking them here and there where they are most needed. It meant a great deal to both of us when our eldest son came one day. Faithful visits of one of his friends—how could words describe what they meant to Jim? Others came, too: pastors from churches we had attended, Christian friends, and three of Jim's former work-mates, one of whom Jim teased yet again about his beard. The owner of the business was unwell at the time, or, as he told me later, he, too, would have made a point of coming.

Another most welcome visitor arrived one day at our request. He is a man of God who knows how to move with Him in miraculous ministry. Both Jim and I had trusted that, if he were to come, God within him would rise up and give that healing Word for which we were praying.

I should have told him *why* we had asked him to come. As it was, he read the natural signs and spoke from them, saying that Jim was going to a "better place," prayed along that line, and gave me the name of a funeral home. Devastating disappointment: death, where we had cried for life! I will never, ever, forget watching hope die in my husband's face. I do not blame that person; he is a busy man, and no follower of the Lord is always on top of things.

It was then that I realized we had been depending on the faith of another, and felt that God wanted us, ourselves, to reach out to Him. Why did I not say as much to Jim? He seemed to have given up at that point. Obviously, I failed to touch our God for my husband. Oh, the searing questions that have tortured me over that!

As Jim weakened, we sometimes played soft, sacred music for him; it blessed us, too. We continued to pray, and also called so many others to request prayer for him. Different members of the staff told me that they did not expect him to live, but always, always, in my heart I met their words with, "But God...!"

Eventually, because one nurse told me that we could all deeply regret it if I did not, I called the members of the family. I really hesitated to do so, thinking Jim would not fail to catch the significance of their coming. That proved to be so. Our daughter came again, with her young son. (One of Jim's sisters stayed with him a lot.) When she told her father that the others were coming, he said, "So they're playing the 'call-the-family' game, are they?" This daughter and her husband paid for the youngest son to come from BC and for the youngest daughter and her five-week-old son to fly from Cape Breton Island. God bless them for that!

We have some treasured pictures of the joy with which Jim saw his youngest grandson; he could not sit up or stand the least pressure on his chest, but I laid the little one in the crook of his arm and, ill and in pain though he was, there was no mistaking his enormous pleasure in seeing the baby. He often asked to see him again.

I continued to stay with Jim day and night, and some of the children also took turns spending nights there resting in the chair, the youngest daughter with her wee one in her arms. Our eldest son and his family came several times. Members of the family also visited in the common room.

How I prayed and prayed for the Lord's touch for Jim! Yet he continued to weaken. We were still able to communicate little things from time to time. Once, when I leaned over and reminded him again that he was *mine,* he smiled a little and with a trace of his old verve mumbled, "Yep, I b'long to you, and you b'long to me." How precious! Another time I spoke into his ear, "I *love* you Jim, *love you, LOVE you, love* you!" He said nothing, but his face spoke volumes. He closed his eyes in contentment and seemed to rest back in that sense of being *loved.* I am so glad for that. What a precious, precious relationship!

A senior nurse told me that it would be best if we were to talk together about his impending death—which I was not keen to do; I was still praying for his recovery. As she was tending him one evening, she tried to open the subject by commenting on how wonderful it was that we had enjoyed so many years together. His reply? "Yes. A few more would be nice." Heart-warming!

We never did discuss his approaching death, though in the time since he left me I have often wished that we had. The closest we came to it was once when I leaned over him and told him softly that we were praying for his healing. By that time he was unable to speak, but those dear eyes flew open and he gave a very negative sort of moan. How I wished that he could speak what he was thinking. But even without words, it was rather evident that he didn't expect to recover. I will always remember those eyes; beautiful golden brown with warm brown flecks, so pain-filled.

As those last days went by, so slowly, yet all too quickly, he continued to weaken more and more until even I sensed the inevitable. I fled to the private family room and cried—for a very long time. One dear Christian nurse came in and sat beside me for a good while, saying little, just *being there*. I could not stop crying even to look up.

Quite near the end, there was considerable pressure on me to put him on midazolam, a medication which would put him into a sort of coma, easing his pain but also rendering it impossible to communicate any longer. I did not want to lose him that way even before he left this earth. The girls thought it should be given to him, as did much of the staff, so I finally consented. I feel that, in a real sense, I practically lost him at that time.

The girls took turns staying at the hospital with their Dad and me. One evening, after one of them had gone back to the apartment for some rest, an attendant came in and found that Jim's blood oxygen had dropped to seventy. They quickly took the moisturizer off the oxygen supply and turned it up as far as it would go, but the downturn was obvious. I called my daughter, who got back to the hospital while he was still living. His breathing became startlingly violent for a time—deep, heaving breaths that actually shook the bed. Then, rather unnaturally, it began to quiet down a little, and there were short pauses between breaths...

Right then I got a call from a doctor who was responding to a staff report that I was not happy with the last medication. I had to cut the conversation short and get back to my husband. Even in the short time that had elapsed, I saw that the breaths were shorter, shallower, and farther apart. All too soon there was a small breath, a long pause, then—one last little breath...

He was gone!

That final, tiny breath: it tore the heart out of me...

I was not very strong. My reason for living, my dearest earthly love had been taken from me. I don't know how long I cried my heart out there, beside the one I loved. When left alone with him for a time, I held his dear face in my hands and kissed him, over and over. I caressed him. I just wanted to stay with his dear form for a while, even though I knew he was no longer there.

I remember while sitting there looking up to the Lord, knowing, even as I knew that God could have healed him, that God could raise him from death. I said, softly, "I guess you don't want me to ask you to raise him up, either." Some faith!

Later, I asked the senior nurse a few questions about details that concerned me, and left the hospital, a widow. The pneumonia had taken his life at seven twenty p.m. on March ninth, 2002.

The days immediately following were another kind of nightmare. Mechanically, I dealt with things that had to be done: funeral arrangements, choice of a casket, purchase of a burial plot, the interment... I can still feel the numbing pain as I, with others, stood by that coffin during the graveside ceremony, after which family members laid deep red roses on the carved white pile of the casket. I laid a white rose above his dear heart last of all. I remember getting back into the cars, then piling out again when one of the boys went back to the graveside. He felt so badly that he had "taken Dad for granted." I assured him that was perfectly normal; we take people for granted when they've just "always been there." I told him that his own children probably took him for granted, too. I did not want him to add blame to the pain of losing his father.

There was the memorial service at the church with Jim's picture at the front backed by red roses; various pastors taking part in the program; solos and congregational singing; tributes; the luncheon, and the way some folk came to talk to me. I felt their kindness even through the fog of grief.

The next while went by in a depth of shock and numbness that was unfathomable. The children left to return to their normal lives. A short time later I made the following notes:

CHANGES:

When Jim first left, the shock, anguish, and grief all but overwhelmed me. Uppermost was the culmination of a life-time of distress at unanswered prayer. The promises, such multitudes of them, all "...*in Him Yes, and in Him Amen*"; the repeated assurances that even "*the desires of our heart*" would be given; that what we ask in His name He, Himself would grant—still hang in the firmament of my heart.

It is now thirty-eight days since he went Home. I begin, just begin to sense the Lord again. The numbness of spirit has been a frightening thing.

I know that the fact of Jim's going will always be. The "home" is so strangely quiet. Nothing moves unless I move it, there is no activity unless I initiate it, and there is no sound unless I cause it. Lonely. Strange. Unfriendly. Dead.

His picture still brings tears. Sometimes tears interrupt at strange and unexpected times and places. I still feel unsure of being with others; for that reason I will not rush it.

Chores in connection with the closing of that era of bliss are still awaiting me, though many have now been attended to. There is still a great deal of weariness—and pain—both physically and emotionally.

Subsequent weeks and months were a blur of agony. I felt the grief so deeply that no words could describe it. Sometimes, in desperation, I would spend my strength in profound weeping. At other times, I would desperately call or write someone whom I hoped might help me. One of those calls led me to someone who had lost her first husband while he was still in his thirties, twenty years before. Out of her pain she had established a Bereavement Center, where from time to time groups of grieving people meet and are guided through some of the worst of their pain. She was a tremendous help. I have had cause to be grateful for the use of a book from their library, *Up from Grief,* by two widows, Kreis and Patti. When my own grief-walk took me through cycles of progress and regression, the understanding that those cycles are normal at least saved me from the fear that I was losing my mind.

Our doctor, a precious Christian whose practice is a real ministry, has been a superb help to me. He has provided wonderful support and advice through this dark time. At his urging, I tried to put down what I was going through. The following words cover the next few months:

MY LOVE...
I went back to your grave today—
Cold, unrelenting evidence of death
That tore you from my arms
And broke my heart.
So much, so very much rests there!
How could it be so small, when all my world
Is buried in that ground
Wherein you lie?

There is no way to plumb the depth
Of grief, or find its shores, or flee its pain
When treasured love like ours—
When love—is gone.
God called you, and you went to Him.
I know, one day I'll be with you again...
But in this painful hour
I weep. Alone.

What strange anomaly is this?
In death, you live; while I, though living,
Know such agony of soul
'Twere rest to die.
And yet, I cannot leave this life
'Til in our Father's eyes my work is done.
Let anguish shape my soul
To do His will!
                                                        – jbl

ONE...
God made us one.
It must have been His hand, and His alone
That brought us gently, sweetly
To a oneness so profound
That every part of every essence of our lives
Was blended, interwoven in a union
Inextricable, inseparable—*one!*

The moment that we met...
Ensuing timid, fleeting times we came
To know and understand
Each other's heart as friendship grew...
The golden day we recognized
That love was budding, though
As yet we dared not say it to ourselves...
The certainty that came, the vows we made,
The joys, the toil and tears of life together...
One—oh my darling, we were *one!*

One! Then how
In all God's earth can I endure
This tearing of my total inner self?
For you are gone!
Torn—ripped from my soul;
From all my life so rudely, cruelly snatched!
"An enemy hath done this!"
What, then, remains for one who's left behind?
Tears, agony so deep it swallows all...
They call *this—LIFE?*

How can I live without my heart?
Father, show me!

– jbl

BROKEN...
It's broken, Lord—
This little alabaster heart of mine.
Hot tears that rush from depths within
I never knew existed
Now flood my world with sorrows
Overwhelming; so profound, immeasurable,
That I am lost within their dark
And heaving tides.

I kneel before You, Lord,
And only ask that as they flow, my tears
Shall fall upon Your feet
Nail-pierced for me.
I bring to You my pain. Poor offering!
Yet, may the simple coming to Your heart
Be something 'kin to spikenard,
Which You accept—and bless.

— jbl

I cannot begin to describe the depth of my grief—the anguish of love lost, swelling beyond time and out of sight into eternity... I have often known "strong crying and tears" that drained me to exhaustion. There were times when the stress went beyond exhaustion into panic attacks. For over seven months there was total stress of mind, emotions, spirit and body, with no let-up. What a dark night of the soul! Eventually the stress took its toll on my health in several ways; back pain returned, weight sloughed off, and an autoimmune disorder developed which is thought to be triggered by prolonged stress, and which no one really understands or for which, knows a cure.

Physical distress was one thing; but far outweighing that was the unrelenting, immeasurable depth of emotional trauma—the grief. I remember once hitting absolute bottom while lying awake through the night. It was as if, quite unemotionally, I were looking directly at two options: either to sink down into death, or to decide to live. I impassively faced both options for a while. Eventually, though I did not decide to live, I did decide not to die. If God had something He needed me to do, I would rather enter eternity having done it than come before Him empty-handed. Besides, there are the dear children; oh, how I long to see them all safely in real relationship with Him!

My doctor later told me that he would not have been surprised if I had died during those first months; apparently I was experiencing a "traumatic grief reaction." He knows of several cases where the survivor has died of grief within a few months of the spouse. *I can understand that!* But as the journal will later tell, God's purposes have begun to unfold...

6

FIRST MILES THROUGH SHADOWS

What an agonizing journey!

Last week I thought I was beginning to find answers to the deep inner pain and confusion.

A.W. Tozer wrote that one of the greatest ills in Christendom today is mistaking mental assent for faith. Is that where I failed? In the report of the Bakers, a missionary couple from Mozambique, I found confirmation of my understanding that God really does want to manifest His glory in the miraculous. They told of a tremendous manifestation of the power of God in that country. Then I read Jim Cymbala's book *Fresh Wind, Fresh Fire* and again felt a witness within that so many "modern" Christian additives are indeed only clutter hiding the Truth. However, as I read the part regarding prayer being powerful—and answered—my heart again sank to my boots. Why did God not answer the deep heart-cry for Jim's healing?

Last night I slept poorly. Ringing in my heart were some of the songs from the Gaither Vocal Band video I had watched with a few friends: songs such as "Oh, Rock of Ages, Hide Thou Me" and "Make It Real." Through the night the old song "The Ninety and Nine" ran through my mind. One sheep lost in the mountains, caught in a thicket through a night of darkness, storm and cold. How I could identify with that sheep! I think I still belong to Him, but I cannot seem to find the Shepherd. Perhaps I should just quit trying, and let the Shepherd find me.

Yes. Romans 8:28 has come to mind:

> *"...all things work together for good to them that love God, to them who are the called according to His purpose."*

All things. That must include both good and bad, success and failure. Thus, so quietly, He brought a measure of acceptance—the beginning of the next step of the journey. He seems to prefer the "still small voice" to claps of thunder and bright flashes of lightening. He was there, all along. Not drawn into my threshing about; just—there. Calmly, peacefully there, waiting, and ready to help. The path ahead remains concealed in mist; it seems that the journey consists of small steps taken one at a time, as He calls.

He does it. Recently, out of my own brokenness He touched another's pain with His love and began a healing process. Father, may it be so; help me to be fully open to your searching Truth, a channel of Your Life.

Purpose: that was suggested to me some time ago, and has stayed in my mind. I want that. If only I can find and follow the purpose God has in mind for me now...

For one thing, I probably need a lot of changing. Let me be willing for that. It seems impossible to lay the label "willing" on Jim's death; it is definitely not what we longed for, asked for, or reached for—not at all. Even yet, I am not at all sure that I have really accepted it. Though the realization is, of course, becoming more and more inescapable, the chilling *pain* of the reality only seems to grow deeper.

The only thing I hope for now is that God will use even this to accomplish something good, such as awakening me, and perhaps others, to the fact of our spiritual poverty in His sight. As I have asked for help from several of His servants, the "logic" of their statements, the lofty level of intellectual philosophizing—the "natural" approach coupled with failure to "walk in the Spirit"—have become more and more evident.

Now Jesus' words to the church at Laodicea take on an alarming aspect. As a generation, have we become so satisfied with our own intellect and way of life that we exude that *"we are rich and increased in goods and have need of nothing..."*? When it comes to living reality in the Spirit, are we *"poor and miserable, wretched, blind and naked"*—and unaware of it?

Scripture portrays a God of power, of love, of faithfulness; One Who, out of love, not only promises but fulfills those promises, providing the answers to our needs according to His Word.

Of this I am sure: the disciples had a quality of *knowing* that we lack. They had seen the Christ. They had walked and talked with Him for three and a half years. They had heard His Words, seen His works, felt His heart. They saw Him tried, tortured, crucified, and buried. They saw Him, triumphant over death itself, walk among them in resurrection glory and rise into Heaven. They knew that they knew Him as the living Son of

Almighty God. And they went out in His Name, and worked His works with His anointing.

They really knew Him.

Do I?

True to His Word, He has begun to send small rays of light into this darkness. One: My children, knowing that I am not just talking, but experiencing this struggle, feel more free to open up to me with their own issues. How precious! More than anything in this life, I want to be used to bless them. Two: The extreme sense of overwhelming agony has forced me, in desperation, to ask for help. Looking back now, I think that my reserve and "private person" approach to life was an effort to avoid being vulnerable. What a crucible it took to begin to break that shell!

Come to think of it, one piece I wrote in trying to express the inexpressible started out, "It's broken, Lord..." Is this new state a blessing? If, as Scripture says, He is able to make all things work together for good, it may well become a conduit for His blessing. The other day a person called in, and there was opportunity to tell her about how God had held me through all of this, and had begun to reach through to me. I even gave her copies of those three pieces written during the early, most incomprehensible pain of my loss. It was new to her that God could be so personal; it really impacted her. May Father draw her all the way into His arms.

Still with me are the realities of the deep, overwhelming darkness of the first while after Jim's death when I had no feeling but anguish, and could not in the least degree sense the presence of the Lord. It was as if light, breath and life were all but extinguished within, and a deadening numbness crushed me to the ground. Yet, when the thought presented itself that "if only I had put on a certain TV program he might have been helped" was about to drive me out of my mind, from deep within my spirit there came firm words, "He was too ill to watch (another program) which might have helped him more." God was in those shadows watching over me and not allowing the testing to be more than I could bear. May I remember this: I do not have to "feel" Him to know His presence as an unshakeable reality, a foundational fact of my life as His child. I can lean on that truth when I cannot see or feel. Father, help me to do that.

Strange! Or is it? From the prolonged trauma there have certainly been physical difficulties which resist treatment. There is a sort of calm now, at least on the surface. The cold fact that Jim is no longer here is irrefutable. Is there still a sort of numbness in the face of this? Or is it a mixture of numbness and despair? Not exactly that, either. Resignation. Reluctant, sad resignation, at least in part; that describes it better. Sadness—so deep that it is ineffable. I was so blest to have shared those years with him. How I loved that person! How I miss him! Honestly, I have felt as if I were dying, or that a large part of me were already dead. Fatigue, the known results of stress as manifested physically, yet more. Inside, it feels as if there is a dark, gaping crater, with a little life around its edges. I wonder: is this a stage of grief? I rather think it must be.

What a journey!

I think I am afraid of Christmas this year. A few folk, not wanting me to be alone, have invited me to their homes. My usual shyness makes it difficult to accept. And, of course, the fall I had on the 16th which left me with very sore ribs and two very black eyes makes it almost impossible to think of going anywhere. I have no way of knowing which would be worst: being alone with others, or being alone with my memories. One thing is certain; the alone-ness will be very keen on that day, regardless of where I spend it. I'm glad the children usually call.

My Jim, I wish you hadn't had to leave me...

"The day" has come and gone. They seem to do that; one gets swept along through the rapids and over the falls, as they say. Time keeps passing, regardless of circumstances. One of Jim's sisters dropped by this morning and stayed for lunch. It was a good break, and we were able to talk about things, which is surprisingly helpful. I dared to give her copies of the first three pieces of blank verse I'd written not long after Jim's death. Should I have done so? She admitted that her divorce experience was a grief issue for her, too. Very difficult in a different way, since part of the hurt was rejection by her husband. I did not try to express the pain I felt when it seemed that God Himself had rejected me! Perhaps the pieces will help her? Lord, it would be wonderful if You were to open up some ministry of writing...

It is a dull day, outside and in. I feel deadened, sluggish, dull. I know that, in part, it is the effect of illness; an auto-immune disorder is an overall drag. The hacking cough pounding bruised ribs is tiring, and possibly the "cold" that I caught is amplifying the blues. But the ache in my heart overrides everything else. The realization that for the rest of my life, long or short as it may be, I will never again know the presence of my precious Jim or sense the tender love we shared—there are no words for the sharpness, the all-encompassing depth of that pain. And the haunting question still remains: why could we not have experienced the healing touch of our God? How can I find Him? Can I go on? Sorry, Lord. Help me!

Ten months ago today; that heart-wrenching interment and memorial service for the most precious person I have ever known. The wild, overwhelming initial shock of grief will be forever seared upon my memory. I do not think that the sorrow has lifted much; it has just gone deeper; very, very deep. It is hard to have to realize that this change cannot be reversed, that the one I love is forever lost from my life. I hope to live long enough to find his singing on old tapes and copy them, and to do a little writing. I suppose this is a time of parenthesis—of waiting through a dark night of the soul. If God has a purpose for me, I would like to find and fulfill it; a sense of meaning would be such a blessing.

A year ago we were really going through it. My dear Jim was so ill, in so much pain. Home Care was sending help to sit up with him at night and help in a few other ways. He had not lain in bed for months—just sat in the glider on a folded sleeping bag, with some small pillows pinned in position for his head. What a nightmare!

I still love him—so much. And miss him terribly! The confusion of spirit is a dreadful sort of suffering. There remains that underlying feeling of being rejected by my Lord, of being walled off from Him.

It is strange; often my spirit so spontaneously wafts its love toward the Lord, and it is genuine, deep. My emotions, though, are still wrung with anguish. Worst of all, there remains such bewilderment in my mind over the contrast between the multitude of strong promises from the Most High and the lack of their fulfillment in our situation. I don't understand it. I just don't. I know that just one Word from the Lord would have completely healed my beloved husband...

When I turn here or there for help in my dilemma—and get all of those "easy outs" men have dreamed up to keep themselves comfortable—it is ever more obvious that what they say is in stark contrast to the Word of God. I am more and more sure that His Word is absolute truth, and nothing else can stand against it. How I wish I could be given understanding as to why we got no answer! The ensuing peace would be so welcome, so healing. Perhaps, then, the physical problems from all the stress could begin to fade.

Deep within there is this lingering, persistent confusion. I begin to realize that it is a very complex issue. Part of the reason that I seem caught in a web from which I cannot extricate myself is no doubt the deep grief—a struggle against the thought of being without that dear one who has been the most treasured and meaningful person in all my life.

Dare I put it bluntly, even to myself? I do not *want* to let go of Jim. God brought him into my life and through him gave it worth. Who *am* I without him? My very identity is in question. To really face "life" stripped of the covering of his love and personality is frightening to the core. At this stage of life, must I again flounder around wondering who I am and why I am here? Where would I find the strength, on any level, to take on that kind of quest?

Oh, Father, the blackness, the anguish—they go so deep, so immeasurably, profoundly deep! I cannot pretend otherwise; they are *the* present reality. I know that you desire truth in the inward parts; you would not want me to pretend, evade, or deny what is true. Thank You for that. Where to go from here I know not—neither what path to take, nor how to think. I have neither map nor compass for this journey. From the depths of my soul I cry out to You, knowing only that You alone could understand, direct, or make sense of my life now. This whole experience has shaken the very foundations of even my faith. Forgive me for that! This sheep is dreadfully lost, caught in thorns, very much in the dark and buffeted by storm. I cannot begin to find my way...

Will there ever be an answer? Will the painful confusion ever end? It is taking its toll on every level of my being. These days tears are much closer to the surface than they have been for some time. The agony has gone *so* deep; too deep for tears. This time a year ago... Valentines Day, next Friday, will be the anniversary of his last day at home. How that man suffered! It was a nightmare to have to see that. There was so little that I could do. I couldn't, simply couldn't see what was happening—could not face the possibility. I remember, while sitting on the floor washing his feet, seeing his dear face almost give way to tears as he said, "I think I'm leaving you; but (as his face cleared somewhat)—not for long." My response? "Oh, *no,* Honey! We'll get treatment."

Without him, the *life* has gone out of my life. I don't know how anyone can find a way of living again after falling into the profound, dark anguish of separation from one so dearly loved. If only the Lord were to meet me in some way! I feel *so* lost, so much of the time.

This is the anniversary of our last day at home together. Valentine's Day. There was no romantic celebration, but there was so much love. And suffering: physical, for the one I loved, and inner, for me.

A year ago today we went to the local Cancer Institute. Memories are painful: my strong husband reduced to using wheelchairs; the doctor's words exploding in my mind, "It *will kill* him!"; the Word rising in my heart, "*But God...!*"

When the outpatient visit led to admission, the staff made simple provision for me to stay with him. I was so grateful for that. I could not bear being away from him.

What strange—and agonizing—chaos. In my spirit I sense Him, love Him, and rejoice with Him when souls find Him as Savior or worship Him. Yet my heart is so heavy, so broken, and my mind confused. Lord, please "*unite and direct my heart*"; bring me into understanding and peace.

Will there ever be an answer?

Two days and it will be one year since Jim was transferred to the Palliative Care wing of the other hospital. It hurts to remember.

And it is painful to carry alone the deep concern for the children. How my heart aches for them! Even before God placed them in our arms, the deepest yearning of our hearts for them was that they really, fully come into a vital relationship with our Father.

May He cover them, shield them, protect them—and deliver them from evil. May He work that miracle in their inner being which will enable them to fully cast themselves upon Him and enter into the wholeness and fullness that flows from relationship with Him. Ezekiel's record of God looking for someone to stand "in the gap" stirs me; by His grace, may I refuse to budge from that place of connecting my children to the Lord. Even when they resist. David wrote, "*By my God have I run through a troop; by my God have I leaped over a wall.*" When I encounter resistance as I pray, may I simply "*leap over*" it to touch You on their behalf.

Perhaps now I have an object lesson to illustrate to a few caring folk the spiritual dilemma in which I find myself embroiled. A few weeks ago when the extension cord for the block heater on my car went missing, I found another, longer cord in the trunk and began to use it instead. For the next while I did wonder if it were working, for the car didn't start as easily as it had done. Yesterday, the battery was too low to start the motor and I had to call the local Motor Association. Their workman cleaned the corrosion off the battery posts, gave it a boost, and voilà, it started. After running it for an hour and a half as instructed, I ran my errand.

When I returned I found that my neighbors had salted and graveled the icy spot which had delayed my start, and one had tested my cord: no life in it. He found that the receptor end of the cord was burned out. That illustrates my plight. According to all known scientific law, when cords are plugged into an electric source, current flows and the expected result follows—unless something is dead, or missing.

God's Word is the final source of authority. It has in it the power to perform the will of the One Who spoke those Words that are eternal. The expected results will follow—unless something is dead or missing. I do not want some human explanation aimed at making me more comfortable; I want to know the Truth. I want to correct what is missing. I want to know my God in the Way His Word describes Him!

I guess it has been there from earlier on in this dark night of the soul—the awareness of God's presence within, my spirit mingled with His and flowing in love to the Lord. I'm thankful for that. There has also been a firm conviction that the God Who made the heavens and the earth and all things therein is reliable. He says what He means; He means what He says. He is well able to express Himself clearly, and He stands behind His Word. Over and over and over again, the fact of His infinite power and unending love are portrayed as unchangeable, though Heaven and Earth should pass away. Repeatedly, He is described as a God of deliverances, of mercies new every morning, of unending faithfulness. He cannot change; He has no need to change.

This morning I remembered a time before Jim and I were engaged when I almost wrote him to end the relationship because, being aware of the growing depth of my love for him, I was afraid that it would usurp my deep love for the Lord. I remember Mother sensing my predicament, and telling me that unless there was some clearly defined area which I *knew* to be wrong, not to write it off. "The Lord is always definite; the destroyer is vague." In thinking about what I was feeling I became aware that, even though my love for Jim seemed to flow from the same depth of my being as did my love for the Lord, the latter went *beyond* love—to worship. That is the way our love remained; strong, full, and unchanging, except that it became richer and stronger through the years. Now that the earthly love of my life is no longer with me, may the Spirit of God cause the remaining love of my heart still to flow, fully, to the One Who authored both.

Continue to teach me; guide my steps, Father.

I have often said through this time that I am so glad that Jim did not have to go through this dark valley. The grief process is such a horrific "dark night of the soul"! I am glad he was spared it.

It is the anniversary of the day Jim went to be with the Lord. I must record something rather incredible. I was searching through an old reel-to-reel tape tonight for Jim's singing. As the time drew near the anniversary of the moment he died a year ago, there was a song describing the joy of being in the very presence of God though endless ages of eternity. Then, of all things, at the exact time of his death one year ago, Jim's voice came from the tape, singing,

> "What a joy 'twill be when I wake to see
> Him for whom my heart is burning!
> Nevermore to sigh, nevermore to die,
> For that day my heart is yearning.
>
> I'll exchange my cross for a starry crown,
> Where the gates swing outward never,
> At His feet I'll lay ev'ry burden down,
> And with Jesus reign forever."
>
> – Chas. H. Gabriel

Isn't that amazing?

My mind often goes over the events of the past year, looking to the Lord for meaning and purpose. At last, some insight into the ways and purposes of God has begun to come.

I am beginning to experience a measure of acceptance, and through that, peace. Relief. Little by little, in small ways, life is gaining meaning and direction. Father, keep me sensitive to Your leading; use me to find and carry out Your will, Your reason for leaving me here. Most of all, draw our children to Yourself.

Now there is a new stirring. For both Jim and I, the one basic, deep desire we carried in our hearts together for over forty years is that all of our precious children would come into living relationship with the Lord. During the last few days the realization has begun to sing within my heart that our Lord has accelerated His purposes in them, using the events of this last year to reach into their hearts more deeply than ever before. Jim did not want to die that soon; I certainly did not want him to leave me. Yet, if we had known that God would use our combined pain to reach those dear ones, we would have *chosen* this path. Yes. *Oh, yes!*

One of the pieces I wrote earlier began with the words, "It's broken, Lord, this little alabaster heart of mine..." That very brokenness, quite evident to those "parts-of-my-heart" people, has brought us closer—has made it easier for us to open up to each other. Dear Father, yes! Please

Dark Valley ...and Beyond

accept our pain as gladly given to You, to use in love and wisdom to accomplish Your good purposes in the lives of those children. Bring them *all the way* Home to Your heart.

How precious are your ways, oh Lord!

Through all of this writhing, heart-searching and agony; where has God been? Everywhere. As in the darkness of despair when facing childlessness, there was an overwhelming blackness of grief when my precious Jim breathed that last, small breath. I have dwelt on that grief experience at length, for I have been bound and imprisoned in it for many long months. There was nothing else within me. Or was there?

Nevertheless, as in that first instance, a gradual awareness of His inner presence did return with renewed stirrings of worship flowing from the depths of my being toward the God I love. It was quite surprising at first, for there remained deep emotional trauma as well as overwhelming mental confusion. How could one person seem to be going three ways at once? I have been told such a state is normal in the grief process.

I still have much to learn—about absolute trust in His Word which frees Him to confirm it with signs following; perhaps, also, concerning the covenant rights of the believer.

Looking back on the entire time it seems that while I was in the grip of agony and calling out so desperately, He and I were as Father and small child; I thrashed about, not understanding, while He held my hand and moved not at all. He knew what He was doing. I only begin, now, to see some meaning in it all. He is strong; strong enough to keep me through that dreadful storm, strong enough to steady my goings, and strong enough to use all things to work out His purposes. Let that be so!

It has been one of those recurring times when there was tremendous pressure of discouragement under the weight of deep concern for one of the children. A time when the flood threatened to push me toward letting go, giving up.

But I must not—cannot! Their eternity is at stake! Again the Word— the inner image—of "standing in the gap" was reinforced. I *can not* fall or fail here! His Word strengthens again, and despite the pressure I renew the determination to just stay put—in the gap. I will, by God's strength, remain unmoved as a connection between the Hand of the Savior and those of my children.

That same evening, one of them called. It was one of those "open" times; he was, in his own words, "closer to coming than he had been in thirty years." He "didn't know what kept him back"—but admitted he

46

knew *who* was responsible. He was receptive as the Spirit enticed Him God-ward. Then the escalating anger of a young man toward his mother distracted him... Father, I can only commit him to You, and just refuse to budge from "the gap." Release Your Spirit into his heart and break every barricade the enemy has set up. Completely free him and enfold him in Your Purpose for his life!

It seemed to come out of nowhere—a terrific burst of grief, mostly over bewilderment concerning the spiritual side of things. Yes, God has brought me to a measure of acceptance over Jim's death; after all, it is done. But though I worship my Father, though at times I sense the sweet moving of the Spirit within my own, there remains *no* understanding of any Scriptural basis for the absolute lack of promise-fulfillment; this, in spite of diligent research and many enquiries of those who claim understanding. The words of those to whom I have spoken just do not have Scriptural backing. I am not content to allow human "wisdom" to fog over the multitude of plain statements from the very mouth of my God. "*Let God be true...*" and please, let me find the Truth as it is in Him. There must be some broken connection between His eternal truth and His kids.

I've just re-read all this. I know I meant every word as I wrote; or did I write what I was reaching for? I do know that the inner pain is still very, very deep. There are still tears, still deep grief—and confusion. Can I even hope that it will change? How *can* it change, when the fact of Jim's death cannot change, ever? Not ever! As time slips away the vacuum seems to increase, to take on a more hopeless, hollow emptiness. Do I face whatever is left of my life in unremitting grief? If there is a purpose to my remaining days, must it be fulfilled in on-going pain? Is there to be no relief? No joy? I've really hit bottom again in the last while: part of the ups and downs which I'm told are to be expected in this journey, but real—and *hard*—nonetheless.

There can be some surprises along the way. Last week *Crossroads* began to offer a message by Philip Cameron, "She Broke the Box," with which they will be sending a little vial of spikenard. That came "up close and personal." I sent one of the people in ministry there a copy of the poem I had written called "Broken..." and asked him to have the above offer sent to me. He gave a copy of my e-mail to the host of the program, who gave my name, commented on it, and asked his co-host to read the poem—on air. An interview followed with a man who had lost a son in the plane that went down off Peggy's Cove, Nova Scotia, a few years ago. I wept all through that discussion; my own grief has made me so much more aware of the pain of grief in others. Later, I learned that someone had written in to ask for a copy of the poem. I hope it helped that one.

After the poem was read out, inevitably, folk who know me made comments—which really made me squirm. I have never liked attention, have always preferred comfortable anonymity. God knows, when I wrote those words the *only* purpose was to try to express the inexpressible agony within, to cry out to my God...

But since *Crossroads* told about Philip Cameron's message, I have begun to realize that I have, indeed, been very tightly "boxed up." God knows; I did agree to live on to finish whatever He had in mind in leaving me here, and I know He will not ask from me larger steps than those for which He readies me. How would I feel when I stand before Him, if He put something in my Box He wanted to release, and I kept it locked up? It may well be that nothing more than that heartbreak poem will ever go out. It may be more than that. Whatever He chooses will be all right.

"She Broke the Box..."

7

PAINFUL CONFUSION

The battle continues to rage. Perhaps part of my deepest pain is feeling that I have failed my Lord in not having the real faith He always seemed to be looking for in His followers. Why can I not find Him?

His Word—His promises—are abundant, clear and, according to His Word, readily available. Many times, out of Jesus' own mouth came words indicating that...

> "*all things are possible to him that believes,*" Mark 9:23
> "*these signs shall follow them that believe.*" Mark 16:17

He inspired James and Paul to say that...

> "*...the prayer of faith shall save the sick, and the Lord shall raise him up.*" James 5:15
> "*All the promises of God are in Him Yea, and in Him Amen, to the glory of God by us.*" 2 Corinthians 1:20

Over, and over and over again. In Psalm 103:3 (Amplified) David wrote:

> "*Who forgives every one of all my iniquities, Who heals each of all my diseases...*"

John's gospel records that in His last heart-to-heart talk with His disciples before He gave His life to purchase our redemption, Jesus told his disciples six times to *ask,* also to *receive,* one reason being just that their joy might be full. It's everywhere. There is no joy like that of answered prayer. Conversely, there is no abyss like that of failure to touch Him when the whole heart has reached out for Him!

Early in my life I was really sobered by Hebrews 3–4, in which the Israelites who refused to enter Canaan were described as having hard hearts, rebelling, going astray, not learning God's paths, failing to appropriate a God-given promise. In so doing they were classed as disobedient, provoking God, trying His patience, greatly grieving Him and angering Him. All of that is equated with—lack of faith.

The writer goes on to say,

> *"Take heed, brethren, lest there be in any of you an evil heart of unbelief, in departing from the living God... Let us therefore fear, lest a promise being left us of entering into His rest, any of you should seem to come short of it."* Hebrews 3:12, 4:1

I am one found to have fallen short!

I know that the "all things" of Romans 8:28 must include failure; "*all*" leaves nothing out. That would take care of past trauma. But what am I to do when it comes to looking to Him for current and future needs? Very obviously, I do not know how to ask in faith, even though I am absolutely positive that just one Touch from Him would have completely healed Jim's body.

> *"Without faith it is impossible to please Him."* Hebrews 11:6

It is very uncharacteristic of me to open up to others, but in my desperate search I have corresponded with quite a few people—and had many strange "answers" tossed at me. Thank God for the Words planted in my heart over the decades I have known Him! As people responded, there was always an instinctive checking of their words against the Words of my God. Always, though ideas came from all points of view, God's point of view stayed exactly the same: eternal, unchanging, unmoved. At first it seemed strange that every comment which differed from what He has said only served to reinforce His Word, causing the contrary thought to fall away. It was as though human views were cancelled and His words "underlined," again and yet again. They have not shifted or lost meaning since they came from His heart. They are sure.

So many strange answers! "Strange," because they come from the human mind in an effort to be comfortable with the status quo—and *not* from His Word. ("*Strange fire*"*!*) I don't just want to be comfortable, I want to find the Truth as it is in Him. I will never find an answer if I am not honest in facing the question. Jesus said, *"When I come, will I find faith on the earth?"* I'd rather face the question now than at His coming.

I have sought help everywhere I thought it might be found. I have cried out to my God, over and over and over again.

Is there no help for me, anywhere?

Recently I again came across Isaiah 45:19:

> *"I have not spoken in a corner of the land of darkness; I did not call the descendents of Jacob [to a fruitless service] saying, Seek me for nothing (in vain, KJV); I, the Lord, speak righteousness—the truth [trustworthy, straightforward correspondence between deeds and words]. I declare the things that are right."*

No human being ever forced God to make those promises; they came voluntarily from His heart of infinite love for His creation—a lost race with whom He wants to restore fellowship. In expecting God to fulfill His promise we are not "putting Him in a box." He has "put Himself in a box," so to speak. He volunteered those promises, swearing by His own Name, since there is none higher. A little later in the chapter are the words:

> *"I am God, the only God there is, the one and only. I promise in my own name: Every word out of my mouth does what it says. I never take back what I say."* (v.23, The Message)

I have built my life on that. The ultimate horror is that I threw myself totally upon His promise—and fell through—as if there were nothing there. The ramifications of that are destroying me. My husband died. I will die... Theories are not enough in the face of that kind of reality.

What—where—is Truth?

One of my nieces was married in July. I'm glad I went to the wedding. It was precious to see the couple look at each other as they did; so like the way Jim and I treasured each other. I talked to my brother a bit. Perhaps, since we are both rather reserved types, it was too hard to touch on deeply inward things.

I wrote to a dear sister in the Lord, telling her some of the struggle, hoping that out of her close walk with the Lord she might have counsel that would prove to be the key to my dilemma; she is a dear, and so joyful in her walk with God. She kept to her joy-walk.

It is much more pleasant to rejoice with those who rejoice than it is to weep with those who weep. I understand that. But those who weep desperately need someone to enter into their sorrow with them and support them as they find their way again. After service two weeks ago I talked briefly with a respected servant of God; somehow I still have the feeling that God could use him to open a way out of this maelstrom of confusion. How many times have I "written to him," and just not sent the letter? It's almost impossible to lay out the entire background of the situation so that someone else could fully understand. Only God really knows it all. And I do not know how to find Him, though I sense that He is there... That is the very heart of the confusion. I sense that He is there, and cannot touch Him!

Why?

I keep scanning the Word that is in my heart, seeing the promises, knowing that He never changes and that His Words are as unchanging as He is, knowing He is no respecter of persons, seeing His will portrayed in His life on earth when He healed all that came to him, when...

> *"as many as touched Him were made perfectly whole,"* Mark 6:56

....when He told His disciples,

> *"...ask and receive so that your joy might be full,"* John 16:24

... when He repeatedly said that He, Himself,

> *"...will do whatever you ask the Father in My Name,"* John 14:14

...seeing that when He performed miracles it brought glory to the Father—always feeling that I have fallen so far short of experiencing Him in that way: short of bringing Him glory, and so very, very short of the joy that is full in the experience of answered prayer.

Hebrews 3: The Israelites who did not enter Canaan because of unbelief were called hard of heart, rebellious, displeasing to God; I have felt as if my failure put me in that category, too. However, they were blatantly refusing to possess the land he wanted to give them at that time, while I was reaching for the promise, yet failed to receive. Still,

> *"Without faith it is impossible to please Him."* Hebrews 11: 6

Jesus often said,

> *"according to your faith be it done to you,"*
> *"your faith has saved you ."*

He commended faith, rejoiced when He found it, sorrowed when He did not find it. I know that one touch of His hand, one Word from His mouth could have destroyed the destroyer in Jim's body. Yet I could not touch Jesus. What horror to look at the situation and feel that my "faith" is vain! Where do I stand before Him? Within, it is as if two enormous tides crash into each other, creating the ultimate confusion. For, in light of His own Words recorded in Mark 16:17...

"...these signs shall follow them that believe... they shall recover."

Obviously, since there was no recovery, there was no faith. There is ongoing war within—two tides in conflict: the verity of the promise / the validity of the faith.

What is truth?

I feel as if everything I have based my whole life on is shaken to the core. My God, please come to me!

Talk about a tempest! At least it is being clarified: there are two opposing, all-out forces in collision. Why can I not receive? Having failed to receive, how can I continue to believe? The abyss at the foot of the second question is unthinkable, a course I *cannot* take. Yet the question haunts me at my most vulnerable point.

Early this morning I was so torn by the storm that I couldn't stay in bed, so I went out to the living room and turned on TV. A speaker was twisting the same question around in a way, saying we can't get (in fact) what we don't have (in faith). That may be so, but how do you move from one point to the other?

The program which followed was led by a young man who has gone through much the same struggle as I in that his father died despite much prayer and reaching out to God. He spoke of leaving the past, of not being locked in it, of giving up the ashes associated with mourning in exchange for the oil of joy.

Just—*how?*

Before leaving for church I was again mulling over Isaiah 45:19, 23:

> *"I am the Lord," he said, "and there is no other. I publicly proclaim bold promises, I do not whisper obscurities in some dark corner so no one can understand what I mean. And I did not tell the people of Israel to ask me for something I did not plan to give. I, the Lord, speak only what is true and right. "For I am God; there is no other. I have sworn by my own name, and I will never go back on my word...."*

I kept thinking of how consistent this is throughout Scripture, and could think of no place where it is contradicted. Until I went to church this morning. The pastor spoke of Jeremiah, and read from Lamentations, where Jeremiah was going through just this struggle; that, I must study. You know, through all of this turmoil there is an underlying sense in the shadows that He must have a plan...

Well, I read through Lamentations. True, some rough things happened—as a result of long-continued disobedience and rebellion against the Lord. I know we had no claim to perfection, but there was no known alienation from the Lord. We were both seeking Him with all our hearts; surely, if there had been something specific that displeased Him, He would have been faithful to make it known to us.

Yesterday in my incoming mail there was an inspirational presentation from Guideposts. As I browsed through the various articles, I came upon one which was most meaningful. A woman wrote of the premature birth of her second child, a little girl, and the struggle to keep her alive which involved surgery, breathing assistance, tubes and needles. When she was finally able to bring the baby home, the child never looked at her. Months passed, and though the mother was very tender and loving toward the little one, she could never get her to look directly into her face. Finally, one pediatrician told her that the behavior is common with preemies; they come to associate care-givers with pain.

A day did come when the little one opened her beautiful eyes and looked straight at her mother, who realized that she, herself, had been doing the same thing with her heavenly Father.

Could this, in part, be what's been happening with me?

Today I prepared to take out the garbage—something I never, ever did as long as Jim was able to do it; that and getting the mail were part of his routine. The unit has a flip top that is easily released. I removed it and, as he used to do, hung it by its edge on a couple of hooks at the end of the cupboard. Just as I bent down to tie the bag, the top released and tapped me on the face. It *was* rather funny... and somewhere in my mind I could hear Jim just burst out laughing. (He had the most infectious laugh—an all-out merriment that just tumbled all over itself when something struck him as funny.) Oh, how sweet that was! I would love to hang onto that echo forever. What an immeasurable void he has left!

I wonder if this deep, deep pain will ever leave. Is inner agony an integral part of this new existence—something which will haunt me until the day that it is my turn to die? Every time I advance the perpetual calendar, I am aware that days are being chipped away one at a time, leaving fewer and fewer days remaining. And it is hard to feel that I am making much headway in completing what I have left to do.

Went out to lunch yesterday with one of the ladies in the apartment building; it was a good time. Maybe there is something I don't yet understand about why I am still here. Today I want to find the e-address of another deeply grieving widow in hopes of reaching her with some understanding.

It is some time since I have visited this Journal, but I have found a target for some of the deep questions which have been swirling around within. For one thing, I have been corresponding with a support person in a ministry. When I ventured to share just a part of my turmoil with him, he gave what answer he could and also said that my questions had caused him to search Scripture and find more firm footing within himself. Perhaps that is part of the reason I have been propelled into this search?

In addition to that, I finally pin-pointed each strange comment which had been given me and set down why I could not accept it; these, with some explanation, I sent to two different ministers whose understanding I have come to respect. One has replied, not with answers, but with compassion in precious proportions. Sometimes I wonder if I should include those things in this Journal. There is another set of statements still to be placed in the hands of someone I trust; then...?

One great joy today: One of my children sent a brief e-mail expressing wonderful *joie de vivre*. How wonderful; a marvelous shift from depression. Is there anything more thrilling than evidence of the hand of God at work in those you love?

I am getting things thinned out a bit. I have sent my questions to two destinations, heard back from one, and delivered the letter to a confidante, with enclosures. He is pressured these days; hope he did glance at things.

This grief process is a long and very deep one. How it stretches out! Sometimes it seems as if there is hope around the edges, some little rays of light in the darkness. Yet there is a huge heaviness/weight/shadow that persists; a weariness—deep pain and confusion, I guess. Maybe, where I cannot see, God's hands are working at some project of His own that will come to light in time to come.

I think that I have completed the summary of all the aspects of confusion; lovely occupation! I hope that answers begin to come out of it soon. The heaviness accompanying the turmoil and self-doubt has a smothering effect on every aspect of living these days.

The days are getting so much shorter now. Which makes the nights that much longer. The dark time is depressing; darkness seems to amplify the *alone*-ness. When days come to a close, loneliness and perplexity have a way of taking over.

I'm learning a little bit, all too slowly. I really question whether any human being will be able to answer my questions. More and more I am turning them to the Lord, asking, seeking, knocking—and waiting. It is exquisitely painful to be rocked back in my faith. When His immutable Word clearly expresses His intent to answer, yet none comes—where does one go from there?

From somewhere back in my subconscious thought an issue still presses for acknowledgement, one which I consciously do not want to confront. I have glimpsed it before: I just do not want to accept the fact of Jim's death.

No.

No!

NO!

My whole inner being screams it. My own existence is inextricably entwined with his. I never seemed to become a real person until his love made me feel safe enough to emerge from an iron-clad prison of self-doubt. My gentle father loved me and always, always encouraged me, but in spite of that, insecurity and self-doubt tortured and constricted me on all sides—until Jim. My very personhood seems only to have come into being in the safe haven of his love. Can this person survive outside of that haven? There is such a sense that, outside that shelter, the storms of life will shred my very self and scatter the shreds into oblivion. How, in all the world, could I *ever* willingly go there? *Alone...*

And yet, One stands in the shadows... I am at an impasse. I fear to let go of my earthly love; I fear to really face that One in the shadows. What does He ask of me? What a stupid sheep I am! Shepherd, I am caught in a thicket; help me...

Such a long time in this "furnace." Reason demands the questioning, the search; yet all the while there is an icy fear of being in this state of uncertainty regarding things which ought not to be questioned. After all of these decades of loving, trusting and resting on the Lord, I feel like a traitor. Oh, God, please find me soon!

This morning I "happened" to tune in to a program I have missed a lot of late, only to hear an account of Francis Sheaffer, whose works I have read. It shocked and in a measure reassured me to hear that before the beginning of his work at L'Abri he went through a time of going back to the beginning and questioning everything. Is even this frightening time part of a Plan? God grant it!

My age; what Plan could there be for one like me at this stage of life? Yet, while recently reviewing some articles I'd saved, I came across an item in which were listed percentages of major accomplishments at various ages, and the senior age group had the highest percentage...

This is a most dreadful, uncomfortable experience. It is most painful, and cold with fear. If it is, indeed, the "furnace of affliction" from which I am to emerge as "gold," I fear that I have a long time yet to suffer, for I am not finding answers—am not making gains that I can discern. If only I could be *sure* again, could *know* again, could understand, rejoice again...

What lies ahead?

Later—
Perhaps I have just seen the beginning of an answer—something of which I have had a sense all along. I watched a television program in which a couple of ministers were discussing renewal movements; they had felt they had all the doctrines just right, but saw no working evidence of the miraculous as promised. They told how they first saw and began to experience the living reality of the actual working of the power of God in accordance with His Word, stating that prior to that, they had known (of) the promise of the Word of God but had "denied the power thereof."
Isn't this exactly what I've been disturbed about, and the cause of my deepest grief?
I keep busy—working on one or another of the things I'd like to finish. Oh, with all that is within me, I wish that the pain in my heart could be resolved. I have sought help from every source that seems to hold some promise. Some are compassionate but empty, others are not even that. Only one remains constant in an effort to help me. I keep crying out to my God for His personal counsel, His personal answers; but, as I've mentioned, though I sense Him in one way, I cannot find Him in another. If only He, Himself, would sort things out for me! I'm becoming convinced that only He has the answers; why does He seem to hide Himself?

The inner struggle continues. Sometimes I am numb, at other times so very close to tears. There are times in the night when panic tries to rise again, and there are times when I feel as if I am on the very edge of a dark precipice of depression. I suppose the short days with their long nights may have something to do with it.
Our son is still hurting deeply, too. He did write about it recently. It was painful for him to write, but, as he said, though he cried a lot as he did it, the process was strangely therapeutic. I've encouraged him to do more writing.

Still finding tears close. This afternoon I set down words referring to the deepest agony of all, that of being unable to find the face of my Lord.

When the three Hebrew children of Daniel's time faced a crisis they said, "He is able to deliver, but if not, we will still not bow." Their allegiance to God was paramount, whether or not He delivered them. They did not escape the fire, but it burned only their bonds, and He walked with them in it. May it be so for me. I am His; I have not escaped the fire of my grief, disappointment, and confusion, but He walks with me. May bonds be burned in the process, so that I may walk free to do His will. *Father, help me to trust you fully...*

More discussion yesterday. The core of the pain is so hard to describe. The love-relationship with my Lord has been so precious, so real—passionately so, much of the time—for decades. It has been foundational, my *raison d'être.* The basis for that relationship is, of course, the recognition of His absolute supremacy in all things, in all ways. He is absolute goodness, absolute mercy, absolute truth, absolute love—always—from eternity past to eternity future, and all time between. Jesus said that He came to show us the Father. His words, His ways, His compassion, His deeds are the perfect, everlasting, unchanging revelation of Who God is, what He is like, and how He operates. Nothing was ever too hard for Him to totally master; no situation too hopeless for Him to work deliverance; no human state outside His compassion. His own Word states that He is still that way. There is, in Him, *"no variableness or shadow of turning."*

His Word, once given, remains unshakeable, unchanging, ever-operative. He never retracts one syllable. He has sworn by Himself that He so stands behind His Word that though the very heavens and earth pass away, not one jot or tittle—not the dotting of one "i" or the crossing of one "t"—shall ever change or pass away. What could be more solid, more totally dependable?

He has created immense universes so vast and complex that the best of human ingenuity has only scratched the surface of understanding them. It has been obvious since the beginning of time that He rules all things, from the immense vastness of space to the intricate minuteness of the atom. There are laws of physics which never vary but are counted upon in so many of man's endeavors; laws of gravity, aerodynamics, electricity... every part of all we know is predictable and dependable according to the laws that pertain to it.

Is there any reason to imagine that the sphere of the spirit is any different? In fact, Paul spoke of *"the law of sin and death,"* and *"the law of the Spirit of Life in Christ Jesus."* How can I help but feel that in some way I have not known how to work with Him according to that law—hence my failure? How can I be expected to happily set up camp in this desolate place, close my mind, shut my eyes, and drift off into a sort of spiritual coma? Would God want that, after the price He paid to bring us to *life?*

When, unknowingly, I used a faulty cord to connect my block heater to the power source, the electricity, though present and ready to be drawn upon, had no effect on my car. It is just a simple fact—law—that electricity will always do what it is channeled to do, when the design is compatible and the flow of power unobstructed. Is it any different in matters of the spirit?

Even the Spirit of God? I do know that sin can break our connection; I know, also, that I am most definitely one of the "all" who have sinned. But Jesus died to redeem mankind, and I am one who has come to Him on that basis. Beyond that, neither Jim nor I were aware of anything amiss; surely, if there had been, the Lord would have been faithful to make that known to us so that we could make it right. Hardness of heart? Not likely, in those circumstances! Unbelief? Yet I knew that the least Word or Touch from Jesus would have brought the victory for which our hearts cried. Lack of faith?

I guess I'm at the point of wondering, "What *is* faith?" Yet, in Jesus' day, besides responding to any manner of asking, any level of believing, He often did His works of mercy seemingly just on His own initiative.

Another part of the deep questioning: if saving faith is literally *"the faith of God,"* i.e. something that can only originate with God, how can He require it as if it were something originating from within ourselves? True, Scripture says *"He gives to every man the measure of faith,"* and that *"faith comes by hearing, and hearing by the Word of God ("the entrance and unfolding of Your Word gives life,"* according to the Amplified Bible). That *"hearing,"* a deeper level of perception, of understanding—the *"entrance and unfolding of Your Word"*—what gives rise to that?

If, as I presently understand it, this is a work of God's Spirit, not mine, a work of Grace rather than something I can generate, then it must come from God. All I know to do is pour out my deep need and simply ask Him to do His work in me. It has often puzzled me that Jesus always seemed disappointed when His followers did not have faith. If our part is to choose to trust, still God-faith must be imparted from God to the seeking heart. Yet, in our calling out for His touch, were we not making just that choice?

Back to the wall again. I need a miracle of understanding, and of peace.

8

SEARCH FOR CLARIFICATION

Although it has been some time since the last entry in this Journal, much time has been spent trying to work through enormous and deeply troubling issues.

Different writers concur that the grief journey is like a roller-coaster; ups and downs, progression and regression. My own experience has certainly followed that pattern. I don't know whether I will ever find answers to the profound questions in my spirit. The need is desperate, and the search has been so very long. Partly, I suppose, because the questions *are* so desperate, they are uncomfortable; few people can resist the instinctive urge to quickly look the other way. It is difficult to find anyone who is willing to reach into the *"horrible pit"* into which I have fallen and really help me walk out of it.

David prayed,

> *"In You, O Lord, have I put my trust; let me never be put to shame or (have my hope in You) disappointed ('be put to confusion')"* Psalm 31:1

What David didn't want, I have. There is no painful confusion like that of *un*answered prayer, particularly when you have cried out of the deepest depths of your being over a period of time. Everything precious in your relationship with the Lord, your hope in Him, your very inner life, is thrown into the most agonizing turmoil imaginable. When from the innermost heart you cry out to Him on the basis of His own Word—and fall through the cracks—there is a horrific sense of being rejected by the One you most love. The bewilderment, the confusion, the anguish—are indescribable. I don't just want to "be comfortable"; I need to know the Truth!

I gave my heart to the Lord as a child, and with the naïveté of a child thought that what God said could be trusted, absolutely and without question, just as He said it. Somehow, though some decades have passed since then, I still feel the same way, and cannot see why I should think differently. Still naïve?

I have reached out for answers in this matter for most of my life. Sometimes God intervened, but often I could not touch Him. What really brought the matter to a head was what became the final illness of my precious husband. As I have recorded, he died a year and a half ago, following a cruel struggle with multiple myeloma.

Both of us loved the Lord dearly, and held His Word as the highest authority—an out-flowing of the very essence of God Himself, an on-going portrayal of Who He is and of His intentions in dealing with His children. To copy all of such references here would entail copying most of The Book. There are so many, many Scriptures that depict our God as a God of Deliverances, a Keeper of His Word, the Redeemer, the Healer, the Promise-Giver and Promise-Keeper. On the basis of the Word and character of the Most High, we both sought the Lord for His healing touch for my husband. Other Christians prayed with us, and elders of the church came and anointed him with oil...

I mentioned earlier our deep disappointment when a man of God read natural signs and spoke death, rather than speaking from the Word of Life within him. In my heart I then thought that the Lord wanted us to touch Him *ourselves*, rather than expecting to touch Him through another.

Why did I not say as much to my husband?

When I did convey to him the fact that my daughter and I were asking the Lord to heal him, though he couldn't speak by then, he indicated that he wasn't in accord with that; apparently he had given up. I continued to reach out to the Lord with all my heart, knowing that Jesus had given His very life to provide that healing, knowing absolutely that just one Word, one Touch from Him would be more than enough to provide perfect restoration.

I still feel that it would have brought more glory to the Lord to have received healing from Him than to give cancer the ultimate authority in such a situation.

Jesus said:

> *"Ask, and keep on asking, seek and keep on seeking, knock and keep on knocking, for every one who asks receives, and he who seeks finds, and to him that knocks it shall be opened."* Matthew 7:7

Psalm 103:3 was another Scripture that I held to:

> *"Who forgives (<u>every one of</u>) all your iniquities, Who heals (<u>each of</u>) **all** your diseases who redeems... beautifies... crowns... satisfies... so that your youth, renewed, is like the eagle's (strong, overcoming, soaring)."*

That Scripture, and so many others, are so all-inclusive!

In reaching to others for answers I found many creative efforts to "reason away" the plain failure to receive. The quick "answers," so far, I have not been able to accept, for I cannot see that they have a basis in The Book. In an effort to consolidate the bits and snatches with which I have been wrestling, I have listed them here in point form.

Some of the strange replies are these:

1. "You must not have asked the right way."

Last month I heard a Christian minister on television speak about Jesus and the fig tree, saying we needed to speak to the problem. I wonder if that is where we failed? Yet during His earthly ministry people came to Him in so many ways.

Another speaker said that in approaching God, to *ask* was to come as a beggar—that we need to come as sons, with authority. I freely admit that to be a rather unknown element to me, yet when I look at the Record, it didn't seem to matter how people approached him. The blind beggar cried aloud after him. Jairus approached him politely. The Canaanite woman asked and kept on asking. The woman with an issue of blood pressed through the crowd and simply touched the hem of His garment. The leper said, "I know you could if you would." The father of the demoniac boy as much as said, "You would if you could." In *every case* He responded with His healing touch.

Scripture records Jesus' healing more often than it records His forgiving. Sometimes He healed when that was asked of Him, sometimes when the needy one was not even sure of His willingness, and sometimes just out of His own compassion He, Himself, initiated the connection and healed or delivered people even without their asking. *"He must go through Samaria"* to reach out to one outcast woman. The man beside the pool of Bethesda didn't ask for anything; on His own, Jesus approached him, spoke with him, and healed him. Without being asked, he released the woman bound for eighteen years, and gave sight to the man born blind. He initiated the healing touch to Peter's wife's mother. When He approached Nain and saw the funeral procession *"His heart broke,"* (The Message) and He raised the widow's son to life.

2. **"You can't base a belief on just one Scripture."** (Referring to Psalm 103:3)

One Scripture? When Derek Prince went through his Bible underlining healing Scriptures with a blue pencil, he said that he ended up with a "blue Bible"! From what I can see, the promise of God's intervention is all through His written Word.

3. **"Don't allow yourself to be tormented with false guilt—don't blame yourself."**

The fact remains that I could not touch God for my husband, even though Jesus amply provided for it in His redemption. When I came to Jesus to receive Him as Savior, I had to be totally open and honest before Him regarding my sinful need. It was not comfortable, but being honest—real—gave Him the opportunity to cleanse my heart and give me His life. Must I not be open and honest in the matter of faith (or lack of it) if He is to be able to make any change? If, to protect myself from inner pain or discomfort, I refuse to let Him show me my own lack before Him, how can He do what He wants to do in me, or through me?

What if His own heart is deeply grieved when we blithely avoid facing even the possibility that we are shutting Him out, while He longs with all His loving heart to give the gifts for which He paid such a price?

4. **"Those mentioned in the last part of Hebrews 11 did not receive, but were classed as believing."**

But "the Promise" they did not receive was the Messiah, who had not yet come. He has now come.

5. **"Healing of the body is not really important, because the body is only a mortal, temporary thing."**

Yet our mortal bodies are marvelous creations of God; He values them to the point of including their healing in the Calvary redemption and promising their resurrection in glorified form at the return of Christ.

Beyond that, miracles of healing are given as convincing proof of God's existence and His love. Jesus said that if there had been miracles in Sodom it would not have come under judgment; people would have turned to God.

When I look into what happened *after* the healing miracles of Jesus throughout His ministry, most often The Book goes on to say that healing brought great joy, and that the people marveled and glorified God. Healing is a physical blessing, but is also a spiritual event. It affects not only the body, but the whole person. Nothing stirs the soul to worship and joy in God like answered prayer. Jesus Himself said,

"Ask, and receive, that your joy might be full." John 16:24

He *wanted* us to have the overflowing joy of answered prayer. Six times in those four chapters of John (His "last words" to them) He told His followers to *ask*, to *ask*, to *ask*... promising each time that He, Himself, would answer:

> "...whatever *you shall ask in My name, that will I do*..." John 14:13

After receiving the Great Commission and seeing the Redeemer rise into the heavens, the early believers...

> "...*went forth and preached everywhere, the Lord working with them and <u>confirming the Word</u> with signs following.*" Mark 16:20

We need the Word.
We need it confirmed.
We need *Him!*

6. "You can't expect to understand God."

God is greater than our human minds can comprehend—until we see Him face to face, made like Him. Yet Jeremiah 9:24 reads:

> "*Let him that glories glory in this, that he understands and knows Me.*"

God said that! It is His instruction, His command.
Paul said,

> "...*therefore do not be vague and thoughtless and foolish, but understanding and firmly grasping what the will of the Lord is*...."
> Ephesians 5:17

In his first prayer for the Ephesian Christians, (1:17-23) Paul prayed:

> "...*that He may grant you a spirit of wisdom and revelation—of insight into mysteries and secrets—<u>in the deep and intimate knowledge of Him</u>*..."

God made his ways known to Moses. Psalm 103:7
Jesus promised that He would reveal Himself to those who obey Him. John 14:21
Paul wrote, in Colossians 3:6,9:

> "... *in the whole world (that Gospel) is bearing fruit and still growing (by its own inherent power), even as it has done among yourselves ever since the day you first heard and came to <u>know and understand</u> the grace of God—(that is) you came to <u>know the grace (undeserved favor of God) in reality, deeply and clearly and thoroughly</u>, becoming <u>accurately and intimately acquainted with it</u>... we pray that you may <u>be</u>*

filled with the full (deep and clear) knowledge of His will in all spiritual wisdom (that is, in comprehensive insight into the ways and purposes of God)..."

Would He not want us to understand Him enough to be able to enter into the benefits of promises He gave us—provided at the cost of His own Son? His Word indicates that He wants us to know Him *much* better than we do.

7. "Jesus didn't heal everyone; what about the impotent man at the Gate Beautiful?"

The Gospels don't say that He healed everyone, but they *do* say that He healed "*all that came to Him,*" and that "*as many as touched Him were made completely whole.*" The Book gives no instance in which Jesus ever turned away anyone who sought Him. Repeatedly,

> "*All who touched Him were made perfectly whole.*" Matthew 14:36
> "*They brought their sick unto Him and He healed them all.*" Matthew 12:15

There are many, many such instances. As mentioned, not only does the Book present a consistent history of these things, it also records instances in which He reached out to heal those who hadn't even asked.

We are warned about adding to Scripture. Or detracting from it!

8. "The only times that miracles were present were during the times of Elijah and Jesus."

That's an actual quote from a well-known Canadian television preacher. He went on to say that, "while God can do anything He wants (after all, He is God) miracles seldom occur now." He did *not* quote the Great Commission, where Jesus said "*these signs shall follow them that believe.*"

Scripture says,

> "*Jesus Christ is the same, yesterday, today and forever.*" Hebrews 13:8
> "*I am the Lord, I change not.*" Malachi 3:6

A.W. Tozer wrote that since He is the "I Am," not the "I Was," what He has said He is still saying.

Since God does not change and the miracle-rich ministry of Jesus was the expression of the Father's will, then in all honesty we must face the fact that He still wants to manifest His love through deliverance. To teach otherwise is to misrepresent the God of heaven.

9. "God still does miracles today; probably if we gathered up all the instances we would have a record much like that of the Gospels."

Miracles were abundant in the ministry of Jesus. They also followed in the lives of the apostles, so that people…

> *"…gathered their sick into the streets so that even the shadow of Peter passing by might at least fall upon some of them."* Acts 5:15

There would have been no need to "search out and gather up" records of miracles to prove their existence. This was also evident in a recent report of the Bakers, missionaries who labor in Mozambique. After they *really met God*, miracles *abounded*. People would walk barefoot for five miles to attend meetings. When a little girl died in a village, the Christians just gathered around her and prayed until she was restored.

10. "Sometimes God says, 'Yes,' sometimes He says, 'wait,' and sometimes He says 'No.' "

I know of no *Scripture* like that.

There *is* one, however, which says,

> *"<u>All</u> the promises of God are in Him <u>Yea</u>, and in Him <u>Amen</u> <u>to the glory of God</u> <u>by us</u>."* 2 Corinthians 1:20

Have we any right to evaluate Scripture by our experience? Ought we not, rather, evaluate our experience by Scripture? Further, note the *reason* for the dependability of the promises: *"to the glory of God."* Note, too, how that glory comes to Him: *"by us."* Jesus said that the need of the man born blind was an opportunity for the glory of God to be manifest in his deliverance. The need was God's opportunity to manifest His glory. The glory was not manifested until the miracle took place—in the man with the need. My need is God's opportunity to manifest His glory. His glory is not manifested until the miracle takes place. Let nothing hinder that outworking of His glory!

11. "There must have been sin in your life."

We—I, make no claim to being without sin; our claim is that the righteousness of Christ was given to us when we confessed our sin to Him. If there had been specific sin preventing God's answer, I believe He would have been faithful to make that known to us. Neither of us was aware of holding anything wrong in our hearts; there was too much at stake!

12. "How old was your husband?"

Where is one promise in the Book which has a qualifying statement with reference to age? There are, however, many places promising special blessing to the elderly:

> "...*they shall still bring forth fruit in old age,*" Psalm 92:14
> "...*even to your old age, I am He.*" Isaiah 46:4

There is even promise that...

> ... "*your youth shall be <u>renewed</u> like the eagle's.*" Psalm 103:5

In Smith Wigglesworth's books there is at least one written account of the healing of a man in his nineties.

13. "There is an appointed time to die."

Yet Hezekiah, when personally told by God's prophet that his time had come, prayed, "*and the Lord added to him fifteen years.*" Scripture says that He is no respecter of persons. And that He does not change.

Jesus said that if we abide in Him and His Word abides in us, we can ask what we will and it shall be done for us.

14. "If God healed us every time we prayed, we'd never die."

He could heal us every time we prayed—and at the right time just take His children Home without their having to be tormented into death.

> "*He taketh their breath...*" Psalm104:29

Since He has borne our sicknesses, since he has taken both our sins and our sicknesses upon Himself, redeeming us from them at His own expense—since He has paid in full—His children should not have to pay again.

15. "It was the sovereignty of God."

If this is by way of saying that God, being Sovereign, has the right to keep or not to keep His promises as He chooses, the statement could be close to blasphemy, for it is in direct contradiction to both His character and His Word. The Message Bible puts Isaiah 45:19 this way:

> "*I am God, the only God there is: I never take back what I say.*"

He has sworn by Himself, since there is none higher, that not one jot or one tittle of His Word shall fail, though the very heavens and earth pass away. Matthew 5:18

"If we believe not, yet He abides faithful: He cannot deny Himself."
2 Timothy .2:13

His own Word concerning His faithfulness to His promises contradicts the human idea expressed in this point. Does God reveal His sovereignty by over-ruling His promises, or by over-ruling circumstances that run contrary to His promises?

"God is not a man, that he should lie; neither the son of man, that he should repent: hath he said, and shall he not do it? or hath he spoken, and shall he not make it good?" Numbers 23:19

16. "You can't put God in a box... "

It would be presumptuous to think that a human could force God to do his will; but how can it be presumptuous to ask for what He has *told* us to ask for, since He has sworn by Himself that He is behind His every Word? It is He, Himself, Who puts the onus on Himself:

"I did not call the descendents of Jacob to a fruitless service, saying, Seek Me for nothing (in vain, KJV), I, the Lord, speak righteousness—the truth [trustworthy, straightforward correspondence between deeds and words]." Isaiah 45:19

17. "We can never tell what God is going to do; we can only do our part (like anoint with oil, lay hands on the sick and pray, as in James 5:14) and then it's up to Him whether He comes through or not."

In other words, we can be counted on, but God can't? James 5:14 *goes on* to say,

*"...the prayer of faith **shall** save the sick, and the Lord **shall** raise him up."*

It does not say that the ritual will bring healing, but that God honors an accompanying prayer of faith. This Scripture bears out the need for faith:

*"...**the prayer of faith <u>shall</u>** save the sick, and the Lord <u>**shall**</u> raise him up."*

One speaker "quoted" from the Great Commission; *"they shall lay hands on the sick..."* then followed with the tired explanation that "we just do what the Word says, and after that it's up to God." He obviously didn't realize that his comment was based on only one small part of Mark 16:18: *"They shall lay hands on the sick..."* while ignoring the other *"shalls"*:

*"...and these signs <u>shall follow</u> **them that believe**... they <u>shall recover.</u>"*

Two things: 1) The requirement of faith, and 2) The *shall* of the miracle. It does seem to narrow down to that. It's uncomfortable to feel a lack—but if there is one, how can God fix it if we won't face it?

18. "You can't question God."

He has told us to seek Him diligently; if we have no need of answers, would He do that? If we are to grow in our understanding and knowledge of Him we must search for Him. In fact, searching is the honorable thing to do:

> *"It is the glory of God to conceal a thing: it is the honor of kings to search out a matter."* Proverbs 25:2

Besides, how can we hope to be changed, if we do not ask Him what's missing? Jesus said, *"Ask, seek, knock... "* Scripture abounds with instances of folk who spoke openly to God about the pain and confusion of their inner struggles. Jesus' own words from the cross, *"My God, My God, why have You forsaken me?"* were a question—a very deep one!

We really need to seek answers from Him, especially when our experience comes short of what He promised.

19. "You can't just claim a promise unless you get a special assurance that you may."

What Scripture backs that up? Such a premise would destroy the very meaning of the word *promise* and make of it only a *possibility.* A promise, especially a promise of the Most High God, is not to be confused with a (remote) possibility. Paul wrote:

> *"All the promises of God are 'Yea' and 'Amen' in Christ Jesus, to the glory of God by us."* 2 Corinthians 1:20.

Surely Almighty God, Who invented language, is well able to impart His thoughts in such a way that they would translate with His intent intact.

20. "It must have been God's will for him to die."

I'm not so sure of that. It could hardly be said that everything that happens in this world is something God wants to happen! It seems more likely that there was some shortfall on the human side of things. Scripture says of Capernaum,

> *"He did not many mighty works there because of their unbelief."*
> Matthew 11:58

If it had been God's will to take Jim, He could have shown us that and given peace about it. He Himself underwrites His own promises, swearing by Himself that He forever stands behind that Word to perform it. He paid the ultimate price in the sacrifice of His only Son to provide salvation from both sin and sickness, and those two great ills of mankind are often linked in the ministry of Jesus and in the rest of Scripture.

Psalm 103:3 says in the same sentence that...

> *"He forgives every one of all my iniquities, and heals each of all my diseases."*

We have no doubt that, in every case, those who come to Him for forgiveness are cleansed from sin; what right do we have, if we use The Book as the basis for our belief, to expect any less consistency in the matter of healing? Both aspects of redemption are in the same sentence!

If God were to be hit-and-miss in healing, would He not also be hit-and-miss in forgiveness? He describes Himself as entirely consistent, faithful to every Word He has said. He does not speak "tongue-in-cheek"; He is not random in keeping His Word; He is not subject to whims. He has said that though the heavens and the earth shall pass away, His Word shall never pass away.

21. "If we are not healed on earth, we will be healed in Heaven."

Scripture does say that there will be no sickness, sorrow, death, or dying there. But since we will not have these physical bodies there to get sick, there will be no "healing" there, for there will be no need of it.

Jim's redeemed spirit was not sick. His sick body *died* because it was *not* healed. His spirit is with Christ; his body lies in a grave in a certain plot in a cemetery north of this city, awaiting resurrection in glorified form when Christ returns. Paul said that...

> *"...the Spirit that raised up Jesus from the dead shall also quicken your mortal bodies..."* Romans 8:11

It was earthly, physical human bodies that Jesus healed during His earthly ministry, and *not* by causing them to drop dead so that their spirits could leave their sick bodies and get to Heaven. (He would not have been very popular if he had done that.) It was mortal, physical bodies that He healed.

Is it because we see so few miracles that we try to change the clear, *literal* record of Scripture?

22. "'The secret things belong to the Lord our God'; we can't expect to understand everything."

The remainder of that same verse (Deut. 29:29) *goes on* to say,

> *"...but the things that are revealed belong to us and to our children for ever..."*

When He has promised healing and purchased it for us on Calvary, is it not one of the things that belong to us?

23. From one who had sometimes seen miracles in answer to prayer: "I don't sense the Lord prompting me to pray for Jim's healing."

There is definitely need to be sensitive to the direction of the Spirit, but with regard to healing, is that direction not already clearly given in His Word? When Jesus, those many times, told the disciples to ask, He didn't tell them to first test their sense; they were to test His Word—to ask based on His instruction to do so and His promise that He would grant what they asked on the basis of that Word. Scripture simply states,

> *"...by His stripes you were healed."* 1 Peter 2:24

24. "You're just ticked off at God for not coming through for you."

Those who are trained in such matters do say that anger is one of the common stages of grief; however, even as I search my heart before Him, I really don't think that I am angry; I love Him too much. But I am terribly confused... There are depths of grief understood only by those who grieve.

25. "You ought to avail yourself of the grace of God, leave your grief at the cross and go on in the victory and joy of the Lord."

The inference in this statement is that one must always be filled with certainty, praise and joy; that it is sinful to come short of that state.

"At the cross." That same cross was the point of ultimate agony for our Redeemer, a point at which He felt totally abandoned by God His Father, and expressed that to Him in the words, *"My God, My God, why have You forsaken me?"*

Earlier, He had told His followers that if any would come after Him, they must take up their cross (not necessarily their picnic basket) ...and follow Him. Might that not imply that, in our journey, there may be times of darkness, despair, and a sense of abandonment—times when we feel that same Father hides His face from us? There is also Jesus' example that it is not only all right, but necessary to express our heart to our Father at such times.

71

The Psalms certainly do not omit grief, perplexity, even anger. Key men of God in Scripture went through times of anguished confusion, which they took to God. *"These things are written for an example to us."* To whom shall we go, if not to our Father?

Grief is a process, a journey *"through the valley of the shadow of death."* One cannot honestly or safely avoid it. Nor can one just terminate it at will.

Not everything will be set to rights before we get Home! While Jesus' offering of Himself as the Man of Sorrows is complete and His provision for restoration full, the fact is that many a sorrowing heart will not understand how to receive that benefit. Another thing: the tares in Jesus' story were left in the wheat-field until harvest before they were separated out and destroyed. And—in heaven there will still be tears that God Himself will wipe away.

26. "God doesn't heal everybody that asks."

Is that what He intended? What Scripture teaches that as His will? Jesus repeatedly told His disciples to ask, with the clear expectation that they would receive:

> *"Ask, and receive that your joy may be full"* John 16:24
> *"For everyone that asks receives...."* Matthew 7:8

Where is the Scripture that ever says that Jesus answered "No!" when asked for a miracle?

Years ago, a young man once rather gleefully pointed out that in one place Scripture didn't say "all," but "many." Yet, in looking at that passage, it doesn't say that He healed many *of* the sick (as if He left some out), but that He healed *"many who were sick";* obviously, not everyone in the crowd was sick.

If we ever get to the point where "many" are healed in our services we will not need to be looking for excuses for our unbelief.

Over and over again in the Gospels it is written that...

> *"He had compassion on the multitude, and healed their sick."*
> Matthew 14:14
> *"they brought their sick to Jesus, and He healed them all."*
> Matthew 4:24, 12:15

I can find nothing in Scripture other than that our God is a God of Deliverances, Who paid the ultimate price to provide forgiveness for sin and healing for our mortal bodies in exactly the same Atonement.

He told the disciples that, in all of these things, He was working out the desires and instructions of the Father. He has not changed!

What is it that now blocks us from His touch?

Are we looking at our God through the wrong end of the telescope?

27. "God knows best."

The comment is based upon God's words to the heart of Isaiah:

> *"My thoughts are not your thoughts, neither are your ways My ways, saith the Lord, for as the heavens are higher than the earth, so are My ways higher than your ways, and My thoughts than your thoughts."*
> Isaiah 55:8,9

I had always taken those words to mean that when things don't work out after the desire of our hearts, He has a better idea. Others, too, have pressed the thought with that Scripture. However, the best commentary on a Scripture is its own context. In the verses following the above quotation from Isaiah it becomes clear that God is actually saying something quite different: His thoughts and His ways are infinitely higher, better than ours in that He is totally able, unwaveringly faithful, invariably working with good purpose—while we fall far short, at best:

> Verses 10-12: "...*For as the rain and snow come down from the heavens, and return not there again, but water the earth, and make it bring forth and sprout, that it may give seed to the sower and bread to the eater:*
> "*So shall My Word be that goes forth out of my mouth; it shall not return unto me void—without producing any effect, useless—but it shall accomplish that which I please, and it shall prosper in the thing for which I sent it..*
> "*For ye shall go out [from spiritual exile of sin and evil into the homeland] with joy, and be led forth [by your Leader, the Lord Himself and His Word] with peace: the mountains and hills shall break forth before you into singing, and all the trees of the field shall clap their hands...*"

He makes no idle promises; He never lacks purpose or power to completely carry out what He gives His Word to do. He works not just for the joy of working, but for provision for those He loves—providing seed to the sower (the means to fulfill his purpose) and bread to the eater (provision for personal need) *bringing tremendous joy* to His people.

That fulfillment, that fullness, is what my heart longs for! Though Romans 8:28 assures that He can even use my failure, I yearn for more of the manifest working of God according to His promises.

28. "The lessons learned through suffering are more important than healing."

Did Jesus ever say anything like that to *anyone* who came to Him? His first words in His public ministry, recorded in Luke 4:18, declared that his purpose in coming was that of declaring the good news of deliverance and healing. What "lesson" could be more valuable than the experience of the touch of His hand in deliverance? That is the lesson continuously evident in His ministry—that God is loving, all-powerful, personal.

29. Some just evade the issue by not responding at all.

30. "There must be something wrong with your faith."

That is just what troubles me. I must not have had enough faith, the right kind faith or…? If, to have received God's touch, there needed to have been an impartation of divine faith, of God-faith, why was that withheld? Why would He not give what was necessary as a basis for Him to work according to His Word?

In the ministry of Jesus, if He required anything, He required faith to release His work, though, as mentioned before, He often did His work just on His own initiative. When He did say, *"If you can believe,"* were people just supposed to turn it on somehow?

If it is not a deep inner conviction that He has the power and that He backs his Word to perform it, what *is* faith? Tozer has written that one of the greatest ills in Christendom is mistaking mental assent for faith. Is that what we did?

What *is* real faith?

What is it that bridges the chasm between the Promise and its fulfillment?

While clearing my desk I came across a Billy Graham newsletter in which Franklin Graham quoted from Matthew 11:21-24 NIV. One part of that quote seemed to lift right off the page, almost shouting:

> *"If the miracles that were performed in you had been performed in Sodom, it would have remained to this day…"* Matthew 11:28

If we, God's children, allow ourselves to remain content with only a form of religion, denying its power—miracle-less—will there be upon our hands the blood of those who would have come to Christ if the signs (the proof) had accompanied our message?

In general, most of the things that have been said to me seem to be based on a feeling that "we are all right, all is well, we have need of nothing ('don't rock the boat...')" **(Revelation 3:17 !)** Somehow, I just *cannot* be reconciled to that.

I am caught in a pit of perplexity and painful confusion.

9

STRUGGLE—AND A FRIEND

Earlier in this storm the words of Romans 8:28 brought assurance:

"God is able to make all things [even my failures] *to work together for good to those who love God... "*

Those words cover the past, but leave tremendous trepidation regarding both present and future, including eternity. Jesus did tell His disciples to seek, which is the basis for all of this writing. There are deep needs among my children, in this whole world, and in my own life, but I am as one with hands that hang down and knees that are feeble—one who cannot please God, for, obviously, I am lacking in faith. Yet I love Him. Strangely, at times worship still rises from deep within me; I marvel, and am glad.

All I know to do is keep on asking, keep on seeking, keep on knocking—and wait.

Grief over the loss of one I loved so dearly has been more profound than words can describe, yet the anguish of this spiritual confusion far exceeds even that. The stress is taking a toll on my physical well-being to a frightening degree. I think that there are some things I should finish before I die, and I am trying to do that; but what will my eternity be, with my heart in such a mess?

In my blackest moments, and there are many of them, I am tormented with terrifying questions: "What if all that I have believed is not true? What if it has all been wishful thinking, a delusion?" "What if the very questioning itself is so heinous a sin of unbelief that it forever separates me from the God I love?" "Oh, what is truth?" Is there no way out of this blackness? I feel as if the pressure is killing me.

What a down time! I know that there are natural factors: short, dark days and long dark nights, physical pain accumulated from the two falls I had last year, the effects of pain medications and withdrawal from them. But I do not think I have been so low in spirits ever before in my life. I drafted (but did not send) the following to one person with whom I had corresponded previously:

> "I am at the end of my rope. I have reached out to several men of God, the Christian counselor connected to your ministry, prayer lines, and God Himself—with no real answers, no help, no real understanding. Sometimes those to whom I reach out for help beat me up before they pass by on the other side; I am like a leper!
>
> Like an old sheep caught in a thorn bush in a severe night storm, bleat as I may, the only sound I hear other than my own heart-cry is that of wolves closing in. Perhaps one old sheep is of little consequence to the Shepherd?
>
> How much longer can I take the strain? If God doesn't help me, either the stress will kill me, my mind will give way, or—there is the temptation to end it all.
>
> I am so ashamed to have sunk this low!"

It is so like Him to send positive things just when they are needed. There have been straws to clutch.

On re-reading *Sentiment and Sediment,* this sentence stood out:

> "Here is something to remember: Jesus was a carpenter; His hands, now nail-pierced, know how to *use* grit to bring out deep, hidden beauty. Trust those hands! "
>
> — jbl

While watching a music video I heard one of the singers speak of the marvelous way the Lord crafted the earth we dwell in, and how that evidence assures His children of His care, His ability, and His trustworthiness as He works His good designs within us through times of struggle. How often He speaks through things He has made!

Then, one radio pastor spoke from Proverbs 16:9 "... *man plans his way, God directs his steps,*" and another reminded his listeners that Jeremiah kept asking deep questions of God...

(Maybe this asking is not a mortal sin?)

Some seem to adjust so quickly to their bereavements, while others, like me, just cannot seem to get their bearings. I wonder why I am so slow, at a standstill, really. I feel so very *lost*. Of course, Jim's death was devastating; it was bound to be, since I loved him so much. I guess I continue to come back to the compounded grief factor in that I seemed to have lost my God at the same time. Oh, for answers! If only He would reveal Himself, His plans, His purposes to me in such a way that those awful questions were answered; then, perhaps, I could begin to deal with the grief over losing Jim.

Several times in the last few days I have thought back to the interesting terrain around Nipawin, Saskatchewan. There is a large natural berm around much of the town, but another feature of the countryside which seems so aptly to parallel my inner journey is a large "sink" outside of town. I remember very clearly the drive through a wooded area and the driver stopping the car for seemingly no reason. There was a well-defined track devoid of vegetation—which suddenly disappeared as if cut by some huge knife. Though we dared not go too close, we could see that, beyond the drop-off, tops of trees were well below the level on which we stood.

So like my life! Suddenly there is no path, just—nothing. There seems to be no place to go, nowhere to set foot. Geographically, of course, we eventually turned back, retraced our steps to the car and returned by the road on which we had come. From this inner journey, however, one cannot go back. And life ahead seems just—cut off. Bewilderment, confusion, a sense of lost-ness...

I really don't like setting this next bit down; it isn't good. Twice this month the pit has been so deep, so black, and so pain-filled that it was right on the edge of being absolutely intolerable. The thought of escape, of ending it all, pressed hard—very hard. *So* hard that, dull though I may be, it smelled diabolic. What a dreadful experience! It is accompanied, of course, by fear, fear of the mounting pressure and fear of what eternity might bring if one succumbed. Sometimes fear is a good thing. Besides risking eternity, such a course would hurt the children, and—leave unfinished whatever it is He has left me here to do.

I am so thankful for the ministry of one person, just one, in whom I can confide:

"Dear Doctor,

"I understand that surgeons sometimes hold patients' hearts in their hands in order to mend them. Though with some trepidation, I'm putting my heart in your hands via this envelope. Doing so is a mark of real trust—and I'm not even under anesthetic! The enclosures, whatever their worth or lack of it, were part of the closeness between Jim and me—

something that often lifted our spirits over the years—something of our own that we enjoyed together.

"One of the oldest of these, 'Say Not, My Soul,' was written in the tenth year of a childless marriage. I once mentioned to you the total blackness of that period for me. It nearly destroyed me! In March of 1969, ten years after it was written, we had adopted the last of our four children…

"In the fall of that same year, Jim's health gave out under the stress of business. 'Tired businessman's heart,' the doctor said: congestive heart failure. When I first took him to the hospital in the next village I was told he might not survive the night! There followed a lengthy period when he could not work, time in which we really sought the face of God. (Very gradually he did regain strength, though always thereafter he had some weakness.) It was during this time that the other songs were written.

"Early in life I made a choice to avoid fuzzy thinking—to try, always, to cut through fog and cobwebs to find solid truth. To evade pain by cloaking it with some sort of prescribed mental attitude that makes for artificial 'comfort' seems dishonest—a form of self-deception that leads nowhere. A person could avoid the pain of surgery by refusing to admit to a problem, but refusing to face reality would preclude any hope of real healing. All I know to do is be open, in all of my struggle, before the God I've loved; to ask, seek, knock—and wait.

"You mentioned that I seem 'stuck' in the grief. I think that's true. I've thought about it, searching for reasons why I cannot seem to get beyond the pain. Perhaps I don't see things in their true light, and there are probably issues I don't recognize or understand, but these few stand out to me:

"1. A very, very lonely youth
"Our family lived in a tiny village in a rural area; most of the school children came from farms outside of town. We had moved there when I was four or five, and it was two weeks before my little sister ran into the house crying, 'Mom, Mom—I saw a girl!' She eventually found a couple of little girls her age, but I never did. Besides that, my mother had been a school teacher and filled in some of my time teaching me to read before I started school. Because of that I was put ahead a grade shortly after starting, and remained the lone child in my grade for several years before being put ahead yet another grade to correct that. Socially, that was even worse, for being two years younger than others at my grade level isolated

me even further. That continued for the rest of my public and high-school years; I graduated from grade twelve when I was sixteen.

"2. <u>A very deep love</u>

"Since my parents felt that sixteen was too young to be exposed to university, I went from high school to a Bible college for the next three years. It was there that I first met Jim. I learned to respect and admire him during those years. He was a sincere Christian with a unique and pleasant personality, keen wit and most infectious laugh. There was a wonderful openness about him; he was genuine—wore no facade; he was real. He showed a lot of maturity and good leadership qualities in the last year when he was president of the student body. He asked me out for the first time two weeks before graduation. I was nineteen; it was my first date.

"We were young, and were careful not to rush into anything. I proceeded to take teacher training, then taught for a year; but as we got to know each other well and really sought the face of God as to His will in the matter we became sure that we were meant for each other. So, three and a half years after graduation, we entered into the covenant of marriage. He loved me! When I gave him my heart, I gave it fully, and forever. I have never, before or since, ever looked at another. The love we shared was more precious than words could describe, all the more because I had been so alone in all those years before he came into my life. Our love filled a tremendous vacuum. He gave my whole life meaning and fullness I had never imagined possible. I deeply, truly *loved* him!

"I have heard that a defining moment can overshadow every aspect of a person's life. That, for my life now, was the moment of Jim's last, tiny breath. That moment is seared into my soul: the moment that tore him and all he meant to me—out of my life.

"I simply can not let go of my Love. I dare not; there would be nothing left of me! (Sounds crazy. I do know that he is gone…)

"3. <u>A lot of rejection</u>

"While growing up, a good part of the rejection came because of age difference, but it was greatly accentuated after I had given my heart to the Lord at the age of eight. In that small village, when thirty-three out of about three hundred people made the decision to follow the Lord, there was quite an uproar—and a lot of antagonism, which most definitely carried over into school life. It never really let up.

"Another facet of rejection (which I feel guilty writing about but feel I must to complete the picture): Both of my parents were loving, but my mother never seemed to catch on to my being basically different from her. As the first child, I got a lot of rather concentrated "mothering" (severe corporal punishment), seemingly in an effort to change who I was. And a significant amount of repression. I know she did what she thought best... At the time I just accepted it as the status quo; it was only many, many years after her death that I gained a different perspective while reading about temperaments.

"Later on, after Jim and I were married, we came back to the village to set up a little business, and after my father died we looked after Mom—made her an extended part of our family. I increasingly became her care-giver during the twenty-four years before her own death. Following her death I felt very painfully rejected when the one personal love-gift she had told me would be mine was denied me. I let it go, and hold no malice, but it hurt. It felt as if she had rejected me.

"Then, when an employee brought down our thirty-three-year business in just six weeks and we were forced into the bankruptcy which was particularly devastating to Jim, our changed social status seemed to put us in a position inferior to my siblings. So—I am still the 'odd man out.'

"But far beyond the discomfort of those relatively minor rejections is that felt in:

"4. A committed faith thrown into confusion

"I am rather afraid to write this next part, but it is necessary in trying to explain why I'm 'stuck.' To me, it is *the* central part of my dilemma, the enormous chasm between my painful confusion and any hope of wholeness.

"Before I loved my Jim, I loved my God. We loved Him together. It was as total a devotion as we were capable of—central to all we were and all we did. We felt that the highest authority on which to base our lives was the written Word of our God. We esteemed it as absolute, living Truth: eternal, changeless, powerful—an out-flowing of the very essence of the God Who gave it. That Word abounds with declarations of faithfulness, mercy, and promises of God's intervention on behalf of His children. On the basis of that Word, Jim and I had both been calling on our God for His intervention in his last illness.

"When hospital staff tried to tell me I was losing him, my heart met the words with: '*But God...!*' Believe me, it was with my whole soul that I cried out to Him, and it was with my whole soul that—I fell through the cracks!

"I feel as if I have been rejected by Him Whom I love most. There is still a strange sense of His loving me at some level, and of my loving Him, but I feel *so* lost...

"King David wrote, '*In You, O Lord, have I put my trust; let me never be put to confusion*' ('*have my hope in You disappointed*' in another translation). I know just what David didn't want; I have it. It frightens me. I really don't know how to deal with it! If it had been a matter of '*according to your faith be it done to you,*' then I am in a very bad position, for '*without faith it is impossible to please Him.*' Yet I knew that just one Word, one touch from the God I loved could have completely restored Jim. What went wrong?

"What is true?

"5. <u>A heightened awareness of mortality</u>

"Death is the inevitable reality that I, too, will face later, or sooner. Each day, when I reset my perpetual calendar, I know another day has been chipped away from the time I have left. Death is a dread unknown; it frightens me, particularly in my present state. What is real? I don't know any more. The only things I am sure of right now are pain and confusion. I don't want to die in this state—or live in it, either. I keep trying to finish some things I've started in the past, and continue to long for some sense of reality. I guess that is partly why I have been spending quite a bit of time in the last months with the contents of this package, reaching for truth, longing for certainty I once had, searching for solutions, hoping that all of this is real. I do sense reality at one level, but rejection and confusion at another...

"6. <u>My temperament</u>

"I am not phlegmatic; I cannot just breeze along, shrugging my shoulders at things that happen. Nor am I an outgoing sanguine or controlling choleric; from what I've read, my temperament is primarily that of a melancholy; I dabble in music and some other forms of art, think a lot, and feel things very, very intensely. (I have never been able to tolerate the tension in drama, even in a Billy Graham film.) That being so, the events of the last couple of years have been traumatic to say the least—not just a storm at sea, but a tidal wave of gargantuan proportions. And there seems to be little let-up, for answers are very slow in coming.

"All of this together must sound like an over-sized pity-party. However, it's because I don't want to stay like this that I'm searching for solid footing, and I am gaining a little—in some areas. In not being able to find my own way out of this quagmire I feel like a failure as a person; weak, stupid, deficient.

"Do you think there is a way out of this, or is it pain that I must just learn to live with?

"Sometimes, remembering the total blackness of those childless years and realizing that God used that brokenness to open our hearts to adopting the children that have meant so much to us, I wonder if there is some constructive purpose in this dark time, too…

"I am afraid that I am being a real pain in the neck to you. I know it is dreadfully uncomfortable for anyone to stop long enough to look at all of this, let alone become involved in it; everyone has more than enough trouble of his own. Yet you have gone more than the second mile with me. I appreciate it more than I will ever be able to tell you. May the Savior, Who did the same thing, take you to His heart in special blessing for walking—in His steps!"

CARING HEART
He fell among thieves.
Beaten, bruised, bleeding,
Broken in body and in spirit;
Robbed of everything that mattered,
He lay near death, helpless to help himself.
Passers-by avoided him;
He was a fearful sight; his pain,
Even guessed at, made them turn
The other way.

But God sent a caring heart!
Kind words fell upon his ear,
And carefully, tenderly
Kind hands poured oil into his wounds,
Lifted him, and carried him to
A safe place where he could heal.

My whole life crashed
When death so cruelly robbed me
Of one I loved with all my heart
So many years. Life lost its lustre;
The dust of death drew t'ward its dulling shade,
Offering escape from agony too deep.
Immeasurable anguish wracked my soul—
My pain made gentle folk uneasy;
They turned away.

But God sent a caring heart!
The touch upon the pain was kind—
And carefully, tenderly,
The very love of God flowed through
Your wise and gentle understanding,
Starting healing in my broken spirit.
Thank God for you, my friend!
– jbl

83

As I have set down my thoughts in the correspondence above, I remain convinced that, as far as our Father is concerned, His healing mercies are openly available to His children and to others, purchased by the redemptive work of the Savior. I do not know what hinders the flow of this mercy, but I feel sure that God wants His mercy to flow. What blocks it? Our disbelief? Our distance from Him in our deepest hearts? Somehow, I think He wants to correct the situation. If the loss of my dearest one is even one small happening He can use to stir up His own, then at least the pain will not be wasted.

Father, grant deep thirst in the hearts of your children which will call out to You until You can open the floodgates of Your glory!

10

EFFORTS TO FIND PEACE

My mentor tells me that I must face pain-points of the past and work through them in an effort to heal from them. He suggests writing as a means of doing this, whether or not the writing is actually mailed. Thus, the following drafts:

Excerpts from the letter sent to the cancer hospital:
"Dear Sirs,

"My husband was admitted to your hospital on February 15, 2002. Many of the doctors and nurses were exceptional; I am grateful for them, but some things trouble me.

"He was in great pain; I suppose it was because of this that he was not moved often enough for his well-being. Partly because of this, and partly because of the next point, he is now dead.

"When he was sent downstairs for X-rays, the woman who pushed his stretcher had a terrible chest cold and coughed all over him repeatedly. She was not wearing a mask, and made no effort whatever to cover her mouth or even to turn her head when she coughed, except for once after I made the comment, 'I hope he doesn't get *that* on top of everything else!' She then turned her head for only the next cough. For a person with a weakened immune system such as Jim must have had, her behavior was tantamount to murder. Though the specialist had told me that he felt Jim could have two or three years with a reasonable quality of life, he lived only a matter of days—after developing pneumonia at your prestigious cancer hospital.

"Nothing can undo what has been done; I know that. But things need not have happened this way. They add to the agony of my bereavement; it need not have come so soon.

"Nothing can mitigate the shock and sense of tremendous loss I feel in being robbed, partly due to those areas of negligence, of what could have been a most precious last few years with my beloved husband; but perhaps my writing can move you to prevent the same trauma from happening to other people..."

In a later interview with a hospital staff member, I was assured that the matter had been dealt with.

To the attendant who coughed all over Jim as she pushed his stretcher in the X-ray department: (not mailed)

"I cannot expect you to imagine what you cost me in agony of grief which followed my husband's early trip to his grave because of what you did that day.

"You must have known better! Everyone knows that illness is transmitted on the breath of anyone with a cough—and you are a health professional, employed at an esteemed cancer hospital. Even some of the patients there wore masks; how much more should you have done so while at work among severely ill people? Surely your training must have prompted you to take precautions. Why didn't you? Your negligence took my husband's life as surely as if he had been murdered.

"I know you must have been feeling most unwell; perhaps you didn't feel you had the energy to do that extra thing. Maybe you felt the mask would make your breathing more difficult. Perhaps, in some way, you carried inner pain as well.

"Nothing can undo what has been done. I forgive you, as I have been forgiven."

To that one whom we had called, hoping for divine intervention (not mailed):

"I have spoken with you about the profound disappointment Jim experienced when you reacted to his illness from a natural standpoint. We had both hoped—trusted—that when you came, He Who indwells you would rise up and from your lips speak the healing word for which we prayed. I know that you are only His instrument; the miracle-power is His. Perhaps the pressure of day-to-day business kept you from listening for His voice, from looking past the obvious seriousness of his condition to the face of God? I cannot blame you; who among us is *always* in full communion with Him? But—how much it would have meant to experience the miraculous deliverance He so often promised! How great would have been our joy and rejoicing in Him, where now there is such deep agony of soul and sense of abandonment!

"But here I must blame myself most of all, for I didn't even know how to touch God for Jim's healing. How much I need to learn! Besides, why didn't I tell you when I called just what we were trusting for? Perhaps one day you may teach me?"

****

"WE NEVER TALKED ABOUT IT..."

Because it was unspeakable!

On a scale of agony, being physically sawn in two could hardly compare with being ripped apart from one who meant more to me than anyone or anything else in the world.

Yes, the original diagnosis of prostate cancer raised the specter of such parting; neither of us faced that head-on. I believe that Jim refused to face that issue when the possibility was first raised; he "lost" the requisition for testing, later claiming to have gone through with it when in fact he had evaded it. When he did finally go to a specialist and got the word that there was enlargement which was not smooth, indicating possible malignancy, he at first went into denial, evading the real feeling of alarm. When further testing made the fact undeniable, at first he didn't want to take the route of treatment. Yet, when I brought him part of the first Psalm: "*whatsoever he* doeth *shall prosper*," he agreed. And after intensive radiation, he did get a clear bill of health for that issue.

I do not know how long the multiple myeloma was brooding before we knew of it. He had lacked his full measure of vitality ever since the episode of congestive heart failure in 1969. Was part of that malaise also this cancer of the bone marrow? After the prostate cancer issue was declared clear, there was anxiety on my part when he showed evidence of anemia, an anxiety I dared not put into words. My turn at evasion? Then there were the broken-rib episodes, especially after the full-length fall when he lost his balance as he turned to sit on the bed; the bone scan showing more than twenty hot spots in his rib-cage which were erroneously read as osteoporosis; the ever-increasing malaise; the growing weakness; home-care...

Then there was the sudden pain in my back as I helped Jim to his feet, which worsened to the point that my doctor called an ambulance to take me from him to the hospital. My heart still bleeds when I remember the totally stricken look on his face as I was wheeled out on the stretcher. Oh, how I hated to hurt him like that!

It was while I was in hospital that word came of Jim's multiple myeloma. I will never forget how it tore me! Hospital or not, I cried my heart out. Later one doctor remarked that it could be treated...

When I finally got home after an interminable twenty-five days (not knowing that I would have only another forty-two days with him), I found him so very, very ill. February 14 was the last day we had at home together. It was far from romantic, for his pain was great, as was my concern. But always, there was the undergirding of our strong, mutual love. The next day a volunteer driver took us to the cancer hospital "for an appointment." When the specialist spoke with us, he confirmed that the illness could be treated—after he said it *would kill him*—but that he should be able to have two or three reasonably good years...

However, even that was not to be. The appointment led to his admission as a cancer patient, where the attendant in the X-ray department repeatedly coughed all over him. He contracted pneumonia, and lived only another three weeks. Later, I wrote the hospital concerning this.

I know, I know—I've been skirting the subject I'm supposed to face.

WE NEVER TALKED ABOUT IT— the possibility of his death.

One of the nurses at the hospital to which he was transferred late in February told me it would be best to talk about it, but I didn't want to. When my father had died suddenly we had no opportunity, and when my mother died she had repeatedly said that she wanted to go, so that it was not necessary. Really, I could not even consider the possibility of Jim dying. The nurse then tried to broach the subject with Jim by commenting on how wonderful it was that we'd had all those years together. His response? "Yes. A few more would be nice!"

When a doctor told me that they did not think he would recover, my whole heart and soul met the statement with, "But God!" There are so many, many promises of God's intervention on behalf of His children—so many! One most specific Word to which I held was from Psalm 103: 3, which, in the Amplified reads:

> *"Bless the Lord, O my soul, and all that is deepest within me, bless His holy name. ... Who forgives (every one of) all your iniquities, <u>Who heals (each of) all your diseases;</u> Who redeems your life from the pit and corruption, Who beautifies... dignifies... and crowns you with loving-kindness and tender mercies; Who satisfies your mouth (your necessity and desire at your personal age) with good, so that your youth, renewed, is like the eagle's (strong, overcoming, soaring)" !*

As mentioned, we had asked a man of God to come, knowing that God moved through him in overseas crusades to perform healing miracles, and feeling that Jesus in him would speak that one Word from God to destroy the destroyer in Jim's body. When he came, he went by natural signs and actually spoke death rather than life. Jim's face registered *tremendous* disappointment; I think that at that point he gave up. Me? I thought that God must want us to reach Him ourselves, and continued to call out to Him with all my heart. When I told Jim that I was still praying for his healing, though he was unable to speak, he strongly indicated that he was not in accord with that.

As his weakness continued to increase and the probable outcome forced itself into my consciousness, I fled to the little private room and cried my heart out for a very, very long while. One precious nurse slipped in and sat with me for some time before saying just a few words and leaving.

At the urging of the staff, I did make the calls to family members. I've told how, when our daughter told Jim that the others were coming, he said, "So they're playing the 'call-the-family' game, are they?" I had been afraid that he would think that, and let go.

The staff pressured me into consenting to the administration of midazolam, which would induce a coma-like state. I had not wanted to do that, for I knew that I would then lose contact with him. There had still been the awareness of each other's presence. Once, when I told him how dearly I loved him, he obviously just soaked it up and rested in that. Another time, when I had called him by a favorite term of endearment, he replied, with a little trace of his old verve, "Yep! I b'long to you, and you b'long to me." You don't ask for an end to things like that! Nevertheless, when the girls added their pressure to that of the staff, I buckled, and began to lose him, then.

When the last tiny breath came—and went—my world collapsed! It has remained shattered to this day.

Yes, I've been evading the point of pain, again. I'm supposed to write what Jim might have said if we had talked about his impending death.

We never talked about it—except for one brief moment while he was still at home. I was sitting on the floor bathing his feet, since he had become too weak to bathe himself. As I washed his feet, his face crumpled and he said, "I think I'm leaving you." Then a measure of composure returned and he continued, "But not for long." My response? "Oh, *no!* We'll get treatment!"

He was obviously thinking about it later when he referred to a certain investment which he advised against; but again, I didn't face his comment head-on. I could not face his death! Perhaps I still cannot.

What would he have said if he had pursued the topic? I know he would have said that he didn't want to cause me pain by leaving me. I *know* that. He wanted to stay with me. There, I've touched it. Pain? Immeasurable! Just that much and the ocean of tears reaches high tide again.

I know that the "articles of faith" would indicate that as of now he would tell me that Heaven is wonderful, that he is free of pain, that he has seen the face of Jesus, that he is re-united with loved ones; perhaps, also, to be strong—to carry on. But, as I have mentioned, though somewhere in the depths of my being I still sense the presence of the Lord, it seems that, in large measure, my faith has collapsed. Everything I have treasured in the realm of faith seems to have crashed, splintered, fallen. Grief over that compounds the grief over the loss of Jim, and adds a torturing, awesome *fear*—and sense of guilt for failing to believe. I am so, *so* lost! I have no idea where to go from here, or where there is to go...

****

Face the innuendo:
"THERE IS NO GOD." How do I feel about that?

Feel! Yes, the first reaction is a feeling—a powerful, complex feeling of shock, horror, revulsion.

I "feel" that I do not want to look at that question. There is such a terrifying, frigid emptiness to even the beginning of the thought that it is repulsive.

I cannot, cannot go there!

Reason demands denial of the premise: The weight of evidence is on the side of Intelligent Design, and that weight continues to increase. I cannot think that there is no God. Things exist—things tangible and intangible—on a scale and in a complexity that defies Chance.

That being so, the idea "there is no God" becomes *the* black hole of contemplation. It collapses inward upon itself—an oxymoron. If there were no Creator, there could be no creation, no existence; how then, could one (who by nature of the premise must not exist) think the unthinkable with no thought, nothing to think the no-thought with, and nothing to think about?

If God did not exist, there would be no existence of any kind. No being. No thought. No life. No love. There would not even be a vacuum.

But—feeling; what do I feel?

My small bone-head must believe that He is *("and is the Rewarder of those who diligently seek Him"*...? Hebrews 11:6) There is instant recall of the words in brackets—the other part of that Scripture—and an all-too-familiar flash of guilt at typing that question-mark.

My head—tells me that He is.

And my heart. If anything unseen is real, my heart has known Him. Was my love for my husband real? Yet this inner awareness of God is stronger, much larger than that human relationship. It is far beyond love; it is worship! The measure that my heart has known Him, even that measure, has been so real, so wonderful beyond words, so overflowing, beautiful, joy-filled; can my heart be wrong? The wonder of being loved by Him, the privilege of loving Him, the joy of knowing the inmost being rising to exult in Him—for this relationship to be thrown into question... Life without Him would be—unthinkable! If what I have taken to be God in my heart were to prove unreal, everything meaningful would implode to ghastly, black nothingness.

Perhaps that fear is part of the painful confusion that persistently haunts—*worms* through the tortured chambers of my mind?

There is such desperate need, somehow, to know what is *real.*

A father told how his little son used to love to jump off the edge of the swimming pool into his arms, utterly confident that his father would catch him. Once the father was not prepared for the jump and both of them were somewhat the worse for it. What if the son had leaped for his father's arms only to see him step back and (lovingly) watch him fall into water over his head—and drown? Now add to the thought; what if the Father were an unseen being? Would it not be natural to wonder if He were really there? That illustrates my confusion.

I made a desperate, whole-hearted leap (faith, hope, or presumption?) and fell into dark, deep water with no arms to catch me, no Word to comfort—and no ability to swim. Suddenly 2+2 no longer equals 4, but 1.279 or some other unpredictable number, or even figs? Rock is no longer rock, but quicksand, or maybe North? Up is down, down is sideways?

What am I trying to say?

When "reality" is thrown into question, there is tremendous confusion, fear, and anxiety. When that "reality" is the fundamental, all-encompassing, basic premise upon which a whole life has been built, then absolutely everything seems to crumble into a screaming void.

Surely the Author of language is well able to convey His thoughts clearly enough to survive translation! When He speaks of promise, can it rationally be construed to mean (remote) possibility? Throughout Scripture promises abound, as do records of those promises being fulfilled.

There is tremendous joy when God answers prayer: an exultation in God.

Conversely...!

When the most precious person in my life was taken in spite of heartfelt prayer based on the promises of Almighty God, there was immeasurable grief on two counts; loss of my husband, and loss of my certainty in God. Unspeakable grief was compounded with the most profound *confusion.* It has been like falling into the blackness of a bottomless pit, where gravity pulls first one way then another, with nothing firm at either extremity and no way to stop the swing from one direction or the other.

Angst. Is that what I am experiencing?

When a man buys a power tool, he expects it to do a certain job. If it doesn't, he looks for a reason for the failure. He may assume that a) the tool has not been plugged into a power source, b) there is something wrong with the power source, c) there is something he doesn't understand about how to use the tool, or d) there is something wrong with the tool itself.

I'm going through a similar search for understanding.

Every observable thing in the universe is governed by predictable, dependable laws. We are told that there is even "*the law of the Spirit of Life in Christ Jesus.*" Would this not mean that God moves in predictable ways, as defined in His written Word? Both that written Word and the Living Word, Jesus, abound in portraying our God as a healing God.

If what I have believed is valid, healing had been provided for Jim. Since he wasn't healed, is everything upon which I've built my life for all these decades—not real? But I know He is real—isn't He? If He isn't, nothing is. Yet there is reality, and I have always felt that He is Reality personified. If what I have thought to be real is not the God of the Bible, what on earth have I got myself into? If what—Who—I've thought to be real, *is* real, then why wasn't the outcome according to His promise?

There must be something wrong with me. Something in me must have blocked the function of the unseen law of the Spirit of Life in Christ Jesus; something must not have been conducive to the healing flow of that "*Spirit that raised up Christ from the dead (Who shall also quicken your mortal bodies).*" Faith. I must not have had real faith, and "*without faith it is impossible to please Him*"; if that's the case, I'm in an awful mess... ad infinitum.

I can't decide that He isn't real, because my heart loves Him too much; and there is too much appeal to reason to allow the thought. Besides, the fear accompanying that consideration is explosive! Yet what I "know" to be real didn't work out the way His Word indicated that it should. Two powerful "realities" directly contradict each other; neither is strong enough to subdue the other and neither weak enough to fold. And I am caught in the middle. I can find no solution.

Angst: "Anguish, torment, anxiety, trouble, sorrow, worry, fear."

Sounds like me!

Yes, the questions bring fear. Fear of grieving Him for one thing, for I love Him and deeply value His love. Also, fear that, like the Israelites of Hebrews 3, my fear will be classified as rebellion (which it could be) and I share a fate similar to theirs when, having angered God, they were shut out of His blessing. Fear, that, if He does exist and I dare to doubt Him, I will "become a castaway," as Paul put it. And, eclipsing every other fear, the fear that He may not exist at all, that I have been caught in a great delusion...

Unspeakable fear. And compounded grief.

With the passage of time, (at times) some of the numbing shock lessens, and, as in the long-ago despair over childlessness, (at times) an awareness of His presence returns—and is treasured—but the confusion, that dreadful confusion still churns deep within. And sometimes it escalates. It is never resolved.

I love Him. I sense that He is near, but cannot find Him. Why does He hide His face from me?

It is much easier to use many words than it is to define with few; I wish I could distill the issue clearly, simply.

I get so-o-o tired of this tug-of-war. Sometimes it seems that both sides of the issue spin too fast for either to be really felt. There is numbness...

Angst. Is that the word?

I know that He is able to bring something good out of this dark night of the soul. But how can I pray now, with any confidence? What do the Promises mean? I feel wicked writing that, but that is my honest confusion. "Honest confusion"—now, that's a strange one.

Sometimes I wonder if there may be part of me taking this detour—chasing a red herring—rather than facing the deep grief over the loss of my Jim. I am afraid of that loss. I cannot accept it. I just cannot! Part of me knows this is totally foolish; the fact is fact, but with all of my heart I don't want it to be. No part of me can accept it. I know this is crazy, but I'd rather be crazy than bereft. Say, how crazy can you get?

I know that while I wrestle with these unyielding issues time leaks away one more day after one more day—with that empty chair, the missing voice, the void. In spite of my non-acceptance of Jim's death, the cold fact of it is daily more evident. In a cruel kind of way, I am forced to become somewhat accustomed to the fact that I have lost my earthly love—and the pain grows, even as I struggle.

The grief regarding Jim's death is still very, very raw. It could be only moments ago that I held his dear face between my hands and kissed him over and over, with no response at all from him, for he was—dead. How can I expect to "get over" that?

11

CORE BELIEF

I know Him, from His Word, to be absolutely unlimited in every positive attribute: He is powerful, faithful, compassionate, unchanging. He says of Himself that every Word that goes out of His mouth accomplishes what He sends it to do, cannot be withdrawn or contradicted, never deviates from its original intent. He has repeatedly confirmed this:

> *"I have not spoken in a corner of the land of darkness; I did not call the descendents of Jacob [to a fruitless service] saying, Seek me for nothing (in vain, KJV), but promised them a just reward. I, the Lord, speak righteousness—the truth [trustworthy, straightforward correspondence between deeds and words]. I declare the things that are right."* Isaiah 45:19

> *"I never take back what I say."* Isaiah 45:23 (the Message),

> *"no one of these details [of prophecy] shall fail, none shall want her mate [in fulfillment] for the mouth of the Lord has commanded..."*
> Isaiah 34:16

From Exodus on through Scripture, He describes Himself as a God Who heals. One of his Jehovah names actually means "God Who is my Healer." Jesus, the living Word of the Father, repeatedly healed all who came to Him, never turning anyone away with a "No." His forgiveness of sin and His healing of sickness are inextricably linked in His ministry of Redemption.

Forgiveness is rarely doubted; how can we doubt the healing part of His work? This is how I know Him from His Word. Why can I not know Him this way in my experience? Is it possible that I do not know Him this way from my heart? Have I had only hope, not faith? *"Without faith, it is impossible to please Him"*!

Background:

How could I define the strange stirring that first drew me to Him as a child of eight? At first it was uncomfortable; it was a turning to One Whom I had, unwittingly, wronged. Yet there was something so real, so warm about that Presence. He was irresistible, even though He was a Stranger to my soul. I faced the discomfort; when I told Him I was sorry and gave my heart to Him, He came into my life bringing light, joy, love—even in the beginning of the relationship. Such patience! Days, weeks, years... He did not hurry me, but led me, like a Shepherd leads His sheep.

Six years later, to the day, the Spirit opened to me so much more of the wonder of Who He is. And as days, years and decades have slipped away, He has slowly, patiently, almost imperceptibly built into my life more understanding, more appreciation, more room for Himself.

There have been heartaches. There have been dark periods of bewildered agony when I could not seem to find Him. Yet He was always there, and only made more room for Himself through those stretching, breaking times. There is nothing more profoundly wonderful, warm, and precious than sensing the sweet, gentle rush of His presence through my soul. In retrospect, the love I first felt, though very real, was such a small trickle compared to the fullness, the widening flow as life goes on. He has become more than life itself to me: essential, precious— the *everything* which carries every other factor of my life. More than breath to my body, He is to my spirit. I have known a wonderful human love, but the love I have for this One from Heaven goes far beyond even all that treasured love could be; it is worship—true, all-encompassing *worship.*

For *this* relationship to be thrown into question...

Can I explain it?

My understanding of God is that He fills all heaven and earth, creates and upholds His creation of all things beyond our comprehension in both extremes of enormous and minute. He is eternal, all-knowing, all-powerful, redemptive, overflowing with loving-kindness and tender mercies new every morning. He is Creator, Savior, Healer, Shepherd, Friend, Light, Source of all Life. He is Truth itself, and the Way to that Truth. Everything that is, in all realms—spiritual, physical, mental, emotional—has its source in Him. His understanding is without measure. His involvement in His creation is total. His authority is unquestionable. His power is infinite. He is unchangeable, impartial, faithful.

His Word is immutable, forever settled in Heaven. He cannot lie. He is fully capable of saying what He means in a way that clearly conveys what He intends it to convey. When He moved Peter to write "*He has given to us many exceeding great and precious promises,*" He could not mean "(remote) possibilities." He means what He says, precisely as He says it. He, Himself, in the fullness of all His attributes, stands forever behind every Word He speaks, for He is in it.

When He speaks, He speaks with intent, and what He intends cannot be turned back or made to fail, but must come to pass. When He speaks, He does not retract or waver in the least degree. His Word is the expression of His very being, and has in it the inherent power of its own fulfillment. It is alive, powerful, quickening, for it is part of Who He is. His Word is God Himself, in motion.

His Word is an expression of His Spirit—not static, but alive. He has said that...

> "*...if the Spirit of Him Who raised Christ from the dead dwell in you, He shall also quicken your mortal bodies through His Spirit that dwells in you.*" Romans 8:11

Jesus, in His person, is the very living Word of God. He came to do the Father's will. He never said "No" to anyone who came to Him for healing; often it is recorded that "*He healed them all.*" He responded to faith. He was delighted when He found faith, disappointed when He did not find it. Sometimes He built up the weak faith of seekers and met their need. Sometimes He went far beyond the faith of the needy to do more than they could have imagined, when all hope was gone. He even went out of His way to meet needs just on His own initiative, driven by His deep compassion. The Message Bible reads that when He met the funeral procession coming out of Nain, "*His heart broke,*" and He touched the bier and brought the young man back to life.

In John 14-17, six times Jesus told His disciples to ask. Ask—and receive.

Requirements: *"Ask in My name (presenting all I AM")"*
                   "Live in Me, and My Words abide in you"

Scope: *"Whatever you ask".*
                   "What you will"

Guarantee*:*   *"I will grant"*
                   "My Father will grant"

Purpose*:*   *"That the Father may be glorified in the Son"*
                   "That your joy might be full"

David said,

> *"Unto thee, O Lord, do I lift up my soul. O my God, I trust in thee: let me not be ashamed, let not mine enemies triumph over me."* KJV. Amplified: *" let me not be put to shame (or **confusion**) or my hope in You be disappointed."* Psalm 25:2

I am experiencing that deep confusion.

My Father is never caught off-guard. I knew it was not at all impossible with God to intervene in Jim's condition; His Word itself, and all He is, bade me join Jim's own prayers and come to Him. I called out to Him with absolutely all my heart, yet I fell into deep water with no arms to catch me, no Word to comfort—and no ability to swim. With the passage of time, some of the numbing shock lessened and, as in the long-ago despair over childlessness, an awareness of His presence returned, and is treasured; but the confusion, that dreadful confusion, still stalks me.

I have felt as if that confusion were destroying me.

I am not looking for a way out of the agony; I am looking for Truth. I cannot hope for God to "fix it" if I evade realities, indulge in escapism, or refuse to let Him search my heart. I do believe that He is utterly faithful, and that if I am unable to obtain the promise, the fault lies somewhere in me, not in His faithfulness. He is God; I am human.

I do not believe that God is capricious; I do not believe that He says one thing and means another; I do not believe that He speaks tongue-in-cheek, inferring one thing and meaning another. He says of Himself,

> *"I, the Lord, speak righteousness; faithful, straight-forward correspondence between words and deeds."* Isaiah 45:19

He has said that He...

> *"...will not allow His word to return to Him void—without producing any effect, useless—but it shall accomplish that which I please and purpose, and it shall prosper in the thing for which I sent it."* Isaiah 55:11

I do not believe that He paid the price He paid without intending that His children benefit from His sacrifice. I do not believe that "we can only do what He said to do and if He doesn't fulfill His Word, it's not our fault..." or "you can never be sure what He will do," as some have said. I believe that He wants His children to know Him. He said,

> *"If a man is to glory, let him glory in this, that He knows and understands me."* Jeremiah 9:24

Paul said,

> *"Do not be vague and thoughtless and foolish, but understanding and firmly grasping what the will of the Lord is."* Ephesians 5:17

Didn't Jesus come to bridge that awful chasm between the promises of God and their fulfillment? What is missing in my life? If I am a citizen of Capernaum (where He could do no mighty miracles because of their unbelief), I want to move! I have sought in every way I know for answers—for a way out of the maze. I take it directly to Him, and wait. And wait, and struggle some more, and wait...

Is there a way of escape?

12

CONTINUED SEARCHING

Could there be...
RECONCILIATION WITHOUT RESOLUTION?

Lord, with the part of my heart that isn't dead, I love You, whether or not I understand what went wrong. Help me, please!

Two truths seem diametrically opposed to each other; how can there be either resolution or reconciliation? On one hand, from the Unchanging One, is the oft-repeated Promise and the unfailing fulfillment of it in Jesus' ministry; on the other hand, my inability to appropriate it. Where, *where*—is the bridge? Is not that same Redeemer the bridge? Why could I not find Him?

Resolution. Reconciliation.

One could, if given the grace, simply accept the fact as it is, trust that good can come from it, and go on. Yet, even then, how could one really have the confidence again to pray for other things? How really trust that He is there, involved, *personal?* And there remains, still, the deeply painful, many-faceted presence of grief...

Perhaps one could assume that, failure or not as it may look to me, He may have some purpose—something He could not accomplish otherwise—to work by this means. If that were accepted as possible, or even probable, there could be a measure of peace, except for future confidence in prayer.

The promise, versus the non-fulfillment of it in our circumstance—in such a case, how can the resultant confusion be resolved? In all sincerity, what reconciliation *can* be made?

Frank E. Graeff expressed well the torment of the soul:

> Does Jesus care when I've said "good-bye"
> To the dearest on earth to me,
> And my sad heart aches 'till it nearly breaks—
> Is it aught to Him? Does He care?

He had this assurance:

> O yes, He cares; I know He cares,
> His heart is touched with my grief;
> When the days are weary, the long nights dreary,
> I know my Savior cares.

Will this anguish never end—in this life? Much of the time the pain is intolerable; yet, in my present state, I fear the next life.

****

What if Jim's death were the catalyst in the life of his son, to bring him to God?

****

Suppose I were to write a...
LETTER TO GOD

> "Search me, O God, and know my heart today.
> Try me, O Savior; know my thoughts, I pray.
> See if there be some wicked way in me—
> Cleanse me from every sin and set me free.
>
> "Lord, take my life and make it wholly Thine;
> Fill my poor heart with Thy great love divine.
> Take all my will, my passion, self and pride;
> I now surrender, Lord—in me abide."
> – J. Edwin Orr

"I think that this will be very difficult, yet I want to be really open to You. You know well how my heart has cried out to You through the years, sometimes in utmost worship, sometimes in tears, sometimes rejoicing, sometimes simply reaching out for more of You. These last two years have been particularly difficult, for I cannot seem to find You. You are not far away, but veiled from my heart's sight, and I long for open revelation of Your face.

"Help me in this exercise; come, by Your Spirit, and walk through the rooms and hallways of my soul, all of them. I give You the keys, hardly knowing, myself, what doors they fit or to what rooms they give entrance. I do not fully know the depths of my own spirit, but You do. Walk with me. Open to my own understanding all that You already see.

> *"Unite and direct my heart solely, reverently to fear and honor Your name."* Psalm 86:11

"Father, am I misguided in my understanding of Your promises? You created language; surely You are able to state your intent clearly,

"so the wayfaring man, though a fool, need not err therein." Isaiah 35:8

"Am I a fool to take Your Words literally, at face value? It really does seem that it would be foolish *not* to do so. In light of Your Words and the supreme sacrifice of Your Son to make the blessing of those Words available, it really seems to me that Your love wants nothing more than to see Your promises fulfilled on behalf of Your children. How could it be otherwise? Are You hurt when we come short of Your love-provision?

"Which would be most impudent: taking Your Word at face value, or inferring that those Words didn't quite—exactly—altogether—mean—what they—seem—to "imply"?

"When You say, '*I Am the Lord Who heals you,*' that Your Word '*is forever settled in Heaven,*' and that You '*never take back what [You] say,*' and people say 'we cannot expect to understand God—it must have been His sovereign will not to have healed,' are they (kindly) making excuses for a delinquent God, or, in reality, trying to protect themselves from facing their failure to touch You?

"Yet, is it a matter of man touching God, or of God touching man?

"What is the bridge?

"The bridge—is it not the Savior? One Who is touched with the feeling of our infirmities? The One Who paid the utmost price to build that bridge? If He truly dwells within, what is it that keeps back the promised blessing?

"Father, You know me—have known me from the beginning. You know my every step, my every stumble. It is no secret to You that I have longed to experience what Your love purchased; it is part of the deep longing of all that is deepest within me to know You. Those times when I have sensed Your presence, known Your touch and seen the miracle of Your intervention—these have been the high points of my life, because they have been times when I sensed that *You* were very near. The lowest points of my life have been those times when I reached out for You with all that is within me, and found You not. It really seems that most of my life has been involved in that search, in varying degrees of intensity.

"You understand how desperate that search was when Jim was so sick. You understand, too, how profound the disappointment has been, how deep the anguish, since he died. The pain has so engulfed me that I can find no escape. It took on huge proportions because it is two-fold, involving not only the loss of that one who has been so dear to me, but also the seeming loss of Your presence; and beyond all else, the confusion of wondering why we could not connect with You for Your touch.

"Miracles belong only to You; yet Your Word, at times, implicates Your followers' relationship with You.

"That immediately puts me in a hot spot. I must not have been living '*vitally connected*' to You; I must have come short of having the kind of faith in You which opens the way for Your Spirit to do Your healing work. I do not like being disconnected from You! Is it because I had not been drawing as close to You as You wanted me to? Yet,

> "*Can a man by searching find out God?*" Job 11:7

> '*Who shall ascend into heaven (that is, to bring Christ down from above) ...for <u>with the heart</u> man <u>believeth</u> unto righteousness...*"Romans 10:6,10

"We can earn nothing; I can only come "*just as I am,*" on the basis of Your finished work. Any closeness to You is a work of Your grace, yet You do require us to seek Your face. Was it my fault? I fear to come short of Your expectations of me! Forgive me; please cleanse me of anything that stands in the way of Your desire to work. Yet, at best, until you accomplish Your full redemptive work at the day of Your coming, can I ever measure up by any amount of searching?

"Father, am I angry with You? Am I? That is a frightening thought, but I absolutely must know the Truth—as *You* see it. Help me not to be too afraid to face whatever You show me.

"*Why* are You silent?

> "*How long will You forget me, O Lord? For ever? How long will You hide Your face from me? How long must I lay up cares within me, and have sorrow in my heart day after day? How long shall my enemy exalt himself over me? Consider and answer me, O Lord my God; lighten the eyes of my faith to behold Your face in the pitch-like darkness, lest I sleep the sleep of death; lest my enemy say, I have prevailed over him, and those that trouble me rejoice when I am shaken...*" Psalm 13:1-4

"Father, come to me. Answer me; show me Your face again—bring me to the triumph David anticipated in the last part of that Psalm. I long for You with all that is within me; my soul cries out for Your face in this darkness. Please, come near again and assure me of your love; grant me Your peace. Speak to me. Give me understanding of Your ways!

"No glimmer of understanding yet. Should I recap some of my inner journey, hoping that, once in motion, You will highlight something?

"Teaching from long ago stays with me: My ideas and reasoning must bow to The Book, not vice versa. In it, You portray Yourself as totally righteous, pure, loving, all-powerful, unchanging, faithful. You both describe and demonstrate that You honor Your Word even above Your name, that Your Word has within it the inherent power of its own fulfillment—Your very Self.

"You have said that as long as heaven and earth remain, not the least fragment of Your Word shall ever pass away or fail. You never take back what You say. You send Your Word to accomplish Your will, and state clearly that Your Word will never return to You empty, but will accomplish what You send it to do. What You say is what You intend. You cannot deny Yourself!

"You have said,

> "*Let God be true, and every man a liar.*" Romans 3:4

"No matter what my natural mind may want to think, no matter how I may want to ratify my own ideas or exalt them above what You have said, I must acknowledge Your Word as true, and allow my own to fall to the ground if there is a divergence between the two.

"Father, why could we not find You when Jim was sick? I want to know how *You* see the whole picture. It is very easy to see a lot of weaknesses in ourselves. We did not know how to exercise 'the authority of the believer,' as some teach. We may, as Tozer wrote, have mistaken our 'mental assent' for real faith, all the while being deficient in true faith. We may not have known how to approach You; so many possibilities.

"Yet, when I turn back to The Book, it is again apparent that it didn't seem to matter how people approached You, only that they did. I have checked and re-checked; Jesus never turned anyone away empty. No one! Over and over again the Record tells that He healed "*all that came to Him.*" He healed all manner of sickness and disease among the people—including those who were maimed. He even raised the dead. Many times He didn't even wait for the sick one to ask; He just volunteered His healing touch out of the depths of His own compassion. And Your Word clearly states that You never change. You are always, forever, consistently the same.

"Was there something within us that blocked You? Something we did not understand? You paid a dreadful price to provide healing as well as forgiveness, and You link both of those deep needs many times in

Your Book. What is missing, Lord? What do You want me to learn? I feel totally bewildered by all of this.

"Your promises, the promises of an almighty God, are recorded in rich profusion in The Book. My heart yearns, *aches* with longing to enter into them and find You there, but it seems as if there is a great chasm between promise and answer, between longing and fulfillment. Why? What is missing, Lord?

"You have followed my search; You know the 'answers' that have come which seem to put a '*Yea, hath God said?*' addendum to Your written Word. Am I not supposed to take what You said just as You said it? Am I too naïve? Lord, I feel abandoned. Please reveal Yourself to me! Have I followed a wrong path? Is all that I have believed about You untrue, unreal? Jesus, You said that You are The Truth—as well as The Way. I need You. Where can I find You? Please, come to me in a way I can understand and recognize. I need You, *Yourself!* Please, find me!

"There is one word in Matthew 10:29: '*leave,*' or permission. Speaking of two little sparrows, Jesus said that, inexpensive as they were, not one of them would fall to the ground without our Father's permission. I suppose, from that, I must face the thought that You gave permission for Jim to be taken.

"In spite of Your promises?

"Because I did not know how to touch You?

"Or—this is *so* hard—because You have some eternal purpose to bring about through this defeat? Oh, that leaves me feeling *so cold*. Help me!

"If only I could know for sure that You were actively involved in the choice regarding Jim's Home-going—that it was not a matter of You not being there, of us being abandoned, or of You withholding Your touch—perhaps, then, I could begin to accept it.

"Back again. Jesus, when Thomas was in one of those questioning moods, You told him to believe that You are in the Father and the Father is in You,

> "*...or else believe Me for the sake of the very works themselves. If you cannot trust Me, at least let these works that I do in My Father's name convince You.*" John 14:11

"If Your own disciples were to be convinced by the works You did, how much more do we, who have never seen You with our natural eyes, need that kind of convincing? How can it be wrong to want to experience Your intervention?

105

"You did say that Sodom would have repented if the people had seen miraculous evidence of the truth. The early church prayed earnestly that Your Spirit would work with them,

"*...confirming the Word with signs following...*" Mark 16:20

"...so that people would believe and come to saving faith in You. That being the case, surely You, too, would want Your church today to have that living faith that experiences the miraculous, both to strengthen Your own and to convince others to turn to You.

"Jesus, in that last heart-to-heart talk with Your disciples You urged them six times to ask the Father in Your name, saying that You Yourself, or the Father, would grant whatever they asked so that the Father would be glorified through the Son, and so that their joy might be complete. In those six times, the only requirement You gave was that they ask in Your name ("as presenting all that You Are"), and that they live in You and Your Words continue to live in their hearts. It looks so straightforward in The Book! Is there some hidden meaning, some unseen level of insight that You require? If so, how are we to find it? Oh, what is that gap between Your Words and their fulfillment—and how is it bridged?

"There seems to be an unacknowledged consensus of opinion these days that all of these things are a beautiful unreality to which we give lip-service, but cannot really expect to experience. That just cannot be Your will. Father, please show me Your Truth, Your Way. If, indeed, Your Word is Truth, it must be alive, and have within it the inherent power to effect what You promise. Let it be so, in me!

"I wish I could cut right to the heart of this confusion.

"Back to the thought of Your 'permissive will,' as some speak of it: Lord, I think that if I were sure that was the case in Jim's death, and that You had a definite purpose in allowing it, I could begin to accept it—and look for your purpose in leaving me here, alone. The fact is, there seems to be a dreadful dearth of Your active working among Your people; a thick, deep blanket of disbelief—and satisfaction in it—which is deeply disturbing. To be honest, I must include myself, for I, too, was unable to reach You.

"The overall situation seems to mirror what You said about the Church of Laodicea: a general luke-warmness—'*neither cold nor hot...*'

"*You say to yourself , We are rich, we have prospered and grown wealthy, and are in need of nothing, and do not realize and understand that you are wretched, pitiable, poor, blind and naked.*" Revelation 3:17

"Advice... You gave advice to the churches after your analyses! What did You say to this one?

"Therefore I counsel you to purchase from me gold refined and tested by fire, that you may be (truly) wealthy, and white clothes to clothe you and to keep the shame of your nudity from being seen, and salve to put on your eyes that You may see. Those whom I (dearly and tenderly) love, I tell their faults and convict and convince and reprove and chasten (that is,) I discipline and instruct them.

So be enthusiastic and in earnest and burning with zeal and repent, changing your mind and attitude... Behold I stand at the door and knock; if any one hears and listens to and heeds my voice and opens the door, I will come in to him and will eat with him and he (shall eat) with me. He who overcomes (is victorious) I will grant to sit beside Me on My throne, as I Myself overcame (was victorious) and sat down beside My Father on His throne. He who is able to hear, let him listen to and heed what the (Holy) Spirit says to the churches." Revelation 3:18-22

"What can I take from this?

"For one thing, Jesus clearly categorized this state of mind as sin: '*repent!*' Let my heart bow before Him, deploring this state of mind and heart.

"How can I 'buy' anything from You? In buying, there is exchange, one value for another. All I have to offer you is myself, my will. Is there something about so putting myself into Your hands for the refining process that what You do in me through the fires becomes truly valuable to You? 'Gold, refined and tested by fire' sounds like value gained by paying a big price—in suffering.

"'*White clothes to cover shame...*' In the surrender, the robe of Christ's righteousness covers us. Our only covering must be Your forgiveness, Your grace.

"'*Salve to gain sight...*' does sight—understanding—too, come only by going through this process?

"'*Purchase from Me...*' How do I find You, and what could I pay You, other than being willing to go through the fires of suffering to find You?

"You say that it is those you love whom you call to reality, urging earnest turning back to You and repentance for having drifted from oneness with You. You said you would come in when the heart's door is opened.

"I long so much to 'see,' to be clothed by You, to receive value from You. Please, set me straight, teach me; show me how to yield to You, to change where You seek change in me. Let me hear you knocking and open all of my heart to You. Come in, take what is mine, and give me what is Yours! If You have use for me, I am in Your hands.

"How little I really understand...

"If all of this trial has been to reveal our crying need of You—a need we have not wanted to see—use it for that. Yet we are so small, so insignificant in the huge scheme of things; how can our pain, our defeat, make any difference in the world at large, or even come to the notice of anyone who could begin to do anything about it?

"Father, I still do not see even my own heart. Am I angry with You? All I can find within is a loud cry from the depths of my spirit after You, a profound yearning for You, a longing to see Your face in this pitch-like darkness of my soul. I long, oh how deeply I long to really know You, to see You clearly, to walk with You! How can I find You? Please, come to me in a way I can understand and recognize.

"*I need You.* Please, find me!"

13

BREAKS IN THE FOG

Last night was a rather sleepless one, but the inner disturbance was one of joy. Over and over again through my mind and heart came that phrase from the Amplified: *"matchless, unbroken companionship..."*

When one has ever known intimate, ongoing communion with God wherein one worships with the whole being, any break in that relationship is bound to be an intolerable agony. That has been what has disturbed me for all this time. Perhaps it was only my perception—that sense of abandonment—brought on by the bewilderment? By the questions? I do not yet understand. The Amplified version of Col. 1: 9, 10b records Paul's prayer:

> *"...that you may be filled with the full (deep and clear) knowledge of His will in all spiritual wisdom (that is, in comprehensive insight into the ways and purposes of God) and in understanding and discernment of spiritual things growing and increasing in (and by) the knowledge of God, with fuller, deeper and clearer insight, acquaintance and recognition..."*

May that continue, and increase! The other part of the night's on-going thought was 1 Peter 1: 8:

> *"Without having seen Him you love Him: though you do not even now see Him, you believe in Him, and exult and thrill with inexpressible and glorious, triumphant, heavenly joy."*

That's life! Intimate love-relationship with Him is the center of being really alive. That's what I have been missing, what my heart cries after.

> There's healing in no other touch,
> Joy in no other Name,
> Love with no other heart but Yours,
> Life, only as You reign.

Thinking back over this past couple of years, I realize that abandonment, confusion and a sense of rejection seem to surface with some regularity. Is there significance in this?

Two years today, as of 7:20 p.m. How meaningless it all seems. How deep the pain! The worst part of the agony is the feeling that the very foundations of my faith seem to have given way. How awful to have questions about the veracity of Scripture! David was inspired to write,

> " Bless the Lord, O my soul, Who forgives (every one of) all your iniquities, Who heals (each of) all your diseases Who redeems... beautifies... dignifies... crowns... satisfies your mouth (your necessity and desire at your personal age) with good; so that your youth, renewed, is like the eagle's (strong, overcoming, soaring)"
> Psalm 103:3...

Such words! Were they God-inspired reality? Or just—sweet sentiment? If *"heals each of all your diseases"* cannot be counted on, can *"forgives every one of all your iniquities"* stand?

I may be very dense, but it seems that if the God of Heaven is behind His Words, He must be behind all of them, consistently, for all time. If we allow ourselves to weaken with regard to any of the promises, they must all go down together.

How do I dare to think like that? Yet, what else am I to think? I am so afraid that I have become a castaway. Please, forgive me if that is possible...! Are You really there, God? Oh, if You are not all that The Book portrays You to be—there is nothing else. Please, come to me, hold me, reveal Yourself to me!

The early church:

> "...lifted up their voices together with one united mind to God and said, '...grant to Your bondservants (full freedom) to declare fearlessly, while you stretch out Your hand to cure and perform signs and wonders through the authority and by the power of Your holy Child and Servant Jesus.'" Acts 4:24–30

...and He worked with them, confirming the Word with signs following. He does not change; His longing to work among His own does not change.

LETTER TO GOD—p.s.

"Father, is there hidden anger in that letter? I don't want to pretend anything with You. What might indicate hidden anger? I suppose that any time a person is saying 'Why?' there is something going on that is not in agreement, that is questioning. Angry?

"There have been those two unutterably dark periods in my life. Two enormous, immeasurable 'whys' that all but destroyed me. The first, childlessness. Even as I touch that area today, the pain radiates beyond my horizons—deep, black. You could have stopped the happening that made it so, as you did Abraham. You could have reversed it. You could have restored, healed, blessed—with the natural ability experienced by so many to share with You the miracle of creating new life.

"But You were silent. Your silence hurt, Father. Oh, how it hurt! You watched my pain, 'if You were there,' and waited. Waited until we went that other route and took into our broken hearts, one by one, the little treasures who needed our love. What joy You gave us in loving them! Perhaps because of the anguish of childlessness we had known, we loved them more than we could ever have loved them had they come any other way. I have learned that You had real purpose for that pain...

"The most devastating anguish I have ever experienced was the death of the one You brought into my life, the one with whom I shared most of it—the one who taught me what little I know of being a whole person. Why did you allow him to be taken away? Why did you let him be tormented to death by that hellish cancer, if he had to go? Why, oh why were you silent when we cried out to You with all that was within us for your healing touch? You could so easily have heard from Heaven and totally reversed that hellish killer—but You remained silent; You did not come to us in that time of dreadful need. Why, Father? Are you really there? Do You see the tears? Do You care?

"What am I to do with Scriptures like Psalm 147:11:

> *"The Lord takes pleasure in those who fear Him, in those who hope in Your mercy."*

"The Book is filled with statements like that. What do they mean for those who cry out to You for Your mercy in their extremity—and find none? Oh, Father, are You really there? Are You really all Your Word portrays You to be? How can I find You? What on earth am I supposed to do when I cannot find You in the darkness?

"I suppose, if I am to go by what I have been taught, I, myself, must have put some barrier between us; if that is the case, how am I to know what it is, and what can I do about it?

"This kind of expression frightens me, for if I put myself outside of You by my questioning...

"Help me—if You have not already given up on me!"

"If You are not real, then life is only empty nothingness. If You are there but we cannot find You, what are we to do? Surely You are there, and, having paid the price You did to restore Your human creation, You must want to manifest Yourself in meeting our needs? So—how does that come about?

"I think that what frightens me most is the thought that I may have become lost from You. Where do these awful questions put me? Father, will You search for this lost sheep? I cannot bear being away from You!

"This frightening 'lost-ness' that seems to engulf me so much of the time—how I wish I could find my way out of it. Yet there are times, like this morning...

"A man from Iran was sharing his testimony of finding You. When he told of the life-change that came to him, particularly when he spoke about being filled with Your Spirit, from deep within my soul there came a surge of great, triumphant joy, like cheering when the home team wins. How can this happen, when I feel so lost? Lord, what is going on here? Please teach me.

"Perhaps, most of all, I need to say to You, purge me with whatever pain You see I need, to be shaped for whatever You want me to do—and bring me out of the shadows when You see fit."

After one discussion with my friend and mentor, I came away knowing he had said something extremely important, something that struck a deep chord within—which I had not been able to remember. I wrote:

> "You really 'hit the nail on the head' during our conversation yesterday. Do you remember me agreeing with you, saying, 'That's what I want!'? What you said so closely matched what was going on inside that—it disappeared into the Rx fog! I'm ashamed to admit it, but it's so. If you remember, and have the time, would you jog my foggy brain? I need to think about it.
>
> Thank you for being where God put you, and for being His instrument in my life. Your being there is one sure indication I have that God has not altogether abandoned me. I am grateful."

Today his answer arrived:

> "The heart-cry you allude to when you said, 'That's what I want' had to do with being so willing and available that we would be guaranteed to get our marching orders on a daily basis if not an hourly basis. Once we live past fear and part of us has died and we are willing to live close on the edge, life becomes very exciting and things start to

happen that we never dreamed of, because we are actually ready, willing, and available to respond to specific direction, having laid aside our own personal pain, our own personal agendas, our own personal pleasures, and our own personal distractions. If we really commit to living life on the edge, we will never be satisfied with anything less again.

God bless you in your healing."

I hope he has written a book!

I do know that, in the search for God, my heart must be fully open and honest before Him.

Since *"these signs shall follow those who believe,"* there has, obviously, been something lacking in the faith department. *"Lord, help my unbelief!"* I remember some years ago being struck with the fact that Jesus *"upbraided His disciples with their unbelief and hardness of heart."* (He linked them together!) Nothing has a worse sting than the realization that, after all this time, the faith level is so low, so ineffectual. And perhaps for that, I lost the one dearest to me!

There has come a startling thought. When my heart was crying out, *"Why are You so far from helping me?"* there came with it a nudge to look it up. I found the reference in Psalm 22:1. It was with some shock that I read what came immediately before the words I had looked up; it was the cry that Jesus uttered from the cross in *His* anguish of abandonment: *"My God, My God, why have You forsaken Me?"* ! Even Jesus went through inner darkness and dismay—and *expressed it!*

That discovery came after certain words from the songs had begun to stand out and stick like burrs: "One like to the Son of God will set my feet where His have trod." He asked us to follow Him; there was no guarantee that we could avoid all of the shadows He walked through. Is this dark night of the soul part of finding God's plan for my life?

Other phrases from the songs followed:

> "a calling out of all that is within"
> "all that's within me, Your will would do"
> "through all the days, Lord, I would be true
> "...one with Your purpose, Your loving plan"
> – jbl

More and more I realize that something within is holding back—unyielded. I have been unwilling to give up my Jim.

I do not want to remain that way. With all my heart, I want to place myself totally in His hands, one with His purpose. Yet I seem to be unable to get there; I don't know how. Father, grant the grace of Your Spirit to bring me where You want me to be!

I didn't take my pain meds last night, because I didn't want to be dull today. Result: not much sleep. However, the inner search continues, as always.

It has been my habit for some years to reach out to Him without words, simply exposing my soul and wholly lifting it from the depths of my spirit, knowing that He understood even the thoughts of the heart.

As I lay down last night I kept thinking of all these things. Sometime in those dark hours it occurred to me that perhaps I should take a little more initiative in my communion with God, actually verbalizing those depths, my spirit in union with His—praying in the Spirit. This I did, not knowing specifically what I was lifting to Him, but aware that I was giving myself to Him for His purpose. Love and worship began to flow as it used to. It was beautiful. I was too stirred to sleep much, so got up early to try to capture what was going on. It was absolutely precious the way the Scriptures opened up regarding Jesus, the Word. The touch brought joy and hope to my distraught spirit.

The meditation:

MIRACLES – *WHO NEEDS THEM?*

I do. In fact, I would not be here if it were not for that initial miracle that gave me life. Miracles abound. They surround us on every side, poured out in such abundance that we take them for granted all the time. The entire creation is the result of miracles—miracles that sprang into being by only the Word of the living God. That same Word upholds the works of His hands.

Jesus, Himself, is that expression of our Father, the One Who portrays the heart of God in His works of creation and upholding of all things, but also in His works of love—His miracles of intervention, healing, restoration. He is that living, Powerful *Word*.

What a Word!

> *"In the beginning, before all time, was the Word (Christ), and the Word was with God, and the Word was God. He was present originally with God. All things were made and came into existence through Him; and without Him was not even one thing made that has come into being. In Him was Life, and the Life was the Light of men."* John 1:1-3

> *"In many separate revelations, each of which set forth a portion of the Truth—and in different ways, God spoke of old to our forefathers by the prophets, but in the last of these days He has spoken to us in the*

person of a Son, Whom He appointed Heir and lawful Owner of all things, also by and through Whom He created the worlds and the reaches of space and the ages of time, (that is,) He made, produced, built, operated and arranged them in order.

He is the sole expression of the glory of God, the Light-being, the out-raying of the divine, and He is the perfect imprint and very image of God's nature, upholding and maintaining and guiding and propelling the universe by His mighty word of power.

"When He had, by offering Himself, accomplished our cleansing of sins and riddance of guilt, He sat down at the right hand of the divine Majesty on high, taking a place and rank by which He Himself became as much superior to angels as the glorious Name (title) which He has inherited is different from and more excellent than theirs." Hebrews 1:1–4

The Living Word. The Word from Whom emanates the throbbing, pulsing Light and Love of God Himself. How alive He is! Oh, to know Him! To really, fully enter into unrestricted relationship with such a One as He, indwelt by Him, and dwelling in Him; walking, living, moving in full harmony with that One Who reigns above all others, that lowly yet exalted One Who is Love and Gentleness and Power beyond our ability to comprehend: what vibrant, vital 'alive-ness'!

"A seeking heart, a heart that yearns to know Thee,
A calling out of all that is within!
A dearth, a thirst, a burning cry for mercy,
Oh, send upon us Heav'ns refreshing rain!

Open now the wideness of Thy mercy!
Open Thou the windows of my soul!
Oh, send the sweet refreshing of Your Spirit—
That heav'nly breath that makes the spirit whole!"
– jbl

Who needs miracles? I do. All of those who belong to the Omnipotent One need Him manifest among them; He is their Bread, their Breath, their Life.

Miracles? His own need them. When Philip wanted to see the Father, Jesus told him to believe that He, the Son, was one with the Father, or *"believe Me for the sake of the miracles themselves."* His own children need such assurance. Jesus also said that healing was *"the children's bread."* Jesus told His disciples to *"ask—that [their] joy might be full"*! Needed, for *"the joy of the Lord is your strength."*

Miracles. Those who have not known Him need them, too. The early church prayed fervently until the house was shaken and they were all filled with the Holy Spirit. They sought the face of God for courage to

115

proclaim the Truth, and asked Him to *confirm* the spoken word with signs following so that many would be convinced and turn to God.

Jesus went about teaching, preaching and healing the sick. There were reasons for the miracles: for Himself, they were expression of His deep compassion; for suffering humanity, relief; for the unbelieving, convincing proof of the living Truth of His message. Jesus said that the ancient cities of Tyre, Sidon and Sodom would have remained to this day *if* they had seen evidence—miracles—as performed in His ministry.

Father, I need You. I need the reality of Your Living Word strong in my soul. Touch me with Your Life. Close the gap, Father; ***come!***

Small steps, good ones.
- more of asking the Lord, Himself
- the lift from my friend's words
- the surge of joy at the testimony of the Iranian doctor/pastor—full, triumphant and alive—*real.*
- the hope that another is seeing the current need
- the rather sleepless night, the renewed joy
- always, the continued reaching, reaching out to God.
- the way He opened His Word just yesterday

And today, all day, the dear, familiar rising of love and worship from my spirit to Him Whom my soul loves.

The breakthrough?

To go over very carefully what has been happening:

From the beginning of this ordeal, my spirit has been crying out to God, a God I could not seem to find. The loss of that close, intimate fellowship was traumatic—as traumatic, if not more so, than the loss of my beloved Jim. It has been a terrifying, unrelenting torment beyond endurance. What painful, all-engulfing questions there have been!

One thing became clear very early on; God Himself put into my life a friend who has been His minister to me through this most difficult time of my life. No matter how hard or complicated things became, it was easy to recognize that provision from the very hand of God. I am more grateful than I could ever say for that one constant, precious reassurance—the friend and mentor placed by God.

A rather profound thought that came from that one early in the journey and has stayed with me all along: it is possible that God has something He wants me to do for Him that could only be brought about in this way. Not an easy thought, yet one which presented some possibility that there might at least be *purpose* in this pain.

As mentioned earlier, a couple of weeks ago that friend began to paint a word-picture of a possible walk with God wherein a person could so blend with the Spirit of God as to be directly led of Him in details of service; that one could literally be His messenger—His hands—to minister to those crying out for Him. I have read and re-read those words many times; they have acted like an off-shore breeze that began to break up the fog.

Then came the surge of joy while hearing the testimony—full, triumphant and alive, *real*—the living, flowing fullness which I have known through most of my life; the discussion with my friend, the conversation with the study leader, the rather sleepless night, the renewed joy! And always, the continued reaching, reaching out to God.

Is this the key— for love's sake, yielding to Love?

14

"MAP CHECK"

I think that each step of the journey has been necessary to bring me to this point; it is not something I could have simply achieved by mental gymnastics at the beginning. Will there be more steps, more twists and turns before He opens up the path He has planned? May He help me walk close to Him, discover his purpose, and fulfill it!

For the last few days, since that touch from God about a week ago, I seem to be on a sort of inner plateau; perhaps a step in the recovery process. Or a resting place before another battle? I wish I had a clearer head; pain meds still dull me somewhat, though I have dropped one of them. Maybe I have been dodging the full impact of the issue by picking up a craft again; tatting keeps my fingers busy while watching some TV programs. I think that the craft provides me with at least one facet of my life where I can *make* things come out right. As such, it is a welcome contrast to the inner confusion with which I seem to struggle in vain for that kind of outcome.

FOG BREAK-UP ?

For most of my life I have reveled in two deep loves: my God and my Jim. In that order.

Both Jim and I earnestly looked for God's intervention in his illness; the Lord's promises are explicit, strong, multiple, and part of the Redemption paid out at Calvary. When we failed to find God in this matter and Jim was taken, I felt as if both loves had been ripped from me.

What painful, all-engulfing questions there have been!

From the beginning of this ordeal, my spirit has been crying out to God, a God I could not seem to find. The loss of that close, intimate fellowship was traumatic—as traumatic, if not more so, than the loss of

118

my beloved Jim. It has been a terrifying, unrelenting torment beyond endurance.

I wrote earlier of His intervention rather soon after Jim's death, when an escalating horror threatened to swallow me altogether when I was struck by the thought that my dislike of a TV program might have made Jim miss a chance at a miracle. In the midst of the tumult came those firm, quiet words to the depths of my spirit which absolutely stilled the storm. Peace!

That storm stopped, and has not returned. For the few moments when He would not let me go down in that tempest, I knew He was still there; then the fog closed in again. Throughout the two years since that time, in a way that surprised me with joy, there came an occasional spontaneous lift of loving worship from somewhere deep within, but most of the time the fog-bank remained constant, a deeply troubling heaviness rife with bewilderment and pain. Each time this lift of the spirit happened, I grasped at some hope that He had not abandoned me.

As I set down my thoughts I remain convinced that as far as our Father is concerned, His healing mercies are openly available to His children—and to others—due to the redemptive work of the Savior.

I feel sure that God wants the mercies purchased at Calvary to flow freely; why else would He have paid such a price? I do not know what hinders the flow of this mercy. Our disbelief? Our distance from Him in our deepest hearts? Are we too satisfied with just enough of God to "get by"? Somehow I think He wants to correct the situation, whatever the causes may be. If the loss of my dearest one is even one small key He can use to stir up His own, then the pain will not be wasted. God, grant a deep thirst in the hearts of your children which will call out to You until You can open the floodgates of Your glory.

I am not alone in this heart-cry; some with whom I have corresponded have also begun to sense the current luke-warmness and long for the fire of God.

I once made reference to Nipawin, and the way the road through the bush just cut off, dropping away into nothingness. That is such an apt picture of what seems to have happened in my life-journey; life as I knew it just—cut off! As I mentioned before, from the geographic cut-off we could just turn around and go back the way we came, but in the journey of life there is no way to go back. When Jim died, I was left with no path to follow, no place to go, no way to move. Then came that precious paragraph from my friend, and things seemed to begin to come together, shaping into the possibility of a new "road."

I have been wondering what next step to take, if there is one. If only I could be fully assured again of my God, of His being there for me—and understand why His promises seemed to fall to the ground—I would love to fully give myself over to Him, to walk with Him like that.

Having set that down, something about the statement does not look right. Perhaps the order needs to be reversed; maybe the full assurance awaits fully giving myself to Him?

I still have the one great love of my life: my Lord. I don't want to feel lost from Him any longer. I want to get back into that life of overflowing joy in His presence.

Marking time. The on-going fatigue: part of the fog-bank, no doubt. I wish I could really feel alive again. Whatever will it take? Will healing ever come?

Heaviness again. I think part of it is physical. I hope that part can be reversed, for feeling like this is not great. I don't have the understanding to be sure, but I think that I am still emotionally wounded or scarred, or part of both; and though at times I do sense the Lord's nearness, I am somewhat disoriented spiritually. Is it a matter of applying more effort in reaching out to Him, or of waiting for Him to reach me? How I would love to consistently soar again with His unspeakable joy!

Help me find Your Way for me, Father.

15

PARABLES

A few weeks ago, the Canadian Edition of the 700 Club told of a woman overseas whose husband died and had already been embalmed for burial when she recalled Scripture telling that women received their loved ones back from the dead.

A man of God was holding meetings in the town. Laying hold of that Scripture, she had her husband's body taken to the lower auditorium of the building where the meetings were being held. There, some of the elders of the church began to pray over him. Realizing that the man had not moved for some time, they also began to massage his limbs as they prayed. He came back to life and is now serving the Lord, together with his wife.

This morning on *100 Huntley Street*, the Bible account of Dorcas being raised from death under Peter's ministry, and two other similar, present-day accounts were given. In one story, a Christian was going past a hospital when he saw a Muslim couple coming out of the building with their dead child. He asked if he could go with them to their home, where he prayed for two hours—and the child's life came again.

In the other incident somewhere in the States, a minister was returning from a Southern Baptist conference when his vehicle was involved in a severe accident, and since they could find neither pulse nor respiration, Emergency Medical personnel pronounced the man dead. A minister friend passed that way a short time later. Though he was waved away by the medics who were trying to retrieve the body with the jaws of life, the friend found a way into the car through the trunk area, got to where his friend lay covered as for dead, laid his hands on him and began to pray, then to sing "What a Friend we have in Jesus." A short time later, Don Piper joined in the singing! His pulse had returned. (I have since heard both of these men speak of this experience.)

These stories clearly underlined to me my own abysmal lack of faith. How well I understand the Scripture in which Jesus "upbraided the disciples *with* their unbelief and hardness of heart"! Realizing the deplorably low level of one's faith in a God one loves is deeply painful.

The other matter, too, of being unwilling to let go of Jim, troubles me. What a mess! And after belonging to Him all these years... I admit to my shortfall, Father; all I can do is be honest about it and put the broken pieces into Your hands. I can change neither the failures of the past nor the loss incurred, perhaps because of them. What a price to pay! Having faced these failings full on and openly before You, much of the storm seems to have settled out of them. Thank You!

16

STEPS IN SUNLIGHT

A few days ago something changed. Perhaps the change has been coming for some time; I trust that it will continue to strengthen and grow. Tears have never been too far away for a long time now, primarily from my desperate grief most of the time, but increasingly when stirred deeply upon hearing of wonderful things God has been accomplishing in the hearts of people. This entire grief experience has, I think done more of that "hollowing out" in my heart that the childlessness had done so many years ago. There has most certainly been an emptying-out process: costly, painful, deep. What if, as time goes on, His handiwork for good begins to show—something for which He may have wanted to shape me? I have asked Him for that.

A little earlier I wrote of an experience during a sleepless night in which I felt a nudge to verbalize the on-going deep yearning of my heart after Him. For many years my preferred manner of praying has been just to continuously allow my spirit to rise to Him past my understanding, expressing the inexpressible without utterance—just a deep yearning—which I knew He read perfectly. This seems so much more intimate than everyday speech which falls so very far short of fully expressing the deep longings of the heart. It is perfectly natural to lift concerns and worship from the depths of the spirit either in yearning, or in everyday speech; perfectly natural, also, to lift them with the Spirit as He prompts. Beautifully natural.

A couple of days ago, this really opened up again for me, most profoundly and deeply. By far, the most important factor in life for me has been the touch of God. Living in union with Him is the most profound experience a person can ever have. The seeming break in that union since Jim's death has been the most excruciating part of my pain; there are no words to begin to describe it. To sense His beautiful presence so clearly again that day was delightful.

Throughout the day following that touch of the Spirit, there were very definite, gentle nudges to do certain things. Oh, how wonderful it would be to live always within the awareness of that warm circle of His will, knowing clearly—and following fully! Let it be so, my Father.

Among other lovely things which filled the day so richly, He gave me something to do which I have not done for a long time.

I am beginning to feel that the great God of Heaven wants to be much larger and greater within His children than we have even begun to imagine. He has so much He wants to do, so very much of His overflowing abundance that He wants to pour out upon His people and His earth—a profusion of His goodness, His grace, His immeasurable God-love. And we timidly offer Him thimbles, hoping that, just maybe, He will fill them at least half full with blessing for which we hardly dare to ask. Oh, Father, enlarge our hearts to understand Your own! His Plan is much, much larger than we can understand. A large machine cannot run on thimblefuls of fuel; large Plans can only be energized by large Glory.

Many years ago as my husband and I were waiting in His presence during another time of deep crisis, He spoke very clearly of His tremendous intent:

> "You come to Him desiring Him, but you insist on bringing something. You have nothing. He would give; He would give lavishly—would pour upon you with overflowing abundance which you cannot begin to imagine—but you will not come empty-handed. You insist on bringing something. The Lord is restrained from giving, because you will not come with nothing."

Some time later I came across these words from Dorothea Sitle which re-emphasize the thought:

> "If my hands are fully occupied in holding onto something, I can neither give nor receive."

No wonder Jesus told us that we need to come as little children...

Just yesterday, someone gave me an insight into the heart of God. With such joy, I gave that one a valuable gift—just because I loved, and because I absolutely knew that it was deeply, deeply needed. Though I appreciated the love for me on their part which made them hesitant to accept it, I felt an uneasy sense of grief at that hesitance in the face of my desire to give. The singing joy in my heart in making the gift needed the dear one's glad acceptance of both the gift and the love accompanying it to make my joy complete. I cannot but think that is a faint echo of how God feels toward His children.

Well, I had that one day that seemed to be just like my mentor's paragraph. How wonderful it would be to understand how to live like that always!

I had, as usual, been thinking a lot, and looking to the Lord a lot, particularly through wakeful periods in the night. When I got up, early, because sleep forsook me, I spent some time with my old Amplified Bible and just communed with God. As the Spirit rose within, I worshiped Him from the deepest depths of my spirit in the language He gave. How beautifully close He draws at such times! It did seem as if the "river-bed" widened during that communion. Then throughout the day I just knew what to do, one thing after another. It was absolutely precious! How wonderful it would be to live like that, always.

Sometimes, when God has met us as we have reached for Him in a certain way, there is a human tendency to feel that if we approach Him again in the same way we will have the same results. Yet I have lived long enough to have experienced that there is no profit in "copying a method" of working with God. If one tries that, it quickly becomes dead routine. It is best to simply be open and sensitive to His Spirit. He always chooses something different; that way He is the Initiator, and the communion is always fresh and new. The main thing is to deliberately draw near.

Lord, help me to follow you, always, in every detail of my life.

My physician gave me a medical slant on the confusion I have been living with. He tells me that pain is subjective: not obvious except within a person. When a patient is suffering great pain, any decision he makes will not stand up in a court of law, simply because the suffering affects perception. At the same time, if medications are given to counteract the pain, they also affect perception and can render void any decisions a person makes under those circumstances. Interesting...

I guess all of this effort to sort issues is having at least some effect on me. In the Bible study a few of us held Tuesday evening there had been a discussion about Mary and Martha, comparing their ways of entertaining Jesus. It came through so clearly that they both loved Jesus. Yet Mary sat at His feet taking into her heart every Word that He spoke, while Martha set about trying to *do* something for Him—and getting overburdened and stressed out in the process.

Mary could not get enough of Jesus, Himself.

Martha wanted to express her love by serving Him. While that is one of the ways love is expressed, it caused her to divert her attention from Jesus to her work for Him. Common? Yes, ever since Cain brought the results of his labor as an offering. Jesus, loving her, told her that she was *"cumbered about with many things,"* that *"one thing is needful,"* and that it is a matter of choice: *"Mary has chosen the better part."* Intimate relationship with Him is the first priority, the benefit of which remains forever: *"...it shall not be taken away from her."*

I couldn't help thinking of a missionary I knew. When he gave himself to the Lord for the work laid on his heart, he determined that his main ministry would be that of prayer, and anything that followed out of that would be secondary. At his funeral the family showed a picture of him which said more than a thousand words: face and hands wrinkled with age, that man of God in an attitude of prayer—so very obviously "at home" in the Presence.

At the next Bible study the person in charge went back to the subject, this time presenting the thoughts of a writer who felt that Mary and Martha would both have been better off if they shared each other's attitudes. That shocked me. Without thinking, I blurted out, "But that's not what Jesus said!" I'm afraid I surprised folks, myself included. But the leader thanked me.

Just yesterday during a Christian program an aged theologian, referring to the current debate about same-sex unions, said that the discrepancy in views could basically be described as choosing between looking at the Scriptures through the lens of the culture, or looking at the culture through the lens of the Scriptures. Aptly put! That also pretty well sums up my dilemma heretofore. There is a strong tendency, in this day of intellectualism and higher learning, to look at Scripture through the lens of our experience rather than view our experience through the lens of Scripture. Lord, set our thinking straight! Let the light from Your Spirit show us where we have departed from Your Truth, and bring us home.

With reference to this journey, what still stands out most clearly in my mind is the recurring memory of an early comment made by my mentor that, just maybe, God had something in mind for me to do which could only be done in this set of circumstances...

Long, long ago, I pressed into nail-pierced Hands a diamond that had been intended for me. At this point in my life, I begin to see that I must press into those same hands a *most* costly gift—my earthly love. Jesus, please show me, lead me into that full release into Your hands of all that is dear to me, and all that I am.

17

"WHEN . . ."

I have been thinking about the two opposites: rejoicing and weeping. It is extremely difficult for people in one category to really empathize with those in the other. Those who rejoice cannot, at the same time, weep; those who weep cannot, at the same time, rejoice. It would be almost impossible for one from either group to really identify with one in the other. Yet Romans 12:15 urges that believers both rejoice with those that rejoice and weep with those that weep. If a caring person were personally at the same end of the spectrum, that might not be too hard; but for those caught in either extreme—what an inner conflict! Only God's own grace could make it possible.

Where am I now in this grief journey? Still very close to tears much of the time; still utterly bewildered at not being able to connect with God when we needed Him so much.

I know, I realize, that Jim is dead; my heart is, too, in large measure. While at times I sense the touch of the Spirit, there is still a huge, black emptiness engulfing most of my inner being. How real is this sense of His presence, if, when it counted most, Jim's illness was not destroyed according to Promises claimed, when all of our earnest calling upon our Father availed nothing? I want more than just a feeling; I want Living Reality. How *real* is all of this which I have taken to be real for so many decades? Have I been living an illusion? How am I to *know* what is real?

Lord, oh, my Lord, please don't leave me in this state. If You don't show me, Yourself, no one else will be able to do so. I have sought diligently of many. Being completely cut off from everyone—being so absolutely alone in it—is dreadful! The anguish is all-engulfing, intolerable. Please show me Truth, as You see it. Make me to *know!*

I am sure that I am not the only one wrestling with this confusion; how can I help those I love who also struggle in this way? Personally, all

I know to do is recognize the need to seek the answers in God. He is consistent; He works according to laws He has set in all of observable creation, including the law of the Spirit of Life in Christ Jesus. I want to understand that law so that I can work with Him in it; then, I am sure, He will work according to His eternal Word of Promise.

It seems that, though at times I have hope of brighter days, those times have not yet become established. I have often written about the conflict between the truths of God's Words and the facts of my circumstances. These contradictions are sometimes heightened to a strange and intolerable level.

One instance of this maelstrom is in the writing of the song, "When..." While at the organ, both of the seemingly opposite conditions warring in my heart surfaced: the anguish, the blackness, the despair on one hand, and on the other, the hope, the deep worship, the profound love toward the God I long to fully find again. It began with an expression of black depths of the agony of grief, proceeded to cry to the God of heaven for His help, then rose to soaring heights of ecstatic worship—which stayed with me through the entire process of determining melody, harmony and text. Sometimes a song can find expression for depths of the heart otherwise unfathomable:

WHEN...
When I cannot understand the way God leads me,
When my night is dark and sharp thorns pierce my feet,
When my soul is troubled deep and my heart fails me,
When the Lord I love I seem to vainly seek...
Then hear from Heaven, God of Ages,
From Your highest throne now hear my soul's deep cry!
For my heart is faint with longing for Your Spirit—
Hear from Heaven, Savior, do not pass me by!

When my Master comes to me o'er stormy waters,
When His voice I hear above the thunder's roar,
How my heart will leap with joy to know His coming,
Knowing He will bring me safely to the shore!
Oh, how I love You, precious Savior,
For You come to rescue even souls like me!
Love o'erwhelming floods my life with healing mercy
Flowing from Your riven side at Calvary.

Precious Savior, God of Ages,
How my trembling soul now worships at Your feet!
How I love You, my Redeemer!
Your sweet Presence fills my soul with joy replete!
How I revel in Your glory—
Flow on, oh Living Light, flow on through me!
God of Ages,
Lord of Love.

– jbl

Worship. There was something wonderfully releasing in that outpouring of love to the Lover of my soul... That euphoria lifted me to a beautiful plane of peace, even joy, which lasted for several days. Then it seemed to dissipate, leaving me once more in confusion and pain.

Worship. Confusion. They co-exist in this clay vessel. Always, I am torn two ways; sometimes there is more of one and less of the other, then it drifts the other way. Always, the large core of my being feels like a bomb crater: dark, void, pain-filled.

There are many factors in this package of pain; above all, the extreme *alone*-ness. For the most part, people avoid those in grief as instinctively as they avoid pain in any other way. Even those who care in a measure cannot, by the very nature of things, walk where I walk or step where I step, for it is a journey of the heart where each one walks alone. It is impossible for anyone else to feel with me exactly what I feel. And I cannot even seem to fully find my God! Is it any wonder that the pain runs deep?

Purpose. There is a suggestion of purpose: things to do, to finish. But must they be attempted, accomplished, in the crucible of pain? Could not the fires be lessened, if not extinguished, and the process continue with at least some semblance of peace? Where is the joy of the Lord, which is our strength?

Scripture reads that Jesus came to heal the broken-hearted. Please, find me!

Show me...

Can I find words to describe the turmoil?

Jim is dead. As is much of my heart! The pain of losing him is immeasurable because we truly loved each other. Being without him has also thrown me back into the world of extreme self-doubt which tormented me before he validated my personhood in his love.

My father always affirmed and encouraged me in his quiet, gentle way but, since he was the bread-winner, most of my time out of school was spent with my mother. She loved in her own way, but could never understand that my temperament was different from hers (more like my father's), and she often disciplined me—harshly, and always in anger. Besides that, in early religious enthusiasm, she cut off activities and associations which might have allowed for personal growth. Inwardly, I still empathize with the bound feet Chinese women used to experience. Only in my years with Jim did I begin to emerge from the inner prison and become a person.

Who am I, without him?

I have read that the grief journey is a series of lows and highs; I can verify that it is so. There are times when I think that I am finding a way out of the blackness; then those times fade—sometimes back into blackness, sometimes into numbness. And all of those opposing feelings keep churning within, each vying for supremacy. Then, confusion! One cannot go both right and left, or up and down, or backward and forward at the same time. I am like a frayed rope in a tug-of-war. How long can this go on before something snaps?

Often it occurs to me that my inner state is like the profound blackness of a deep, jagged pit; sometimes the sun shines, sometimes it is cloudy, and always, there is recurring night. Add to that, the turmoil...

I do not understand these ups and downs. I am rather sure that the grief is real; after all, Jim is gone. The times that I glimpse hope—when I experience what I used to feel was the touch of the Spirit—how real are they? Highs. Lows. Are both of these "feelings" nothing but physical chemical reactions? Manic? If this is a neurosis, how can it be resolved unless there is new understanding of the issues? Am I crazy? Yet how can it be irrational to weigh promise against lack of fulfillment? But that leads to questioning the ultimate reality of truth—in a personal God—and tremendous guilt in doing so.

If only I could be sure of God again! He is the one anchor I felt I had even before Jim came into my life. He *must* be; the intricacies and consistency of laws governing the universe allow for no other conclusion. But... personal? I have known times of supreme joy—ecstasy—when His Spirit welled up within and overflowed. That must be real. Yet, what am I to do with the fact that we could not find Him when Jim was sick? I seem to spend a lot of time at the bottom of that swimming pool. I want to know the Truth! It will absolutely destroy me if He is not real. Even the question is eating me up—with horror, and with guilt.

There must be something about His ways that I do not understand. I guess I want to come under Paul's prayer for the Ephesians:

> *"... that He may grant you a <u>spirit of wisdom and revelation</u>, of <u>insight</u> into mysteries and secrets, in the <u>deep and intimate knowledge of Him</u>, by having the eyes of your heart flooded with light, so that you can <u>know and understand</u> the hope to which He has called you and so that you can <u>know and understand</u> what is the immeasurable and unlimited and surpassing greatness of His power <u>in</u> and <u>for</u> us who believe, as <u>demonstrated</u> in the working of His mighty strength, which He exerted in Christ when He raised Him from the dead and seated Him at His own right hand in the heavenly places, far above all rule and authority and power and dominion and every name that is named, above every title that can be conferred, not only in this age and in this world, but also in the age and the world which is to come. And He has put all things under His feet..."* Ephesians 1:17b-22a

Oh that I knew where I might find Him!

There is continual change. Very shortly after I had written this I went online and almost immediately one of the children started instant messaging about a matter of concern, and I was able to help. While engaged in that, caller ID indicated that a neighbor was calling. When I returned the call later, the conversation turned to a spiritual issue, which I was able to address. That meant a lot to me. Purpose. There would be such fulfillment in that.

He is more real to me when He uses me, even a little.

18

OLD ROOTS TO PAIN?

The thought was presented to me that it is possible, in light of the constraints of my early years before marrying Jim, that I never had opportunity to "individuate," to find myself. That could very well be. Part of my struggle since his death has certainly been that of wondering who I am without him, of having to become a person in my own right at a rather late stage in life. And that is a *process* rather than an *event*. Ouch! Obviously, there can be no five-minute fix. It looks as if it will be a day-to-day, tiny-gains kind of thing. For the rest of my life? It does not look easy.

As to the "crazy" part of my concern? "Crazy in love with Jim!" I guess I can accept that.

It seems that my confusion and sense of unreality in some areas are bona fide evidence of deep grief—and my grief has been *most* traumatic. I watched my dear one die a most agonizing death. And in one fell swoop I lost my first love, my committed love and, seemingly, my deepest Love: my God; all this, apparently, in a state of never having found myself.

I think that I must continue the reach toward God, not being surprised by the ebb and flow of strong, mixed feelings. Evidently it is normal to have that wide rage of emotions, and lack of them, in this kind of struggle. Do I have the strength to climb this mountain? Father,

> *"Infuse inner strength into me."* Help me to
> *"draw strength from my union with You."*   Ephesians 6:10

Yes. Part of the confusion regarding the grief has been resolved— leaving more room for the grief itself. It is quieter now, with better understanding of the issues. Without the pain meds, my head is clear; with lessening of the confusion, my mind is less cluttered. But as with fog fading, clouds clearing or dawn breaking, real issues now take on definition and clarity which intensify their impact. The pain—the totally engulfing agony of soul and spirit—is also clearer, sharper, more intense. It has no boundaries. It goes beyond my horizons. It permeates all of who I am and spills across all of time: past, present, future. Talk about a "crucible of pain..."!

And I had thought, from time to time, that I was coming out of it! I am beginning to understand that while one can be grateful for those brief interludes of relative relief, they are by no means the end of the journey.

Sometimes I think that I begin to understand at least the issues involved in the struggle; at other times, I am sure of little other than the on-going malaise. I do know that I want truth, not just ideas. And for me, that truth must coincide with the Words of the living God, He Who said,

> *"God is not a man, that he should lie; neither the son of man, that he should repent: hath he said, and shall he not do it? or hath he spoken, and shall he not make it good?"* Numbers 23:19

Why on earth do Christians in general feel that they must shield God from seeming inconsistency when prayer is not answered? Will we ever make progress with that kind of evasion? Would it not be more to the point to ask where we fail?

There must be something lacking in our ability to receive which thwarts the healing flow of His Spirit from His heart of love. As long as we persist in this evasion—self-deception—God will not be able to do what His heart longs to do among His people. His miraculous intervention is meant to be convincing manifestation of His reality and of the depths of His love. The down-to-earth revelation of His intervening Love is intended to convince the unsaved and strengthen His children for the growth of His kingdom. That was the New Testament pattern. Let's get honest before God!

19

GOD SAYS / MAN SAYS

Yesterday I gave a letter to the wife of a man who is engaged in the same battle that took my beloved Jim. May God give them the inspiration to lay hold of the Word of the living God despite *any* input from *any* contradictory source; may that Word *come alive* in their hearts!

God Himself said,

> *"Call upon Me in the day of trouble, and I will deliver you, and you shall glorify Me!"* Psalm 50:15

I went to the evening service at church yesterday. The discourse was well done, nicely polished and well thought out—with human reasoning. Quotes were from various philosophers... Oh, my God, have we strayed so far from You? What would have developed if the speaker had used only Your Word?

*Father, please, by Your Spirit show us where we are, and above all, show us **Who You are!***

Last night some of us watched a video of Allan Vincent, a man who was drawn to the Lord by searching Scripture to refute false doctrine, then went to India where he met God in a very real way.

In the film, he told of a man named John Babu, who in a desperate search for help had gone into a Hindu temple and cried out to the gods. There, Jesus Himself appeared to him and told him that He is the only true God, and that he must put his trust in Him or be lost. John responded, then left the temple in a daze. Thereafter he began to share Jesus, knowing only that whenever he laid his hands on the sick, they were healed.

"Knowing only *that!*"

We "know" *so* much more than he—but we don't know "*that.*"

Allan also told of a woman who had died from cancer. According to Hindu custom, her body was laid on a funeral pyre to be burned, and

134

throughout the day various ceremonies were carried out. Before lighting the pyre, the people asked the local, illiterate Christian pastor to pray a blessing on her in her after-life. As he prayed, he was moved by the Spirit to pray that she be raised from the dead—and she sat up! The villagers scattered...

When Allan spoke with her six weeks later, he asked her what her experience had been. She told of feeling her spirit leave her body and go into great darkness, then of seeing a Man stand before her in clothing that was shining white. He had one hand extended toward her, and she could see that there was a hole in His hand. The Man told her that He is the only God there is—that she needed to put her trust in Him. She said that she simply responded to Him as He spoke. Then He told her He was sending her back to tell others about Him.

At that point, she felt herself going back into her body. She sat up, and saw the village pastor standing just where Jesus had been standing in her vision, with his hand extended toward her in just the same way. She told Allan, "Then I knew it was Jesus in that man Who had called me back to life."

Jesus in that man!

Jesus indwells us. *Do we really understand Who He is?* Tozer has written that the greatest ill in Christendom is that of "knowing" Him intellectually, without knowing Him in our hearts.

I expressed some of this to the group. (And, as usual, later regretted opening up.) Someone quickly countered all I said: "God is working. Everything's OK." And peace—or was it coma?—reigned once more.

Father, we need You to reveal to us Who You really are; we need to know You in our deepest hearts. Bring us close to You; know us; help us to know You!

Oh, God! You said that You would build Your church; only You can restore. Only You can raise the dead.

But You can!

I've been thinking more about the Sower and the Seed. More and more, I come to realize that this may be the really key issue in this whole journey. The thought became still more confirmed as I spoke with someone this evening. The Seed is the Word, according to the Master; He is the Sower. Those Words are Life itself, for they proceed from Him Who is the Life. Jesus warned that the enemy exerts every effort to steal that Word after the Lord sows it. Father, help us to recognize his every effort, and use Your Word to defeat his every move!

I look back over my life and recognize that all along the way the good Seed had been planted, and so many, many times it has been stolen when it had only begun to take root.

There is a most vivid memory of the first time this happened to me.

I gave my heart to the Lord as a child, and eagerly drank in the Words of Truth that were presented. The love of God was a living wonder; the miracles of Jesus, most thrilling evidence of that love; the promises of God, bright, shining, and alive. Until I overheard two adults discussing them: "It's so hard to believe!"—as if "fairy tales" were one thing, and "facts" quite another. Shock waves hit my soul. Perhaps they still have echoes...

Especially for a child, the words of adults, often well-meaning folk, are given a lot of credence. In fact, we are taught not to doubt what our elders say.

And through the years, increasingly as decades pass, just a little here and a little there, the living Word of Almighty God is diluted, negated, and weakened in our hearts until its all-out power and authority, its eternal reality and its glory, are invalidated where we live our lives.

What would change in our thinking if we were to recognize the thief in whatever form he comes and discard every whisper of what he says? What would happen if we were to entertain only the Word of the Living God in our reasoning? If we allowed that Word to grow, to produce its living fruit by the Spirit Who waters it?

What would change in our circumstances?

"Let God be true..."!

"*And every man a liar*"? (Romans 3:4) What man can ever claim to speak with absolute truth in every word he says? Because we know only in part and understand only in part, there will be elements of untruth and partial truth in the words of every human being until we are made like Christ when we see Him as He is. We can safely accept what men say that entirely represents what God said; but we must learn to discern carefully any addition to, or subtraction from that Word from God, and reject all divergence from its truth.

There will always be a tendency to follow deviations because of our human limitations, and because we do love to be comfortable. God's Word is like a "*two-edged sword, rightly dividing*"—and swords are not feather pillows. The Laodicean Church of Revelation said of itself, "*I am rich, and increased in goods, and have need of nothing.*" That was wonderfully comfortable. What Jesus had to say to that same church was most *un*comfortable! "*You do not know that you are wretched and miserable, and poor, and blind, and naked.*" The Master had stern

Words for that comfortable group. They needed to repent—or face His judgment!

Jesus said that if we abide in Him, and His Word abides in us, we shall ask what we will and it shall be given us. What we long for is the fulfillment of His Word, of His Promise. The desired result will be the fruit of that Word which is to abide in the good soil of our hearts. Jesus said that the Word that was received into good soil—and not stolen from it—would bring forth Life, to an abundant harvest.

Father, give us hearts that look and long only for Your glory; help us to hold Your Word deep in our redeemed spirits and refuse to allow it to be stolen from us in any degree. Bring forth in us the harvest of Your Life at work there.

This truth has been stirring in my heart still more since dawn today. Looking back over the heart-cry of this Journal in light of this thought, it does seem that the entire struggle may well have been over the disparagement between what God said and what men say. Has this journey been one cry of anguished dismay as I have allowed the Word to be taken from me?

Oh, my soul,

"*Receive* with meekness the **engrafted Word**" James 1:21

Receive it! As your heart leaps up at its intent, receive it—never let it slip away. Let the painful wound of your circumstance be a point of entry for His Word; hold it close to your pain until it becomes part of you, grown to you, grafted to your spirit.

"**Let** the **Word of Christ** *dwell in you richly...*" Colossians 3:16

Let it! As the Sower scatters His Word over your heart, let it stay. Allow it to remain. Do not see how good it is, only to keep it on the surface of your mind whence it can easily slip away or be snatched from you as "birds" come your way on some other wind of doctrine. Let it sink deep into your heart!

Let it—dwell there.

Let it—dwell richly. It will take root, for it is alive. And it will yield a harvest of Life; it has come from the Sower's hand, which is nail-pierced.

"*And take the sword of the Spirit,* which is **the Word of God...**"
Ephesians 6:17

Take it! It is all right to be more than passive as the Word of God comes to your heart.

Take it! That is the reason it comes to you—that you might take it! How else can you wield it?

Take it! And take all it is, for all time. In this battle you need a firm grip on your sword! Let your hand cleave to your sword, as did the hand of Eleazar, David's servant, when he fought the Philistines,

> "...*and the Lord wrought a great victory that day.*" 2 Samuel 23:10

The Word of God is a sword, an effective weapon in this war. It is a sword not of metal, nor of mind; it is of the Spirit. Its substance is the essence of the God Who gave it. It is crafted in the very heart of God. It is alive!

Tozer once wrote, "God is not a God of the past, nor is He a God of the future: He dwells in the eternal present; what He has said He is still saying."

When the Spirit brings His Word to your heart, receive it.

Let it—dwell in you—richly.

Take it. Grasp it, never let it go.

Wield it. It is alive. It is powerful. It will triumph—in you—to the glory of your God.

Father, let it be so—in each of us. For Your glory!

This concept is not enough in itself; I must not get stuck here. As thought, it is comparable to seed. I must not be diverted from it, even to argue for it; I must quietly wait in Your presence and allow your Spirit to work it into the depths of my spirit, as well as into my understanding. Guide me in watching over Your Word in my heart until You water it with Your Spirit, and, by the warmth of Your living Love cause it to spring to Life. Then bring to fruition the result, the harvest, that was in Your heart when You sent it. Accomplish Your work in me, my Father.

A few days ago on a television program, Dale Lang said that when God's children encounter evil, it is not a power encounter, but a truth encounter; the child of God speaks Truth, and the enemy has no choice but to submit to that Truth. I did not understand this when I needed it most. I still do not understand how this can come about. Father, make Your Truth become so *alive* in me that Your life may triumph, even over death itself.

Today on the same program a Jewish guest said that Gethsemane literally means "olive press." He commented that the oil of the olive is only produced when the olive is crushed. Crushed? Nothing in all of life could have crushed me more than losing Jim! Is there to be oil from that crushing? I feel compelled to certain tasks—but really wonder if there is any value in their outcome. Will I stand before my Maker with only a few dried leaves to show for His investment in me?

"Line upon line..." From time to time another vignette of truth lights another candle for my understanding:

A quote at a recent meeting: "Don't give up; Moses was a basket case."

A guest who was raised a Hindu: "Every man or woman who has a relationship with Jesus—who has experienced His love—can rise up, have the same anointing, the same power Jesus had in His life, and experience the same miracles Jesus experienced 2000 years ago in His ministry on earth. Until you and I demonstrate the power of God we can never reach others for Christ. You can praise Him, you can experience Him in your life. If you want to see if something works, you have to experience it (as with a computer). Give Jesus an opportunity."

Ruth Graham: "Failure is never final. God specializes in restoration; it is His best work."

Janet Walsh: "My brokenness has been a far better bridge than my pretend wholeness ever was."

Over and over again it is demonstrated that God has a way of bringing something real, something good, from hard things we go through.

20

GLIMMERS OF UNDERSTANDING

Yesterday I came across one of those small piles of papers that Jim used to accumulate in his shirt pockets. Grocery lists, "to do" items, notes from his sisters and other such things. Among them was a dear little love note to me.

How does one who was really loved handle loss like this? My father was an encourager, but no one ever affirmed me the way my husband did. I am thankful he was in my life for those years—but his death has now left a *huge* vacuum in so many areas of my life.

Would it help if I understood how a person is put together? Yet I wonder if that is possible. I have been reading *In His Image* by Yancey and Brand. The complexity of even this temporary house of clay is absolutely amazing; how much more so, that of the human spirit, mind and emotions—and how they all fit together to make each unique human being. I wish I *could* understand, though; it might do much toward resolving my bewilderment.

I have noted that though so confused and seemingly set adrift within, something in my spirit leaps with joy upon hearing of God's working, of people accepting Him as Savior, of what I have always taken as Truth being manifested. All of that, while lost-ness, confusion, guilt, and lack of understanding of my own journey weigh heavily somewhere else within. How can rejoicing at the work of God co-exist with wondering where He is in my experience or—face it—wondering if He really *is*, if all I have treasured as Truth through these many years is really real, or some sort of mirage? How can joy leap within, even while guilt over those questions haunts me? That is the deepest grief of all! Shepherd—how long will You leave me caught in this thicket?

Tuesday, one of the dear folk in the building came to my door fresh from her doctor's office, in tears because of a diagnosis of cancer. Oh, how I could feel for her! I could love her, try to give her hope, offer her a cup of tea, pray with her. But what she needed was someone to *"lay hands on the sick, that (she) might recover."* I did not have what she needed.

My Father, what is lacking? Why do we stand helpless, with hands hung down in defeat, when You, through Jesus, finished the healing work; when You have put all things under His feet; when all powers are made subject to Him, the ultimate Conqueror; when Your Word declares that we are "more than conquerors" through Him Who loved us and gave Himself for us?

You said that when Your Spirit came, he would lead us into all truth; He has come, He indwells us—and still we stand powerless before our enemy.

Why?

According to Your Word, it ought not to be so.

When Peter and John met the crippled man at the Beautiful Gate, they didn't pray for him. Nor did Peter stop and pray for those laid in the streets so that his shadow *"might fall upon some of them and they be healed."* They didn't pray. Peter said, *"Such as I have I give you."* They—*had* something...

You told us to ask—and receive. We ask, but do not seem to know how to receive. Why do I remain so weak and confused? Why can I not be a conduit for Your mercy? What is missing? Lord, I cannot give myself understanding. All I can do is look to You with yearning in my soul, and ask you to set things right. I want to see You moving freely, according to the pattern in Your Word. Only You can fix things; but You can! Please, *do.*

A short time ago I watched a video clip in which Dr. Paul Yonggi Cho told of early experiences. He had been a Buddhist. Death from tuberculosis was imminent; he had been told he had six weeks to live. He had exhausted himself praying to Buddha and began to reach out to the Supreme Being—One beyond the Buddha. God met him, healed him, and now uses him to lead over 500,000 believers in Seoul, Korea. When questioned, he said that all people are aware, in the back of their minds, that there is one supreme God.

Is this what has kept me from giving up? But I want so much more than that! What I have thought to be the sense of His presence... I need to know that is real. I want an unrestricted flow of His Spirit: constant, full, effective. I want to know my God!

The pain is very real, a natural outcome of the horrific sense of very real loss. The inescapable fact of Jim's death underscores the reality of the foundation for all of the inner anguish. Then—how real is that antithesis? Through the years prior to his passing I interpreted that familiar "lift" as a welling up within of the indwelling Spirit of God. It has been most troubling to have that certainty tested as it has been in the face of losing Jim. I have felt so abandoned by my Father since my deep heart-cry for help was not answered.

Could it be that worship is the avenue of release, as in the song, "When..."? (Chapter 17)

Today I broached the matter of the confusion with one who understands these things. He told me that in trauma, quite literally, a portion of the brain dies (!) making room for development of something new, that the brain is always changing.

He also told me that each person needs three basic things: love, significance, and a sense of belonging.

I lost all three—double—in losing Jim, for part of that trauma was the sense that I had also lost connection with my God. All of that, without a clear sense of personal identity.

One of our sons was here for a precious few hours this week. It was wonderful to see him, be with him, talk together. He, too, is still hurting over his father's death. Lord, how we need Your redeeming love, Your power to deliver singing in the depths of our souls.

While he was here, he referred again to his near-death experience after being bitten by a brown recluse (fiddle-back) spider in a desert area of Arizona. He described watching the doctor and nurse trying to resuscitate his body as it lay on the bed. Awareness was incredibly heightened; there were no questions; everything was viewed from every angle, with complete understanding. The confines of the human body no longer a factor, the spirit seemed barely contained within the room. The experience was like being released from a cocoon; he felt set free to be really alive, keenly interested in new sensations, and aware of tremendous new potential. He heard the nurse ask the doctor to try again...

He knows that the hereafter is incredibly real. Savior, send Your Spirit into his mind and heart to bring him fully into Your plan for his life!

Sleepless night. Again. Will peace never come? As usual, wakefulness allows the mind to drift to the ever-present dilemma. Yesterday it came to me that one analogy to this grief process is imprisonment in solitary confinement. Once there was beautiful, free-flowing communication between two people who loved each other and appreciated the experience; now all of that has been stripped away. It is cruel. Inescapable. Deadening. It is a dark, empty prison cell, an emotional vacuum where there is not even an echo of all that was warm and alive with love.

Another comparison: while the relationship lasted there was a constant, beautiful "flow" of understanding and appreciation. Day or night, whatever else was happening or not happening, there was a wonderful, soul-watering current of love, caring, tenderness. When that was cut off, all that remained was the dry stream-bed, all worn, rock-strewn, and barren. The life-giving, refreshing "river" is gone— forever—leaving only a scarred landscape more dead and empty than if the river had never flowed.

Is it possible to survive this kind of devastation? Is it possible, ever, to really live again? I cannot see how it could be. Or how it could be worthwhile.

Lost in a black night on a stormy sea—and the bottom has gone out of my boat. My God: where is He? How I long for Him to manifest Himself to me!

Today I drove off to keep an appointment, arrived safely, and parked the car. As I made my way into the building a better parking space became available and I decided to move the car to take advantage of it, but couldn't. The car resisted movement, and when I gave it more gas it reluctantly, sluggishly, did allow me to back out of the stall, but dragged, lifting slightly at each rotation of one wheel. Steering was virtually impossible. I realized that, quite probably, the weak tie-rod had given out. This proved to be the case. The Motor Association sent a tow truck when I called after the appointment, and I rode with the driver to one of their recommended garages. When I commented that I was thankful it hadn't happened on the street, the driver heartily agreed, saying, "Yes, it's a very good thing it didn't; God likes you."

I replied, "Yes, I know He does. I like Him, too." He gave me a strange look...

Later, I cried out to my Father, "Thank you for preventing a car wreck, *but what about this traumatic **heart-wreck?**"*

143

21

PURPOSE ?

Another day of deep reflection. I still struggle with thinking that seems to go three ways at once. My mentor continues to assure me that this is consistent with trauma. Not fun! There are times when I just can't feel sure *what* is real anymore. Sometimes I sense again what I used to feel was the rising of the Spirit—warm, wonderful; then it fades away, leaving me in the pit again. Oh, *if only* that close relationship with my God would come clear and constant again!

I shared with my mentor the strange mixture of feelings which flowed during the writing of "When..." It opened discussion in which I sensed another heart desperately hungry for reality in God. We both felt that there is a deadly apathy in much of the church today. I was told that there are increasing numbers of souls who, like myself, are under great pressure, experiencing confusion, and engaged in this battle. There is deep crying out to God for Him to move. Is this deep yearning after Him part of God's preparation in the hearts of His own which will open the way for that out-pouring of His Spirit at the time of the promised latter rain? That would put meaning into the suffering...

There is still a carry-over of release, an inner core of peace, from the sharing of yesterday. There is also one area of concern which will not go away. Do I need to respond to that? Guide me, Shepherd. Oh, how very necessary it is to stay within the bounds of the prompts and checks of the heavenly Guide! Just now, as has been the case for most of my life, there is such a sense of the sweetness of being guided, of being sensitive to the mind and will of the Master. Could anything in all of life be compared to being in the center of His purpose?

Purpose. How often that has been a subject for reflection. It would be so wonderful to know what God's purpose is for what's left of my life. It would be marvelous to know that what one did really counted in the lives of others. To have value, something real and definitive as the driving force of one's everyday existence—how wonderful that would be.

Yet I am aware that God does not see as we do. He has need of small, unseen vessels as well as those more obvious and appreciated. I only long to feel fully satisfied in the knowledge of the outworking of His will for *me*.

Today I had to re-read my friend's paragraph. In it he spoke of being utterly willing to take orders and go with them. If I am to fulfill His will in my remaining days, self-preservation must be sacrificed when He asks something of me. If my life is to have real meaning I must learn to clearly discern His will and simply fulfill it. I do think that, just maybe, self-preservation is far less important than it used to be. How I need His Spirit to make me one with His heart, His will, His purpose, and to strengthen me to know His will—and do it.

Help me!

It has been a very down time, yet again. Partly weariness, no doubt, and lack of sleep, but it has been deep nonetheless.

I attended a seminar this week-end, which was a bit much. One new possible reason for the no-progress state of affairs could be "broken will." Other than that new thought, though the course was interesting and informative, there was not a great deal that was of personal benefit in the study. There was, again, that dark pressure toward just giving up. However, reference was made to the Scripture stating that *"He Who has begun a good work in you will complete it."* (Philippians 1:6) He is the Shepherd; our safety is in His hands, not ours. Somehow, in the midst of that inner darkness I was able to side-step the pressure, leaving the outcome up to my Lord. It's true; He is my refuge. My fortress, too, and my God, in Whom I will trust.

Another Word which came to mind was *"the testing of your faith... is more precious than gold, which perishes."* Gold, too, is purified by fire...

Today I saw a possible benefit from my journey through the valley. Another very troubled soul reached out for help after our early Sunday meeting, but those with her looked baffled, uncomprehending; obviously they had never been in that state of confusion.

I could understand!

In the plan of God, will there be times in which that understanding can be used of Him?

22

FOUND – A TAPROOT OF THE PAIN

PAIN FROM EARLY LIFE

My father was gentle, kind and wise; always an encourager. He died when I was twenty-seven. Mother was loving, in her way; after all, I was her child. Much of the time things went well at home. In spite of periods of illness she provided a good home: good meals, clean environment, learning activities. She allowed pets and some of the messier crafts that other mothers preferred not to allow. We could talk to her about almost anything that interested us.

There were lots of good times when she would answer questions, read to us, or show us how to bake our favorite cookies. Her former vocation as a teacher enriched our lives in many ways. I think that she enjoyed being a mother. But there were some very basic differences in our personalities.

I was born long before "temperaments" were understood or thought about. I do not remember why we clashed but I have vivid memories of times when we differed, and her response was anger, always. She would clench her teeth, bang her heels on the floor on the way to the stairway to get Dad's razor strap, then return to whip me severely into absolute submission. Total surrender was demanded. I learned to stop protesting or even crying, just to have the beating let up. Sometimes I would show her the red welts that rose on my legs as a result of the lashing, but she would just shrug it off, saying that I "had it coming."

I think that those discussions were, on my part, a search for understanding. Once particularly, as the crisis point drew near, I longed for her to just come and put her arm around me; it would have melted me. But, as usual, there was that angry journey for the strap, and the whaling that followed.

Children learn to live with the status quo; I never began to realize how deeply this scarred my spirit until more than twenty years after her death.

I realize that she had been a school teacher, when strict discipline had been the norm. In at least one case, the superintendent told her on the way to a new appointment that the unruly class at her next assignment had driven out several previous teachers. He had warned the students that the next one was a "bear-cat," then instructed her to "act that way and you should be all right." She did, and she was.

Besides that background, she was the fifth child and only girl in a family of six children. Her parents had almost lost her at the age of two. She remained rather frail, and while growing up quite possibly had her own way more than would otherwise have been allowed. In any case, she was the type who knew only what she felt; that was her reality, and it followed that, naturally, that was—reality. There was never room in her thinking for an alternative outlook. She never sensed the different personality type in her eldest child, never realized that her treatment of a sensitive nature could be harmful.

The most outstanding and perhaps most painful instance of this confrontation I remember vividly. It was not long before my marriage. I do not remember what caused her to remark, "I feel sorry for Jimmy!" I *do* remember those words piercing me like a dagger, and the thought that formed in my mind but remained unspoken: "Jim doesn't bait me like you do." Thank God, Father was in the kitchen with us at the time and immediately protested to Mother over what she had said, and she backed down.

The relationship changed after my marriage. When Jim and I moved back to the home town to go into business not long after marriage, we had a good relationship with my parents, and after Father died we watched over Mother during her twenty-four years alone. She enjoyed being Grandmother to our children. During her last illness, she gave parting words to each of her children. Her words to me were, "You've been *so good* to me, Beth." I'm glad to remember that!

I am old enough to realize that no parent is perfect; each one, myself included, is flawed in one way or another, and no matter how hard we try, we cannot put out a perfect performance in our parenting. Thank God that we can call on Him to be the perfect Parent of our children and guide them where we cannot measure up.

I know that Mother did a lot of things right and would never knowingly have damaged me. I do not hold those difficult memories against her. I know that she had no intent to wound, but in recent years I have begun to realize that through those many early episodes I was really traumatized. I do not know how to analyze it—do not really want to. But it now seems that something about that part of the past could be interfering with my inner healing in this grief process.

I don't know how to proceed.

23

PANIC !

It was suggested yesterday that I put Jim's pictures away, face down in a bureau drawer.

I panicked!

Why did I react like that?

It isn't as if I spend time gazing mournfully at his photograph. Seeing it doesn't make me cry, though the deep sadness over being separated from him still resonates through the core of my being. The period of my life which was spent with Jim was warm, wonderful. He was not perfect, but he was real. We were blest in that we focused on what we appreciated in each other.

JIM IN MY LIFE

Why would the prospect of hiding his pictures frighten me? Perhaps it is because it seems to symbolize removing him even from my memory.

I would rather have been a miscarriage!

Apart from the time with Jim there is very little in my life that is not painful to remember. Before him, I lived in an emotional straight-jacket—isolated, despised, ostracized—shy, lonely, and with a very eroded sense of self-worth. Only within the shelter of his love have I ever found meaning for my existence. To remove all traces of his place in my life would leave me worse than dead. I would rather join him in our common grave!

I have mentioned some of the trauma of my childhood home-life. In many ways I had a good home. Mostly, Mother was an excellent parent; but there was something about some of her dealings with me which I still do not understand, which traumatized me—which traumatize me to this day.

The torment of being a misfit all through public and high school also created a deep, painful emptiness—a vast reservoir of inner discomfort and self-doubt.

I realize that any attempt to portray to another the all-encompassing painfulness of that kind of reality is an exercise in futility, for inner suffering is—subjective. But perhaps even a shadow of the reality could begin to portray the preciousness of the total acceptance I found in the shelter of Jim's love. I never even *began* to feel like a person before that relationship with him. I had been so bound up that it was a good two years after our marriage before I could actually allow it to sink in that— he really *loved* me! For the first (and *only*) time in my life, I began to feel safe enough to emerge from my prison, to live, to be me. In many ways I am still very locked up.

Part of my current lost-ness is definitely a matter of not feeling like a whole person without him. I think that I never have been whole apart from my identity as his wife. The years that I shared with him are the only years of peace and fullness that I have ever known; the rest of my life has been a howling, empty wasteland that is painful to remember.

Where on earth do I go from here?

In setting down my reflections through this Journal, I have been very honest in admitting that I do not want to let go of Jim, though I am fully aware that he is gone. I do not try to pretend that he is still here. I am trying very hard to be real, to face what facts I can find and deal with them. But facts and feelings about those facts are not on the same wave-length. I cannot control either.

To remove all traces of Jim from my life would be to strip me of almost every shred of wholeness—of all that has been good and wonderful—leaving only the constricting pain of the past and searing awareness of my personal deficiencies.

It would be equivalent to removing every brush-stroke from a beautiful landscape, leaving only the suggestion of some basic background colors on the canvas. It would be like removing every possession from a home, then trashing the interior—leaving it a dark void with only a few piles of debris to indicate anyone had ever been there. It would be like the deformed ashes remaining after fire had destroyed a lovely forest; like a song-bird's decaying remains crawling with larvae and beetles, the song long gone, forever. It would be a living death.

How can I deliberately add that kind of pain to what is already intolerable?

Upon reviewing "Jim in My Life," my friend was kind, as usual, and recognized the writing to be *real*. I appreciated that. It has been an on-going effort in my life to be that—real. There is something so shallow, so empty about pretense; there is an essence of dishonesty in it which is repugnant.

I tried to express the inexpressible: the fullness of life within the relationship we had in contrast with the painful, constricting emptiness of life before and life's bleakness after it. I know that my best efforts can portray only a shadow of those realities.

When I came home I played through TV programs recorded earlier in the day. In one of them there was an interview with a couple who had lost a daughter. Some of what they said found answering echoes in my own pain: the depth of grief, the lost-ness, the weight of darkness which enveloped them. Those facets of their grief parallel my own experience, though they did not mention the spiritual confusion which has compounded the pain of my journey. The close of their conversation almost replayed the words of my friend that somehow, some way, I must find a way to go on.

How?

Where?

I honestly do not know where to set my foot for the next step.

There are times when I yearn to break out of the prison walls that confine me. Sometimes there is a tremendous longing to open up. To whom? With what? Something deep within which I do not quite recognize cries for expression. It is profoundly real; I think that is why I thirst to write. Is there more?

Does God have some plan into which He wants to fit me? At my age? In my situation? What options could there be? Besides, perhaps the deepest pain of this dark time is the bewildered sense of being somewhat lost from Him. Are there more unresolved issues within which I must first search out and open to my God? If there are, I want to do that, with His help. And when He has prepared me, I want to do His will.

I have often felt it would be much easier to die physically than to go through this emotional/spiritual kind of dying; yet there is a sort of realization that if I am still here, there must be a reason for it. My children: how I long to see them find all they need in God! And the God I love—I want to fulfill any purpose He may have for me before I go to meet Him.

Oh, Father, help me! Change me where I need to be changed, and please—use me.

24

A SHIFT ?

After leaving my mentor a couple of days ago I had the sense of a partial shift within. He had said that behind the suggestion of hiding Jim's pictures there was no thought of removing him from my memories, that he will always be there. The thought was to urge stepping into the new phase of "life."

I have thought about that.

I know that to remain fixed in this mode is courting death. The thought is not unattractive; this struggle is very, very painful. To have the struggle cease, to be with Jim again and with the Lord I love, to rest—is a prospect not without appeal. But I understand that my time to die is to be His decision, not mine. Besides, death itself is *the* great unknown. Accompanying the prospect is the immediate sense of two great deterrents: I would not want to reach that Home and face my Lord without having finished whatever He has in mind for me to do. (There would be no "Well done!"... or even "Done!") And I do not want to leave my children while they may still need my support.

To look the other direction, that of finding some new kind of "life," brings its own set of qualms. It is such a bleak prospect—that of going on into a completely unknown future, *alone,* in the most abject sense of that term. That unknown is not attractive, not friendly, cold. And going into it in that all-encompassing *alone*-ness—without love, without companionship, without support—is not a welcome thought.

There is no warm, welcoming path that beckons.

When I was a child, a missionary told of one trip through the jungle when their party was overtaken by the deep blackness of an African night before reaching their destination. It was a dangerous situation! As they looked to the Lord, they noticed a stick on the ground glowing at one end. They picked it up, and it lit the path for the next step, then the next, until they came to the end of their journey. Does that memory surface just now as some indication of what I am to do?

Steps. Projects? Those I have in mind could perhaps fill a few more weeks. I can proceed with them. Then...?

There is no strong drive to "move on"; how could there be when that would take me farther from the last I knew of my Love? I am so weak! But I wonder if I am supposed to just make a cold, calculated decision in some way, without waiting to feel like it?

Just in case that is what is required of me, I did make a rather difficult, small, but indicative choice. One gets so used to things being in the same place that they no longer stand out or attract much thought or attention; it was so with the ribbons from floral tributes at Jim's funeral. I had saved them. They were hung over the shade of a small lamp on top of my roll-top desk, the white one with "Husband and Father" in gold letters prominent among them. Before I went out today, without really wanting to, I packed them away. I hope it will be all right to keep the bouquet of dried roses. How I did love that man!

The sense of lost bewilderment regarding my relationship with the Lord continues to weigh most heavily. From time to time I am encouraged as a glad "Yes!" wells up within at some account of folk coming to Him. Perhaps this indicates that the relationship is still valid at the spirit level. It is difficult, however, to remain confused in my mind and to endure the on-going devastation over my loss. Three-way split. Three ways: three parts of my inner being, each functioning in a different way? Spirit, loving God, reaching after Him; soul, still pained by loss; mind, still searching, reaching for understanding?

Jesus did speak of loving God with all of our heart, soul, mind and strength; it just could be that each of those parts of the inner being respond to trauma in different ways, hence that sense of confusion, the three-way split of the inner person at such times.

"Unite and direct my heart..." Psalm 86:11

In the last few days I have again heard Rolland Baker speaking of the marvelous outpouring of God's grace and power in Mozambique. I wish I could get in touch with him. One who has experienced that reality would know so much more than those with only theories. Yet, the real depth of my longing is to hear from my God Himself. It is not just truth I crave, but *Truth.*

"O that I knew where I might find Him." Job 23:3

Words of another confused sufferer. My longing is for that same One. Perhaps not so much to *find* Him as to have Him reveal Himself to me. I sense Him in my spirit; I love Him—but I am in this deep perplexity of heart and mind. He is near, but I cannot touch Him. What is this murky veil between? I do not like this veil. My heart hungers for oneness with Him, for closeness beyond nearness. I long to be enfolded in His love—one with His heart, His mind, His will. Nothing short of that will be enough. Oh, how I yearn for Him!

At the small service this morning, the one to whom I had given "I Worship At Your Feet, Lord" came and thanked me for it, seeming to have caught something of what had welled up within as the song was given. When he asked the inevitable "How are you doing?" I admitted to on-going struggle and told him that the core of it was confusion over being unable to touch our God when Jim was ill.

He started to give the usual "Don't blame yourself" line, but I expressed the concern that my experience had not been according to the Book, and that I felt I must remain open for God to change me where I had fallen short; that I was part of a Body not living out the expressed purposes of God. He agreed that there is something missing. Maybe the longing for a move of God is spreading. I do hear of others crying out to Him for the same reality. Come, O Lord, and breathe Life into Your Church!

It is ever thus. At least, so it seems. Not long ago I felt a slight shift toward going on; I think that is still with me, but I hit an emotional low again last night. I wonder, if there is a plan for these remaining dregs of my life, just what it is.

Yesterday I went to *church.* I have been going to an early, informal service for some time now. There are about thirty folk who meet in the church basement for an hour or so before the regular Sunday morning service to sing the old hymns and choruses, share testimonies and sometimes speak from Scripture. Among those who come are a retired pastor and his wife. Sometimes he leads the singing while playing his electric guitar, beautifully—wonderful chords and runs with no discordant sounds. (At one time he studied classical guitar. Would that all lovers of that instrument chose to benefit from the same preparation!) And, occasionally, he also speaks.

Yesterday was one of the days he did both. From the first moment there was a wonderful fragrance of the Spirit's presence; oh, how sweet it was to sense Him near—and leading. There was such precious worship, such an awareness of Him in every song, in every word that was spoken. How I have yearned for that! The message he gave centered on the theme of walking in the Spirit, thereby fulfilling all the requirements of the Law without being "under the Law." And in all of it, music and message, the Spirit sang. As did my heart! My soul cries out for Him. There is no substitute—absolutely none—for God Himself.

I think that is the cry of every heart, whether or not they recognize it. From that desire, the tendency these days is to try to "drum it up," literally, with drums, loud guitars, and a beat borrowed from the world. Folk try to stir the depths of their spirits from the outside, though the human spirit can really only be reached from the inside, by the indwelling presence of the Spirit of God. In their desire to be warmed by the Fire of God, there is danger that they work up a "false fire" with external stimuli of their own making.

From time to time we hear the words, "remember Lot's wife." Perhaps we ought also to "remember Nadab and Abihu," who, rather than serve God with the fire He had sent from Heaven, offered their own fire in the Holy Place—and were struck down for their presumption.

True heart-hunger can be satisfied in no other way than by the flow of God's Spirit through the human spirit. This can only happen as the whole heart is open to God, which involves willingness to face personal needs and short-comings and let them go. This can be uncomfortable in the beginning, but the divine flow which follows is well worth the cost. If substitutes in the form of soulish stimuli are thrust upon the hungry-hearted, those things *cannot* meet the need and may actually hinder that opening of the soul to God, and confuse or divert real heart-longing after Him. Spirit must touch Spirit for the soul to really live. Spiritual intimacy with the living God is the *only* deep reality. Substitutionary intimacy is adulterous; no wonder the sons of Aaron incurred God's wrath!

Oh, Father, help us to waive all else in our search, our thirst after You. Come upon us by Your Spirit and reveal Yourself as You really are to hearts that cry to you day and night for—Yourself!

Another small happening: A friend who knows of my struggle came to me before the service began, asked the inevitable, "How are you? Then, before I could reply, said, "You're fine, aren't you? You're here!" It was just a light-hearted greeting...

I know that a broken spirit is not enjoyable, either for the broken one or for anyone else. As noted previously, it's great to rejoice with those who rejoice, but everyone shies away from weeping with those who weep. "Jolly up!" seems to be the prevailing response. They mean well, but I am working through some huge issues—not just of grief, but of spiritual confusion and a sense of being abandoned by my God. I am working through them, not just camping in them. They cannot be dismissed without resolution.

During this time of walking through the fire I have understood in a new way that Jesus Himself was a Man of Sorrows, and acquainted with grief. Would anyone have gone up to Him as He grieved over mankind and said, "Jolly up, Jesus"? He longed for His disciples to understand, to stand with Him. It is not wrong to grieve. I know He understands, for He has been there! He has the answers. I will wait for Him. I do not want simply to escape from the furnace; I want to find *the* Truth as it is in Him. I want to find *Him*.

Through the years some have pointed out that mature Christians often go through severe testing with less visible evidence of the Lord's presence than that which young Christians may experience. The young in Christ seem to need more answers to prayer, more miracles, to be continually reassured of the reality they know in Christ. Who would not rather stay on in that state? Especially if we don't realize that our God does His most precious works within us through our testing times.

Even difficult things can be borne, for a time at least, if there is continuing sense of His presence through them. The test, the fiery furnace, reaches maximum heat when that *awareness* of His presence is withdrawn.

That really seems to be the case for me in this journey. Much of my distress through this dark time has been bewilderment at the seeming absence of my Lord. The Psalmist and others, even Jesus, have recorded such times in their experience. Seeing some parallel between the record of their journey and my own begins to calm my fears and enable me to look past them into the face of Him Whom my soul loves.

Whether or not I felt Him near, I now begin to understand that He has never left me, even in the hardest times; in truth, He drew nearer then, though I knew it not. My soul instinctively reached for Him in my extremity; the very testing pressed my heart toward Him. He allowed the testing to be extreme—most extreme—until it seemed to push me past the breaking point at times, but He never let it overwhelm me. I pray that

He will fulfill His purpose within me and so make me one with Him that I may be used by Him as He chooses. This time of darkness and anguish, in His hands, must yet prove to be used of God to shape me for His purposes in some way. Let it be so! I wish I were a better student...

Jesus' suffering cost Him everything, a price He was willing to pay because *"He so loved."* The suffering left scars; scars He chose to keep. They were solid proof to His disciples that He was truly their Lord. Perhaps, in ways I do not yet understand, scars—the lasting evidence of painful circumstances gone through—are evidence that I am His. Paul called his scars the bond-marks of Jesus. (Galatians 6:17)

> *"Except a corn of wheat fall into the ground and die, it abides alone, but if it dies, it brings forth much fruit."*
> *"He who loves his life shall lose it, but he who hates his life in this world will keep it unto life eternal."* John 12:24, 25

There really is a cost, if we are to walk close to Him. Was there a turning point when this line of thinking helped me look beyond the pain itself and glimpse the possibility of purpose in it?

At my age?

In any case, I think that in this time of reflection there came a point at which I stopped struggling against the brokenness. After all, I had written "It's broken, Lord..." and made an offering of my pain. I want to hold to that. Lord, help me to *accept* the brokenness. I do not want to kick against it any more.

At the time of this meditation my heart said, "Yes, Lord!" Something lifted, then. There was release, freedom from some of the confusion. Like a spring of light welling up out of black pitch, joy swelled up within as I felt Him near again! Such clear, pure joy—as I had known it before this nightmare.

156

25

"LANCE THE PAIN"

REACH FOR UNDERSTANDING
"Dear Mother,

"I wish we could talk together today—really open up to each other—and gain mutual understanding that was never quite complete while you were here. I know you loved me; I am sure you knew that I loved you. In most ways our life together was very good, even in those early years. Certainly, we had a great relationship after my marriage. You were a wonderful grandmother to the children God gave us; they treasure their memories of you to this day.

"So many things come to mind as happy parts of the past. The way you would read to us. (You were a wonderful reader!) So many Sunday afternoons you gave up what could have been a time of rest for you to read books to us, entering into the story with great zest and good humor. You developed in us a real appreciation for literature which not only enriched our lives but opened our minds to learning throughout our school years. You taught us to read before we went to school. You took occasion to teach when you were doing things—even cleaning and drawing poultry; in so doing, you enriched our understanding and stirred our minds in a way that many children never know.

"You always cared for us so well. Good, healthy meals. Clean home. Clean clothes—even when hard times necessitated that they were neither fancy nor abundant. I know that it must have taken a great deal of dedication and effort on your part to be so faithful in spite of your poor health. Thank you! The way in which you took your own mother into your home to care for her in her declining years was a wonderful indication of the caring person you were.

"There were few topics which you would not discuss with us when we had questions about life. Only once, before we knew the Lord, did you ever evade an issue that troubled me. Remember how you cringed, then got very 'busy' when I commented on the fact that 'people are born, grow up, and die—then more people are born, grow up, and die; what is the purpose of it all?' Once we met Him, that, also, was an open subject. When you turned to Him, you turned fully; there was no looking back.

"You had such a ready wit, too. I still smile when I remember having you and a friend come to our home for home-made ice-cream, and asking you to return thanks. You smiled, hesitated, and complied. Then you said, 'I felt like saying, "Lord, bless this food to our bodily excesses!" ' And we all had a good laugh.

"You insisted that we faithfully practice our piano lessons. Your children are grateful to you for that. Music has been such an important part of our lives ever since.

"When Jim and I came back to the hometown after our marriage, we had a really great relationship with you and Dad. And when he was taken from you, you continued to mean a great deal to us, and to the children God gave us later in life. It was a precious trust to watch over you more and more as you grew older and your health declined. You meant so much to me, increasingly so as the measure of role-reversal increased through those last years of your sojourn here.

"The one thing that troubles me—still—is the severity of the way you punished me when I was young.

"Why was that, Mom?

"What was there about me that made you so angry at times? I must have irritated you very deeply. Was it because we were two different personality types? Or was there something more? Some of the time, I know, your irritation grew out of times we talked, with escalating disagreement. Why did we argue?

"Was I being willful? Stubborn? Rebellious? Looking back, I think I wanted to reason things out...

"I wonder if you ever knew what those beatings did to me. When you reached the boiling point and stomped off to get Dad's razor strap, oh, what a sinking dread came over me, knowing the pain that was to come. And come it did! Memory is keen as I remember. The stinging burn of that leather against my bare legs was beyond description. And it came again and again and again and again and again, so many, many times—until something in you was satisfied. If I cried out or protested in any way, you redoubled your efforts until I was utterly subdued. It was a time of helpless horror for me; a time of being overpowered by the anger of someone much stronger than I who was the one main person in my life meant to nurture and to love me. Etched in my mind is one time in particular when, if you had simply come to me and put your arm around me I would have just melted. But you went for the strap. Again.

"I remember showing you the red welts that rose on my flesh from a whipping. There was not the slightest wisp of pity in your face, voice, or manner as you shrugged and said lightly, 'You had it coming.'

"Another strange moment: with a smile on your face and in a most light-hearted manner you once referred to Hebrews 12:10, in which the writer spoke of earthly parents who *'chastened us after their pleasure...'*as if it were your right to have pleasure in that activity.

"I don't understand. Perhaps, don't want to.

"I remember you telling how your father used to regularly whip your brothers when they didn't settle down at night, while you shook with fear under your blankets. I know that Dad's father, too, particularly when drunk, would beat his sons with such severity that their tiny mother would step between him and the boys to stop him. It was a way of life in those days. From what you told me, though, I don't think that you were ever subjected to that.

"Your teaching days—especially the time the district superintendent told you to act like a "bear-cat" to keep things under control—must have contributed to the mind-set.

"Your parents almost lost you when you were two and you had poor health as a child; perhaps you were allowed your own way much of the time, especially as the only girl in a family of six. I don't know what lay behind the way you handled me. Was it just that I was a bad kid? I know there were many times when I was not a happy camper. Was I rebellious?

"Was it partly because I was your first-born and you were taking your parental responsibility too seriously the first time around? I know that you seldom, if ever, whipped my younger siblings.

"What you probably didn't realize is that it was not just my flesh that took a beating. My spirit did, too. To this day I remain cowed; so locked up inside—so unsure of myself—that there are few things which I dare venture to do which anyone might notice. It is crippling. And frustrating! The natural drive to live life—to do things—rises up at times, only to be automatically negated, time and time again. There is that sense that if I were to reach out to try to do something, my arm would be cut off. Maybe I 'cut it off' myself rather than risk having someone else hurt me again. I am in an emotional straight-jacket which nearly suffocates me. I dare not try to escape. I have no self-confidence, little self-worth. I should be used to it after all these years, but my soul still screams.

"I have come to realize that this inner situation may be largely responsible for the lingering trauma accompanying Jim's death. His love-shelter allowed me to escape from my prison at times; without him in my life I am like a shell-fish robbed of its shell, with no protection from the heat of the sun, the grit of the beach—or the gulls that circle overhead.

"Mom, I realize that I am still very limited in understanding, for I am earth-bound, in a clay temple. You are with Jesus now; there, you have fullness of understanding for you are like Him, having seen Him as He is. I wonder what you would say to me if we could really have a conversation now. From what I understand, one of those things would be that both of us are glad for the forgiveness, the cleansing, the redemption that Jesus brought into our lives. Whatever was wrong in the past has been forgiven—exists no more.

"I do know that you had no intent, ever, to really damage me. I never really doubted that you loved me. I am sorry for whatever it was in me that so frustrated you. I do not understand what was behind the way we clashed in those early years. Were we just essentially different? Was I just basically difficult? I wish I understood. Perhaps you acted out of some inner pain of your own. Whatever lay behind your anger at those painful times, even if you were in some way partly at fault, Mom, I choose to forgive the hurt you inflicted on me in the past.

"Since you are in His likeness now, you will understand that I am not trying to lay a guilt-trip on you; in fact, this whole exercise has been distasteful to me and difficult to do. I am just—desperately—trying to find a way of escape from this prison, this pain.

"Most of my life is behind me, irretrievably beyond my ability to make anything of it. Days are dropping away so quickly. How many remain for me before I will face the One who sent me into this world for some purpose? What will I have to return to Him for His trust? I have held back so often... I know—our worth in His sight is really dependent only upon the One Who is worthy, Who covers us both, forgiving all our short-comings. Yet He did say He wanted us to bear fruit; I do not want to fail Him.

"Perhaps my only hope is the work of the Spirit within to heal, restore, and lead. In fact, I am sure of that. May He find a way to accomplish that in this shaky child of His!"

The day after I wrote about seeming to "cut off my own arm rather than risk rejection," I brought my troubled little friend in to see Grant Mullen's tape, *Rejection*. It helped us both. He described my situation to a "T"—withdrawn, afraid to venture or mingle with people, perpetuating past pain of rejection by continually rejecting one's self.

A few days later, I heard Gary Chapman speak about the five love-languages and how they apply in marriage—and in parent-child relationships. That may well be a pivotal issue in the whole matter. We *were* "wired" differently; perhaps we didn't understand what the other person needed in order to feel loved.

Later:
What if... all of that turmoil somehow fits into God's plan? He certainly knew it would happen. He prompted Paul to write "*All things work together for good to those who love God, to those who are the called according to His purpose.*" He has a wonderful way of using everything—even our messes—to make something beautiful.

If I had been strong and free to be out-going and involved in many activities, there is little doubt that I would have developed into a different person than I am today. Did He have a plan in allowing that door to be closed so that, locked within those "walls," I would grow in other ways? It is fairly certain that if I had not been "imprisoned," I would not have become a reflective person, would not have been inclined to think things through, to ponder deep issues—even to write? "When God unrolls the canvas..." how fascinating it will be to fully understand!

Lord, at times my faith is very weak. Let Your strength enfold me. Do not let me fall or fail!

In going through this with me, my mentor made some very meaningful comments. He noted the good things Mother invested in my life: love of literature, musical training, teaching. She also taught by example in home-making, respect and care of her mother, honoring her husband and her God.

He noted that parents are most disturbed by traits in their children which mirror things in themselves they have not yet overcome.

Though he acknowledged that the kind of severe discipline described was the fashion of the times, he clearly labeled it *physical abuse*. He spoke of different parenting modes, explaining that sometimes a parent has only one way of parenting. To illustrate, he said that if a hammer were the only tool in a tool-box it would very likely be used many times when another tool would be much more efficient. He mentioned that often different parenting modes are required for best results with different children; that it is wise to discover the way a particular child will respond in the most constructive way. The objective should be to train a child to develop self-control—by guiding, rather than by breaking the spirit.

When he realized that I was the first-born, he nodded with understanding, noting that for the most important role of a life-time there is no training; most parents learn on the first child—at the child's expense.

My feeling of being imprisoned was labeled as the condition of a closed spirit. I gathered that the only way out of that was to venture out of my shell, perhaps in small steps. *That* will be no easy trip! But I must not stay this way. I think again of the paragraph written by that same friend and mentor, in which he described following the inner prompting fully, having "died"—caring no longer about one's self, but only about following our Lord...

My mentor found interesting, and agreed with, Doctor Mullen's self-rejection theory.

It was noted that I had really sought out reasons for the difficulty, though he did not like the fact that I searched for reasons to blame myself. To him, I was the child; she, the parent. He felt that the "discussions" arose out of my need for more understanding, more information: perhaps, more than she was ready—or able—to give. Did she feel threatened if the discussions got into territory unfamiliar to her or made her feel insecure?

What struck me in a most shocking way was a question raised regarding the horror I felt during those beatings at being overpowered by one so much stronger than I—one who was most responsible for loving and nurturing me. Having read that, he asked, "Do you think that is what lies behind your sense of being abandoned by God at the time of Jim's death?" ! Could it be? There certainly is a parallel. It is, indeed, possible that what I sensed in an earthly parent could translate into what I mistook my heavenly Parent to feel. That will take some thought!

Having dared to look directly at this issue, I am certain that it is a much larger matter than I had first recognized. It is not just a wound that left a scar, but a mutilation that changed who I became.

Upon reflection: Our earthly parents aren't perfect. They can't be. We need to be realistic about that. We also need to face the ways in which their imperfections hurt or damaged us, for evading truth is never right or good; it is a form of self-deception. Yes, admit their faults. Specifically. Recognize how they affected us. We do not need to love them less! Be frank about those issues; discuss things with them if you can. If the relationship is on-going, try to work out ways in which those happenings are minimized. And always, in following the Lord, we must go that "seventy times seven" measure of full forgiveness that Jesus described to Peter, for only in that way will we, ourselves, be freed from the prison of inner pain. The Master's urging, example, and enabling direct toward actual reconciliation if they still live, but certainly inwardly making peace, as He lives within.

What a huge, huge time of learning! There are no words to describe my gratitude for this enlargement of my understanding, and the caring spirit in which the help is given.

My mentor gave me a lot to think about. He told me how he had once cried out to God for His touch, and soon afterward suffered a painful injury which gave him some down-time during which God ministered to him. That brought home to me again the concept that God does *use* pain to bring about His purpose in a person.

Could it be that what has felt like abandonment by God has really, in some strange way, been part of His plan? Does He have some real purpose for the situation as it is now? Perhaps there *were* no loose ends?

Yet—*the promises...*

When I failed to receive from His hand, did He put in place a Plan B? But Romans 8:28 had come to mind long ago, and though it held out hope of God's ultimate good purpose, it did not turn the tormenting tide at that time.

I have not been a willing, let alone an eager student in this classroom. Whether or not Jim's death was due to lack of real faith and the ability to connect with the Healer, it happened. It is a stark fact that will never, ever change. My whole heart cries out in protest. Talk about *dying*—everything within me goes down with him. The future looks too bleak and painful to contemplate! Must every step be filled with pain? Yet, I know that if I stay in this place of pain and confusion it will destroy me. There is the ache of grief, looking either way. The only other option is to look up—into the face of my Father.

This *dying:* how does God want to use it? Is this inner pain a scalpel in the Hand of the heavenly Surgeon? If so, how can I draw back from it?

If He has a real purpose in all of this—what is it? What is He trying to change?

26

MUSING...

What a night! This time, I could not sleep—for joy. It seemed as if the veil had dropped away and His precious presence enfolded me once more, washing through my soul like a river. Could anything, ever, be more precious? How wonderful to sense Him close again!

I do not know what caused the veil. Scripture does speak of times when the Lord hides His face...

There is also the trial of our faith.

Much of the trauma arose from confusion over not being able to touch Him when my Jim was dying. I know that I have not been willing to accept losing him. Was there some rebellion in the grief?

I still do not know what the perfect will of God was regarding Jim's death. I believe that what He gave His life to provide is always intended for His children, and that we grieve Him by falling short of appropriating it. Nevertheless, *He* is beautiful, wonderful! There can be no doubt that, even if weakness kept us from His best, He can use even our worst to birth beauty.

"Beauty... for *ashes.*
The oil of joy... for *mourning.*
The garment of praise... for *the spirit of heaviness."* Isaiah 61: 3

The separation from Jim is still painfully real. The heartache will remain, I know. Darkness still lurks, tears still form. It is strange that the anguish of grief, confusion of faith, and springing joy could all exist in one person at the same time.

Lord, I am weak. Hold me in Your strength. Let me be one with You. Please, keep my heart from looking back; it is hard not to be drawn back into the pain.

In the last short while, I have actually begun to see God's hand directing some of my steps:

Wanting to take something to a troubled young woman, and finding that she was unexpectedly free to attend an informal prayer session at the church, I met her there. The quiet prayer ascending from a number of people gathered there provided a wonderful atmosphere in which to reach heavenward. Beautiful! During this difficult journey, it has seemed hard to pray through the shadows; it was sweet to mingle my heart-reach with those of fellow-believers.

On the same day of the following week, I took my car in for servicing at a station a few blocks from the church. The work was finished a bit early for the prayer service, but I thought I would go up anyway and wait. It so happened that a very small group was meeting in a side room to pray before the main gathering, and they asked me to join them. Again I felt the touch of God.

After noon prayer at the church, I unexpectedly met the woman whose pain had drawn my heart to her. We talked for a bit; she unburdened her heart, and I tried to encourage her. That short time was so blessed.

Then, the Mullen tape. Lead on, Lord!

Deep yearning and heart-cry to God for a son. He had hit bottom—again—and had become aware that this is not what God planned when He created him. Your Spirit is at work, Father. Your redemption is complete; Savior, may that redemptive work have full scope within my son's heart, and then in his life's direction. Guide him into Your plan for his life, into fullness, overflowing joy, and great fruitfulness; let him indeed be the instrument in Your hand to accomplish the purpose for which you sent him into the world.

He seemed so hungry to let go to God, then closed up again. Father, he is Your project. I cannot work the miracle; that is Your province! I put Him—again—into Your nail-scarred hands, commit him to the work of Your precious, powerful Spirit and claim him for You against every power that is arrayed against him. Jesus, let your blood avail for him at his deepest point of need and draw him fully into Your purpose for his life. So be it—for all those dear ones!

There has been joy in the quickened sense of others' needs; it seems natural to reach out to them. Let Your life flow freely. The precious joy still flows. May I walk softly in that Presence. Oh that it might never be interrupted again! But even if it should be, hold my heart steady, Lord. Keep me close.

Is the "high" receding? Does it take continual choosing to keep my gaze on my Lord? Hold me steady, Savior.

The joy remains. It is strange that confusion, anguish and joy can co-exist...

The joy remains—except when the reality of all that I have known about my God is thrown into question.

How often attacks come when one is most vulnerable; and how invariably they come armed with some truth, and aimed at what is most precious! Through the night hours the great question hit hard again, releasing a panic-level of such intense *fear* that I was instantly jolted wide-awake. If only that issue could be completely settled, once for all! Then I could go on in settled assurance through anything else that life might bring.

Yet, does testing ever really cease?

Often in the last few days I have thought back to a day in Bible college, when one of the instructors spoke of spiritual battles. I remember thinking as he talked that one could face battles with complete assurance, having the inner assurance of Christ's presence and, by His Spirit, confidence in the final outcome...

Then there was a prophetic word saying, "...the battle will be *within* you..." That was unsettling! Not long afterwards, the first of such battles arose. There have been others through the years, but never, ever, any with such diabolical intensity or duration as that in which I have been engaged during these last three years.

Must the rest of my life be twisted and tortured in this way? Is there no way of peace and on-going joy ahead of me? Faith. The trial of my faith: Peter wrote that we are not to find it strange when we encounter it. The problem is, how long can one endure those fires? Yet the Lord has promised that we will never be tested beyond our strength—strength that He provides.

There is joy, there is peace, when my heart is strong to believe Him. How can I find permanent shelter in that state?

Would the God Who placed within us the ability to think expect us to fly in the face of reason, to shut our minds to the obvious and choose to persuade ourselves to "believe" some line of thought which is not backed by the Word of the living God? I think that there must be some confirmation from Him, from His Word, concerning matters that trouble me. As I have outlined previously, there is such a tremendous weight of Scripture behind the thought that God is a God of deliverances, a God Who hears His children and answers them according to His promises. After all, He purchased redemption from both sin and sickness by the offering of heaven's best: His own Son. There is such a problem trying to reconcile logic and faith when we fail to receive!

As I understand it, the only things that could thwart the loving purpose of God are ignorance of the promises, sin, failure to ask, or unbelief. We knew the promises, we harbored no known sin, we asked, based on His own Word of Promise—which we knew to be true. Yet we went down! Belief: I know there is a head-knowledge which can be mistaken for faith. Was that our situation? Yet Scripture says we have all been given a measure of faith or we could not come to Him. Can the "faith" He requires ever be present if He does not impart it? And, if it can only be present if given, how can He expect it unless He gives it? I do not believe that His nature would withhold His answer because He withheld the faith to receive it. God would not double-speak in that manner! Lord, please teach me the Truth as it is in You.

There is a growing awareness that this life is not the main purpose for existence. We are involved in something much bigger than we know.

I am sharply aware of the loss, the confusion, the anguish—not knowing what He is trying to accomplish with it. He has promised to give His strength to the weak; how I need that! If He can fill my shattered life with *His* purpose, there could be reason to go on.
What is that purpose?

I mentioned need of confirmation from His Word regarding unanswered prayer: there was one incident when people (whom Jesus loved) called for Him, yet felt they had "fallen through the cracks."
Lazarus.
His sisters sent word of his illness to Jesus. He stayed away, purposely waited, fully aware of the details of the situation, until Lazarus had died. Then He came to them, and used the circumstance for His greater glory—and their greater joy!
There is trusting Him to fulfill His promise. There is also—trusting *Him.*

There is much to think about in that account. Lazarus and his sisters were dear friends of Jesus; "*he whom You love...*" Mary and Martha knew that if Jesus had come their brother would not have died. And they were right. Yet, in spite of His real love for that family (or—because of it?) He deliberately stayed away. They must have been confused, even hurt. He stayed away, every moment knowing exactly what was happening, until Lazarus died. *Then* Jesus came to them! His absence did not mean He had abandoned them. It did not mean that He overlooked them. It did not mean that He was uncaring or unaware of their need, their pain. It meant that He loved them so much that He wanted to do something very special for them, even if, for a time, it caused them anguish.

Scripture says that He is no respecter of persons and that He never changes in the least degree. I can trust His intent in my life! I can make my pain an offering through which He may show His glory...

My counselor referred again to the "closed spirit," saying that it is usually a survivor mode. He said that adversity causes a person to close up, much as, in the old fable of the contest between Wind and Sun, Wind caused Man to more tightly clutch his coat; or as prying causes a clam to hold itself more and more tightly closed. In the fable, Man took off his coat when Sun warmed him. Likewise, a clam will open easily when set in warm water...

I cannot seem to feel the "Sun," and I am not sure how to find "warm water." It must be a process; searching for my God, being found of Him, following as He leads. "He gently leads those" who find the journey difficult. I love Him.

I am so thankful that my earthly guide through this valley loves this same God. I know he reaches out to help with hands and heart that understand inner pain. May God truly minister to him!

There were some tears through the last few days. They are never too far from the surface at any time. When I happened to hear the old love-song, "I Love You Truly," I melted; that was something I often played with Jim in mind—and within earshot. He truly was my heart's love. When sitting in church I remember sitting near him there; songs remind me of him—and laughter, and the tears of a tender heart, and caring things he did and said. Everything in life reminds me of him. Yes, memories are most precious; but one lives—now. And this *now* and the loving *then* are in painful contrast!

How I wonder just what my purpose is from this point. It would be wonderful to sense some real reason for being here. Is there something more than a day-to-day existence to fill with slightly useful activities? Has all of this pain really been a prerequisite course for something important, as the counselor has suggested? How wonderful it would be to find significance—meaning—in the remainder of my life!

I do treasure contact with my children. When Jim was here, their spiritual welfare was a joint concern. I think it still is; Scripture tells that God stores up the prayers of His own, and Jim did a lot of praying for them. And I know that the parental yearning we felt over their souls' welfare is only sharing in the great eternal yearning of the heart of God for them; that will never lessen.

27

WHAT *IS* REALITY?

The beginning of another year. Just where am I now, and where am I going?

There was a good breakthrough not long ago, a release, a beautiful awareness of the presence of my Lord with the surge of joy that always accompanies His nearness. Then came a terrific pressure of things-to-do and matters requiring immediate attention. Now there is a lull in the hectic rush, and time to assess the current status of underlying issues regarding my adjustment to life alone.

There is still a lot of fluctuation between good and not-so-good times. The beautiful "high" has leveled out again.

I have been tormented by questions concerning the reality of the intangible, the unseen. Yet even to the mind (itself an unseen reality), how can that reality be denied? Surely the inner (unseen) agony I've been going through is just as real as any physical pain, itself something unseen.

There are, obviously, different levels of "real." Different realms, different worlds—affecting different aspects of our inner selves? In this world of tangible realities where things that we can touch and see seem so much more easily proven real to us than things of mind and spirit, it can be difficult to keep unseen realities in perspective. Yet, if we are to take literally the teachings of Scripture, unseen things are much *more* real, being eternal. To the thinking person, these matters of the spirit *must* be real. We are more than physical entities. What is it, after all, that gives even the physical part of a person—life? When that essence, whatever it is, leaves the physical body, something, an unseen reality, is definitely—gone. And there is most definitely a profound reality in the unseen inner anguish experienced by those left behind!

In this shake-up of everything I have ever known, this testing of reality, there really seems to be nothing new to consider. When surfing channels in the dark hours of the night, there are still only three essences in anything that is portrayed: human issues, and behind some of them either a revolting sense of evil, or one of uplifting good. Nothing else. This parallels the teaching of Scripture.

Why is there still such an unsettled uneasiness about the "reality" of all that has been the foundation of my life for so many decades? Naturally, there have been factors of shock, profound grief, and adjustment. Troubling, unsettled issues from the past contribute, too, but I still think a good part of it is that old problem of not knowing how to receive from God.

On the natural level, an NSF cheque raises legitimate question as to the reality of a bank account. In the same way, failure to receive from God raises logical question as to the validity of the promise, a thought which strikes immediate shock, horror, revulsion—and despair over the state of one's faith. Such dreadful confusion! Oh, how I would appreciate real understanding...

On another level, I sense that He is very real. Where do these divergent levels meet? Whatever the reasons for the failure, there is a longing that He will pick up the pieces and somehow accomplish something beautiful with them. I must learn to trust that my God still has good purpose.

I have circled that problem over and over again in this journey, never coming to a satisfactory conclusion. Circled... There flashes into my mind the Word to the Israelites after their long sojourn in the desert: *"You have circled this mountain long enough... "* When God said that to their leader, *He* proceeded to direct the next move. They knew exactly who they were and where they were going, and they knew their God was real, and *with* them. And they had circled that mountain—in the will of God—until He had prepared them to go on.

Grief is no ordinary journey. Many who describe the grief process use the analogy of "circling." C.S. Lewis, for one, wrote, "...in grief, nothing 'stays put.' One keeps on emerging from a phase, but it always recurs. Round and round. Everything repeats." (*A Grief Observed,* p. 67).

What "next move" is there for me?

Where am I now? My heart leaps up when hearing of the work of God prospering in someone's life, yet there is still this huge lack of understanding. There are still tears, still deep sorrow and lost-ness in being parted both from Jim and from that wonderful certainty I used to know in God. And sometimes, the joy in His nearness. There is an acute sense of "alone-ness."

So: spiritually, there are times of wonderful awareness intermingled with long periods of numbness, or worse. Mentally, there is still great confusion regarding some spiritual issues. Emotionally, I feel bankrupt. There is deep pain, lost-ness, emptiness, limbo. Rejection is still a hugely raw issue—peers, siblings, Mother? *God?* Why should I not reject myself? At times there is still pressure toward the ultimate self-rejection...

There is heightened awareness of the pain in others.

28

CYCLES

MORE SHADOWS

This has been a difficult day. Long before sun-up, one of those fiery darts hit the "low" mentioned earlier. Later, my mentor began to describe again that "life on the edge" when one senses the whispers of the Spirit and, led by Him, ventures—sometimes into strange places at strange times—to find pre-arranged divine appointments in which one is directly used of God to meet needs. The contrast between that blest state and my black hour broke me. Is this "life on the edge" available for everyone? For me? At my age? In my state? Or am I one of the nameless, numberless multitude who breathe awhile, only to replenish the dust of the earth?

The question was again raised about anger at God. I could be wrong, but I really don't think anger is behind my blackness. My guess would be that it is the *rejection* factor that has riddled my existence in almost every area of my life—except my years with Jim. Peers. Siblings. Church people. Mother? As Mullen says, one who is rejected begins to reject himself. The anguish of unanswered prayer could very well, subconsciously, strum the familiar, painful chord of rejection—this time, by God. Part of me knows that is not so, but the oft-recurring sense of being worthless tends to interpret new pain the same way.

What triggered this particular downward spiral? My thoughts: For one thing, normal cycles. Years ago I read about biorhythms—normal fluctuations in a person's sense of well-being. There are also emotional rhythms: James Dobson wrote concerning these, "anything producing an extreme 'high' will set the stage for a later 'low.' And vice versa." It is well recognized that there are also grief cycles: in their book *Up from Grief,* Kreis and Patti liken the grief process to a roller coaster. Also, C.S. Lewis, as previously quoted, wrote that phases of grief continually recur.

Other triggers: <u>Pressures</u> in every-day life. <u>Physical problems</u>: pain and general discomfort are not exactly inspirational. <u>Embarrassment</u>: the day before that last discussion I made a complete idiot of myself with my most trusted friend—with yet another wad of paper. And "<u>last-discussion-blues</u>": the thought that it could be the last discussion (another cut-off, though not malicious) pushed it over the edge.

What a contrast: "life on the edge"/ "over the edge." I am such a fool!

If something within me needs to die, I wish I knew what it is, and how to co-operate. *Dead* would be much more comfortable than *dying*. Why does it go on so long? I don't know how much more I can take.

Is that the answer—the breaking point? Or would that be the absolute end: disintegration?

I don't know what to do!

"Life on the edge": so wonderful to contemplate, but so far from where I am imprisoned. Will my Deliverer come?

29

THIS REJECTION THING...

It is virtually impossible to go through life without experiencing some rejection along the way. Sometimes it is incidental to other happenings; sometimes it is inflicted without too much thought on the part of peers or even parents; at other times it can be vicious—and intended. It can come from surprising sources. Always, it leaves its mark upon the soul. It can have a most crippling effect upon the development of a child or even upon the welfare of an adult. It is destructive! Like acid, it eats away at the sense of self-worth, often producing a paralysis which renders the victim incapable of fulfilling his God-given purpose in life.

I wonder how much of the pain in the hearts of mankind really stems from rejection. Could there *be* inner pain without some element of it? Even the anger that is said to be a common facet of grief—could that not stem from a sense of rejection? For those secure in their sense of self-worth, it could trigger anger as a defense mechanism. For those whose self-esteem has been broken down by a lot of earlier attacks, perhaps there is not the inner strength to rise to one's own defense. Surely, the inner anguish that propels a wounded soul toward self-destruction is an expression of *self*-rejection; can that develop without a sense of being despised by others?

There can be little doubt that one stung by deep rejection will have great difficulty in dealing with other painful happenings in life.

It seems that one such rather profound rejection is complicating my struggle to find my way out of this grief trauma. Physical abuse in my childhood and on-going ostracism and rejection throughout growing years left me rather defenseless when it came to a new crisis. In turn, that trauma would, for some time, paralyze the effort to heal following the deep grief trauma later in life.

Raw grief runs high at the death of a Mother. There is something about the loss of that one who has been a heart-home for her children which leaves them particularly bereft. It is like no other loss. Actions and reactions of all concerned can be abnormally stressed.

Perhaps I was the most vulnerable of her children, for Mother had spent the many years of her widowhood living nearby and was very much a part of our young family. When Father died, I, as the eldest child, distinctly felt the mantle of his care for Mother settle upon my shoulders, and for decades did my best to be faithful to that responsibility. More and more, as Mother's age increased and her health began to fail, my role as care-giver grew. How many times, when she didn't answer her 'phone, did I go over, find her ill, and get her to the hospital? The bond grew with the years. Other siblings loved her, too, and would certainly have helped her—if it had been their lot—but it was I who actually did carry the responsibility.

From time to time throughout those years I saw mother give away her treasures, though sometimes it was hard for her to part with them. It truly didn't bother me.

One day while we were talking together in her garden, Mother offered me her diamond ring. There was no way I could let her take it from her hand at that time, but I told her I was thrilled at her expressed intent. It was a promise, a treasured love-exchange. I had not asked for it, or for any other thing.

Many years later the family gathered at Mother's side as she lay dying. During the vigil I was called away briefly to attend a sick child. While I was away another asked Mother for that ring, also, the expressed reason being the desire for a larger diamond. Ill though she was, Mother clearly stated that she had intended me to have it. I would wonder later why Mother's expressed intent was not *simply accepted...* Instead, that one pressured Mother until, as had been the case several times before, she gave in, this time shortly before drifting into her final coma. There is reason to believe that those extracted *last words,* all things considered, were not Mother's *last wishes,* but her *last capitulation.*

The rings were placed in my hands after Mother's death. Technically, I suppose I could have kept them, but as I did not want what they symbolized to be sullied in any way, I placed them in the hands of the executor of the estate. I think I hoped that the ring would be returned with the blessing of the rest of the family in acknowledgement of the many years in which, on their behalf, I had watched over Mother. The rings went to the other person.

There is no way to describe how that *devastated* me! Yes, the ring was lovely, though one of the least of her treasures in monetary value. Its worth to me was symbolic: the token of my parents' love for each other. And of hers for me.

When the decision was made to place that one last treasure, too, with someone else, I felt like an outcast. To me, the decision seemed like rejection by Mother at the hands of the others. Though I had been the one to watch over her for the twenty-four years of her widowhood, I alone was left with no love-token from her. Perhaps the servant is of a lower caste? My place in my mother's love, my place in the family, and *my value as a person* were dealt a deadly blow. The profoundly painful sense of being worthless to those closest to me struck deeply. Something absolutely died within me, and has never risen from the ashes. The *joie de vivre,* the inner song, the natural buoyancy of spirit, just... died. I cannot think *that* was Mother's *last wish.*

I remember looking with deep anguish into my Savior's face. The decision seemed so terribly *wrong!* My heart *could not* give that one tangible evidence of Mother's love for me into the human hands that reached for it.

Sometime during the agonizing weeks that followed the decision, I remembered my father's reaction when the machinery was taken by his partner. This helped me to begin to look for ways to let it go.

My heart *could not* release the ring—until, in my spirit, I looked into the face of my Savior, and told Him I could release it—to Him! I could let it go, when I deliberately placed the diamond in the palm of a hand that is nail-scarred. He alone could absorb the pain, robbing it of the ability to destroy. The only "treasure" left to me I held, not in my hands, but in my heart. Perhaps, on a different level, they are more valuable than the ring: Mother's seven last words to me, "You've been *so good* to me, Beth!"

If only I could have gathered all of my heart onto that little ledge!

To me, the ring had been a symbol of approval, of acceptance. In relinquishing it, I subconsciously also relinquished what it stood for in my mind, thus validating the perceived rejection from my family. From then on, a most painful sense of worthlessness lodged in the profound reaches of my spirit.

The trouble with wounds of the spirit is that, naturally speaking, they tend to remain raw. Mortal wounds of the body quickly allow escape from pain by way of death; mortal wounds of the soul offer no such release. Deadly wounds of soul and spirit can still bleed long years after the event. Severe enough, they become watershed moments, changing the course and quality of life from that point.

Only now, decades later, do I begin to understand the serious error in my thinking at the time. It was wrong of me to rest my basic worth upon my own evaluation of it, or on the perceived evaluation of any other human persons; only the One Who made me has the right to set a value upon my life. Only He truly knows what He created, and what He wants to accomplish through that creation. The focus of my heart must be the infinite worthiness of my God, and joy in just being His.

We make mistakes. Nevertheless, He is the Redeemer! He has a most marvelous way of accepting what is given to Him, even the broken pieces and the messes of our lives, then using them to bless us later on. When I turned this matter over to the Lord, I had no idea that many, many years later He would use memories of this very time to help me in the most crucial loss of my life.

If there is a way to peace and to wholeness it is the way of turning to the Lord Who so loved that He bore every ill of mankind within His own heart—then pressing the broken pieces of our lives into hands that bear the prints of nails. He alone is more than enough to carry us, to heal, and to restore.

Rejection. Those whose normal self-esteem enables them to cast off the rejection heaped upon them by others may well find it impossible to comprehend the horror that can swallow up one whose sense of self-worth has been eroded before such an attack occurs. It is sharply, painfully, destructively *real*. The misunderstanding of stronger souls only adds to the intensity of the pain for a weaker one who falls. It is as if the man who fell among thieves in Jesus' story were to receive a few swift kicks to his wounds before the priest and the Levite passed by—on the other side. That wounded one was unable to heal his own wounds, was so weakened by the attack upon his person that he was unable to help himself.

How precious, how valuable are those with the heart of the Good Samaritan!

Rejection. What must the horrors of hell be—the ultimate, eternal rejection by Almighty God Himself, brought on by a person's own rejection of Him. *Father, send Your precious Spirit to work powerfully in the lives of those I love, to bring them into right relationship with You.* And—bring me out of this mess!

Rejection. In contrast, how beautiful is *acceptance*—by ourselves, by others, and by God.

Speaking of emotional scarring, Dr. Wilf Kent, Ph.D., D. Min., a respected family counselor and psychotherapist of many years' standing, says, "Many will never heal."

Jesus said that His Words are seeds. It would not seem to be stretching truth too far to take it that all words are seeds, for ...

"...death and life are in the power of the tongue." Proverbs 18:21

Father, so indwell us that we shall be kept from wounding others. Let us be, instead, those who speak Your peace.

How can rejection be handled? The immediate thought is that Jesus knew rejection. It hurt Him, too! Knowing that He *understands* is amazing comfort. His management of rejection is bound to be best: He neither bowed nor broke under it, never assented to it—nor did He fight it. Knowing Who He was, He stood tall and just carried out the purpose and plan of God for Him.
And He forgave...

Yet, even He still bears the scars...

Earlier I recounted the story of a mother whose premature daughter had endured many painful things in order to survive. When the mother was finally able to bring her tiny girl home she was distressed to notice that the little one would not look at her. A pediatrician explained that preemies often came to associate care-givers with pain. The day finally came when the wee one did look directly into her mother's face...
It is to this point the Shepherd gently nudges His hurting "little ones."

As I mentioned earlier, "on another level" Mother's words might be more precious than the symbol of her love. That other level, the unseen, eternal world of soul and spirit, is difficult to keep in perspective in this everyday world. Wounds on the inner level go profoundly deep when one's sense of worth is limited to the evaluation of other people. Perhaps the only remedy is the turning of the soul toward that One Who called us into being, looking deep into His eyes of love, and asking Him to help us understand just who He created when He formed us.
It is clear that our "worth" as people is measured by three standards: our own, that of others, and that of our God. The only reliable standard is that of the One Who designed us in the first place. Our own understanding of our worth can take a huge beating, or in

some cases be over-inflated, if we accept the rating of other humans who know us only superficially.

If we can look past the way others perceive us and allow our Father to re-define to us our identity as He sees it, then we may come into relative wholeness. Knowing, in some measure, who we are to our Father will change who we are in our own sight; that understanding will strengthen and normalize our ability to be who He meant us to be. Only then will we be in a position to fulfill the calling of God in our existence.

30

WHO LIVES HERE?

So often through the years—the decades—of my life, I have wondered, "Who am I?"

Especially in the early days of my walk with Christ, because of the very great emphasis put on "fighting our sinful nature" as it was called, the search for self was largely comprised of looking for flaws. That is always a successful search. Fallen human nature, even after receiving the Savior, ensures success in that direction. We know the truth that Jesus forever cleansed us of our sin when we accepted Him; nevertheless, we tend to wallow in our shortcomings. It was so, early in my relationship with Him; it has also been the case since my husband died.

Lately, though, I began to wonder what positive inventory might be tallied. This morning in the Seniors' service, the minister spoke directly on that topic. One outstanding statement was that if we do not love the person God called into being when He created us, if we continually allow our thoughts to be manipulated into cutting ourselves down—to be masochistic—we render ourselves practically useless in the service God created us to give! With beautiful clarity, the thought was presented that if God's people would allow the truth to set them free from that pattern of thought they would be liberated—to live, and to joyfully venture into the full plan of God for their lives.

How much more would God be able to do if His people were to come free in this way?

So, who lives in this house of clay? The house itself is rather weathered; we won't go into that. Inside, who is this person who has, for the most part, hidden in shadows? She tends to be elusive...

From early childhood, we could find her pondering huge issues, thinking deeply. She has, it seems, carried that trait through life. Never satisfied with superficial thoughts or values, she has always had a desire to think straight, to penetrate to the core of issues, to keep balance, to reach for truth and hold to it. In later years, the search for truth would lead to writing; she finds satisfaction in that form of expression.

She is timid, far from out-going, yet can stand firm in difficult places in defense of truth. She is loyal. When she gave her heart, it was forever; there was no wavering in her commitment to her earthly love. She went through times of questioning her greatest Love in her 'teen years; that, looking back, was a matter of going through all that she had accepted as truth with childlike simplicity, re-evaluating, and making it her own—a normal part of maturing. There have been tests of faith in different ways through the years; indisputably, the most totally severe being that following her husband's death. The persistent search continues in that area, driven by that inherent longing for reality, for Truth as it is in God.

There has been willingness to hold to Truth, even when it brought derision and rejection. *"To whom shall we go..."* if not to our Redeemer? However, many years of that rejection, and others, left deep emotional scars which have kept her in an inner prison.

Rather than contend for place in public service, she stepped aside, allowing another's ministry to flourish. Later, she stepped aside again to thrust young people into use of their talents; that seemed most definitely the right thing to do. It has been good to see those young people develop ministries as a result.

Later, when her entire worth as a person seemed to be stripped from her in an inheritance issue, she put the matter into the hands of Jesus. The only treasure she held was her mother's words. That huge rejection cut very, very deeply; it altered who she became from that time.

In temperament, she is not out-going. She is neither a control freak nor an easy-going drifter. Perhaps she is more of a "melancholy," for she has a love of music and of beauty and—there is that pondering aspect of her personality. She tends to use logic when trying to penetrate uncertainty and find core issues in search of solutions.

She has a quiet way of trying to encourage people, of helping where she can. Especially her children! She treasures love shared with family and friends.

That seems to be about all. Not much, is it?

Yet, Another dwells in this house, too. That indwelling Presence makes even the smallest things different: purposeful, meaningful in His terms. There is no limit to the glory of the One Who dwells with me in this temple. He continually renovates, builds, rebuilds, redesigns the interior. The day will come when He will unveil what He has wrought within. He will give each of us a new name! What will mine reveal of His craftsmanship?

31

HOW DOES *GOD* SEE ME?
How can I Understand the Times, Understand God?

That question has haunted me for more years than I care to admit. Up to now any attempts to unravel that mystery have been rather futile. If by any chance it is time to discover who this person is, there will have to be help from the One who had the idea in the first place, for I have been unable to find the answer on my own.

How does God see me? I do not think much of that information is available this side of the veil. There is promise in the final book of the Bible that He will one day fully share that knowledge with the Redeemed. To overcomers He will give a white stone upon which a new name is engraved which no one will know except that one and the Giver. Until then, how much *can* we know?

Yet there is an innate longing to know ourselves. In Psalm 139 David was inspired to describe the unique workmanship of God Himself in the creation of every new human life. The immeasurable value of each person in the sight of God is clear in just that truth; each person is a work of God. Books by Paul Brand and Philip Yancey describe in awesome detail some of the absolute wonder of the human body; add to that the inexplicable marvel of mind, soul and spirit, and we are left in awe at the handiwork of God in fashioning each life.

We often tend to downplay our value even to ourselves. What would change in our lives—in our world—if, instead, we were to marvel at the handiwork of God, discover who God made when He called us into being, and fully enter into His purpose for our lives? Jeremiah wrote (29:11) that God knows "*the thoughts and plans that He has toward us, to do us good, and not evil, to give hope for our final outcome.*" (That does not say much about the process of getting there... There are joys in life; there are also great difficulties. God uses both to shape our hearts and press us close to Him.)

The fact that God designed mankind after His own image and likeness must certainly indicate that He intended to establish communication between Himself and humankind. His own evaluation: "very good." Even before that creation, He planned a costly redemption from the results of general disobedience which He knew would take place. That definitely manifests the fact that He placed great value in what He had made. This is confirmed in Jesus' statement that one man's soul is worth more than the entire world. The magnitude of that concept is beyond my ability to grasp. Obviously, the subject is far larger than we are intended to comprehend on this side of eternity.

I know, these are generalities; generalities of rather great magnitude! How, just *how* can I begin to narrow it down to—*me?*

I find it difficult to try. For one thing, self-identity has always been a mystery to me. Though there is an innate longing to reach beyond present understanding, I have tried to "find" myself many times over the years, always concluding the search with little more than a question mark.

Bruce Wilkinson, in his teaching *Going Beyond Jabez,* says that the boundary which we long to "go beyond" is *fear;* fear of going outside our comfort zone. For me, that fear begins at the thought of self-recognition. Here again, it seems that multiple, long-term put-downs (rejection) have deeply ingrained into me the sense that I am of no value; I am afraid to look at the mess. I remain cowed, introverted, fearful, and filled with self-doubt. If God has some use for me, He will need to work some pretty big miracles just to eliminate the "minus" quantity (or worse) which I fear must be at the core of who I am.

Because His Word says so, I am to believe that He designed me, with some purpose in His mind which He wants me to fulfill. How, at this stage of my stunted development, do I find out enough of what He had in mind to even begin to please Him?

Who am I?

I really don't know!

Decades ago when I first walked into the kitchen of the country teacherage, I was rather appalled at the décor; they had used cream-colored paint—as far as it went. A large, irregular area behind the coal-and wood stove was left robin's-egg blue. After a few weeks I never noticed it at all. In much the same way, I have lived with me for so long that nothing seems to stand out. Other than a few things I like to do, I am rather hard-put to describe myself, even to myself.

So, what do I like to do? I like to make music, as much as I am able. I somewhat enjoy baking; after all, it is what I did in lieu of playing with friends, since I had none (no children in town, too young, "religious"). I have done a little oil painting. And sewing. I enjoyed being a wife and mother, especially after those ten killer years of childlessness. I have enjoyed being hostess to friends (much more than being a guest; safety in "more control"?) I once drew up very successful floor plans for both our home and our business facility. In the last few years, I have realized that I like to be challenged to think. I like writing as a means of sorting out my thoughts.

Thinking. How do I think? I cannot remember a time when I did not search for truth, for *reality*. If an issue were cloudy, I did my utmost to cut straight through fog and murk to find core essence, solid truth. I have never wanted to fool myself or try to twist reality to fit what I wanted the truth to be. (That, it seems, is the way He starts people off.) I am glad for that, though often it has drawn me through rough waters, down the rapids and over the falls so to speak. No doubt this tendency was greatly accentuated by many years of manual accounting; I tend to search for answers that "balance" or make sense in all directions. Once, when I went through an IQ test on tickle.com, I was labeled a "precision processor."

Temperament, I have read, somewhat describes a person. Again, it is hard to read one's self, but I think that I may be basically a "melancholy," since I really like music, especially harmonies; something within me really flows with changing harmony. Melancholies, it is said, tend to logical thinking, feeling, and some creativity.

Personality? I am too much of a mixed-up mess to be sure. I like to study people, but don't get involved at close range until very, very sure it is "safe." When I commit to someone, I am very loyal. I think I am gentle, sensitive to what others feel, and caring. I would really, really like to live a life that counts, in the plan of God, to accomplish some good.

Spirit. Any level of spirituality is in question at the moment. I have always wanted to be utterly sincere. I yearn to have close fellowship with God by His Spirit, to live in Him and experience Him in me on a moment-to-moment basis. I do not like the doubts, fears and questions which have plagued me over the last many months. I do not like the ambiguity, the "limbo" in which I seem frozen at this time. There is such guilt and fear in having to admit that I have slipped into this state, and bewilderment as to what to think or what direction to go, if I can move at all.

I cannot say that I understand myself, other than that I am sure that I fall far short of what God must want me to be. Still, I know that He is patiently at work within.

How does God see me? A vessel that He made. A dwelling-place for His Spirit. A sincere heart, one that wants to hear Him. Some of the things He has brought with Him: gentleness, sensitivity, concern for others. He also sees the unfinished, broken-down areas of heart and mind; the fears, the questions. He sees where I have doubted Him, where

I have questioned Him, and the fear which has accompanied that straying from intimate connection with Him. He sees the deep cry of the heart after truth, after reality—living, working Reality.

Perhaps, also, He sees the longing for, yet fear of, freedom from things which have bound and restricted me all of my life.

That "me." What is it? *Who* is it? What was it meant to be? Under the "Frank's Slide" that buried it, bound it, smothered it, what exists? What—might have been?

I think I mourn that "me."

Other than that muffled cry of something stunted, something *imprisoned* deep inside this aging frame, I do not know how to recognize it (me). At times I feel a longing for release, a deep, half-smothered yearning to break free. Why, after so much of my allotted time has fled, do I sense this protest, this wish to stir, still fearing the loss of the shield (the hiding place) those bonds have been? Is there to be some kind of release before that final one in death? Could there yet be purpose for that deformed, misshapen, stunted spirit?

Is He allowing this strange time to answer, in ways I have not yet imagined, a longing He put within? What would it be like to fully be what He had in mind when He made me? It would be wonderful beyond description to sense His hand holding me, *using* me...

Is this stirring only another facet of grief: a vacuum, a longing for a sense of purpose I once had and lost? Or is it more—much more?

This may prove to be of great importance in sorting out my thoughts:
This morning I found myself thinking about Jesus' natural occupation: carpenter. For a tree to become the finished product planned by the Carpenter, much of the natural form must be trimmed away. To fashion what He had in mind, the tree first had to be cut down, have its branches lopped off, its bark stripped, and its wood dried. Then He cut away everything but the shape He had in mind. Perhaps He used sandpaper, too. The tree's natural shape and course of growth were incidental; it was only *part* of the real substance of the tree that He used—after He got rid of whatever perfectly good, sound wood that was not useful to Him.

Parable? Could all of the facets of my life be—planned?

In reviewing the Journal I have kept, I repeatedly come across expressions of desire to find *purpose*.

Twice in this journey there have been instances when, for a few brief moments, there were glimpses of Purpose—accompanied by flashes of acceptance—regarding Jim's demise. The first was when I saw God working in the hearts of the children as a result of the shadows of this valley. At such times, there is no avoidance of the reality of eternity, the issues of life and death, of mortality itself; I sensed a quickening in their hearts of God's truth as it related to them. Also, my own brokenness has seemed to make it easier for them to face something less than perfection in themselves, leaving them freer to open up to me. If it takes this agony to break through to them spiritually, *it is a price neither Jim nor I would refuse to pay.*

The second instance came when someone mentioned that they felt that the process had been planned, arranged, from five years back. Then, too, my heart said a quick, almost eager "Yes!"—if God were using it. Cost fades into insignificance if, through it, God works something beautiful in His sight. Purpose. How precious is a sense of real purpose!

As to understanding the times:

My struggles have made me very much aware of my own great shortcomings in the sight of God, and in my flailing around for help I have found that to be the general condition. There seems to be a tremendous dearth of living reality in the church today. *"When I come, will I find faith on the earth?"* Who really, truly walks in that vital union with Christ which makes way for Him to work in the Great Commission way? Far more desperately than we know, we need an out-pouring of God's Spirit.

There is a fierce battle raging in this world which matches the description of end-times, when Satan will come down to earth in great wrath knowing that his time is short. The battle is vicious, ugly; but the outcome has already been determined: the King of kings will triumph!

The gaze of our soul must be on that Rider of the white horse; He has told us that when these things begin to come to pass we must look *up*, knowing that our redemption draws near. We allow ourselves, in our spiritual peripheral vision, to be aware of the activity of the evil one, and we stand against him wherever we can; but our gaze, the gaze of our souls, must be fixed upon our Lord. We look up, for He comes!

Understand God? Who can? Yet He has told us to search out truth regarding Himself, saying,

> *"Let him that glories glory in this, that he knows and understands Me."*
> Jeremiah 9:24

Moses knew God's ways. Psalm 108:7

Solomon wrote,

> *"It is the glory of God to conceal a thing, but the honor of kings is to search it out."* Proverbs .25:2

Jesus said,

> *"This is eternal life, to know You, and Jesus Christ Whom you have sent."* John 17:3

He also said that He would reveal Himself to those who choose to obey Him:

> *"The person who has My commands and keeps them is the one who really loves Me; and He that loves me will be loved by my Father. And I, too, will love him and will show (reveal, manifest) myself to him—I will let Myself be clearly seen by him and make Myself real to him."* John 14:21

Paul wrote,

> *"Do not be vague and thoughtless and foolish, but understanding and firmly grasping what the will of the Lord is... "* Ephesians 5:17

Why do we hold back?

During a precious recent discussion it was pointed out (as I had begun to wonder) that those years with Jim must have changed me, that I am not the person he married. How can I determine just who this person is now? And what my Father has in mind for His child now? There must be some reason that I am still here.

In Bruce Wilkinson's teaching *Going Beyond Jabez,* he made statements which reinforce what has begun to form in my own mind; God may be working to break down walls and fences which have constricted me all my life. As I wrote above, I am aware of faults; I am afraid to have the walls destroyed. But what if that impression is yet another ploy of the enemy to hinder what God wants? What if God sees something different, something on which He has been working, unknown to me? If He has worked something of Himself into those cramped areas through the years, and especially through the trauma of these last troubled times, He may yet produce something which bears the print of His nail-pierced hand.

The huge question is—how do I discover it?

32

WHY CAN'T I... ?

Why can I not "end" the marriage that was "terminated" at Jim's death?

Simply because he had become part of all I am.

> "How rich the texture of two lives long twined by time!
> So many threads have made the pattern what it is:
> Laughter, tears. Sunshine, shadows.
> Anguish and ecstasy, sorrow and joy, pain and peace—
> How deep we've drunk of light and dark along the way!
> The love that fills our life-way has flowed silver,
> Now flows gold,
> And there is even joy in growing old;
> For we are still together, hand in hand...
>
> "My heart is full of gratefulness and joy
> As on this anniversary of gold I tell you, once again,
> With heart grown full from all the living of these years,
> **'Dearest one, my own, *I LOVE YOU!*'"**
>   – from "Golden Anniversary," jbl

The intermingling of two lives for over a half-century can never be reversed. My life has been forever impacted by Jim's presence and influence. That cannot be undone, any more than study, physical work or activities over all those years could be undone.

> "...*One* . then how
> In all God's earth can I endure
> This tearing of my total inner self?
> For you are gone!..."
>   – from "One..." jbl

In 1,135 days, the *fact* of his death has been pretty well rubbed in. The initial shock has worn off, and the trauma level has lowered to a dull ache. I have become relatively used to the emptiness of heart and home. The sharp peaks of grief have largely leveled out into a constant, underlying sadness. I miss him. I love him. That cannot change; the past is always part of the present.

> "No one departs this life without leaving something behind. The things said and done become living memorials. It is more than a memory. Left behind are the dynamics of that life."
>
> – Lester Sumrall.

"The dynamics of Jim's life..." remain forever in the lives of those he touched. He touched none more than he touched mine.

At the first session at a local Bereavement Center, the director told of her own loss, and went on to say that part of our hearts will always belong to one we have loved. We just learn how to go on.

As my counselor says, an amputee "learns how to go on," but will always miss that part of him that is gone. No amount of mental gymnastics can change that.

If only I could find peace regarding the spiritual aspects of my bewilderment! Even yet, critical aspects of a faith being sorely tried lurk in the shadows of my mind; over and over again the questions try to rise to torment and test all that is within. Such a strange mixture: the deep confusion which does not budge, but also a most profound response to reports of any move of God, any soul finding Christ, any working of the Spirit. Mention of "Life on the Edge," or a report of prophetic calling brings an explosion of intense yearning deep within.

My heart cries out to Him continually; will He, sometime, make it clear?

Shortly after I walked into church this morning a memory stirred once more. Not long after Jim was admitted to Palliative Care, I heard myself saying to another, "Sometimes we need to *trust* God, not necessarily *for* something." I think I am being nudged back to that point.

I need to visit Mt. Moriah! Lord, help me to find the willingness to give back to you the treasure that was Jim. Nothing can now change what actually did happen; help me to surrender to that change, in some way to give myself to You—in spite of losing him. I do not think that I can do this by simple choice. I need You to overshadow me and birth a work of Your Spirit within me.

33

WOUNDS

Last night I spoke with a friend, daring to share the depths of my despair and the dark pressure to escape...

How could words express what it meant to hear him say that he had experienced exactly the same painful pressure that I was feeling? When words come through wounds, they are real; so real—anything but the trite phraseology of those unscathed by personal anguish. Words from one who has known the same kind of anguish find an openness in the hurting heart of one who hears them. When words bleed, they are powerful.

God does not waste pain. He uses it.

(Mine... too?)

Later, thought shifted to Another. This Friend, also, was wounded. It was His wounds which rendered Him infinitely effective toward those He longed to rescue. It was through His wounds that He provided redemption for every soul of all time.

His wounds: to those dwelling in a tangible world, the most obvious are physical; the wounds in head, hands, side and feet. But there were deeper wounds, too; wounds of soul, and of spirit. Every trauma of human-kind was carried in the Person of our Lord Jesus! Isaiah prerecorded them all. (Chapter 53).

He chose to take on human form lacking any special attraction. He was unappreciated. He knew grief. He was despised. Forsaken. Judged. Wrongly condemned. Mocked. Rejected, by His own whom He had come to save. Forsaken, by his friends and by His Father, God Himself. Every part of His being was profoundly wounded; He experienced the absolute depth of every kind of sorrow, grief and pain.

It was *our* griefs, sickness, weakness, and distress that He carried. It was *our* sorrows and pain of punishment that He took on Himself, yet we turned from Him as if *He* deserved this judgment by God. Talk about being misunderstood! Imagine the anguish of being maligned by the very sinners whose punishment He bore...

Upon Him was laid every test that the human race has ever known, and He *never failed.* There is no anguish we experience which He has not experienced. He empathizes with our pain! His love took Him through all of that anguish on our behalf—to redeem us. When *He* speaks, *how* His words bleed!

He continually intercedes on our behalf before the Father's throne, and when we come before that throne with well-deserved confidence in His love, we...

> *"...find grace to help in good time for every need; appropriate help, well-timed help, coming just when we need it."* Hebrews 4:16

What an overwhelming revelation of God's great love, understanding, and provision! And of the fact that God finds purpose in pain.

My pain overwhelms me because I am so small and do not understand the reason for it. On a very much smaller scale, is there some good purpose for my pain? Is it the scalpel of the Surgeon? The carving knife of the Sculptor? The smelting furnace of the Goldsmith? The wheel of the Potter? Sometimes there is a sense that He is working in these shadows, that His hands are accomplishing something I cannot see. And that somewhere in this painful process He is birthing something of His own design...

> "...I bring to You my pain. Poor offering!
> Yet, may the simple coming to Your heart
> Be something 'kin to spikenard
> Which You accept—and bless."
> – from "Broken," jbl

They come back to me, words set down in the newness of my grief. They have deeper meaning now. I have been wrestling with the pain, trying to understand it in order to escape it. Perhaps simply opening it to Him, relinquishing it to Him...?

Earlier I spoke of scars, and the fact the Jesus still bears the scars of the rejection, the wounding He experienced. Scars. We think of them in terms of disfigurement.

Why does Jesus still bear His scars?

Surely He could cause His glorified body to be fully restored, unmarred, gloriously beautiful. Yet He still bears the prints of nails! He must deem them valuable...

Is there worth, also, in our scars, as He sees them? Scars are the evidence of wounding, which validate what we say to others wounded in the same way. "God doesn't waste pain." We have heard it. We have said it. To witness it, to see God minister to other hurting souls through our scars, our wounds, is an awesome thing.

If this pile of words ever amounts to something to help another traveler through Dark Valley, it will be in large part because God trusted another of His servants—with wounds. Directly through those wounds God ministered life to me at my lowest point. I am grateful to Him, and to that wounded minister of hope.

Won't it be amazing, on the other side, to see how He weaves things together?

34

"DEEP CALLS TO DEEP..."

A couple of days ago while watching a Christian program, I heard a missionary-minded young couple tell of a time spent with Bruce Wilkinson, a speaker/writer who had an experience with God which remarkably clarified his calling. He helped them to recognize a profound interest which had lain in the depths of their hearts for many years. Shortly after that, a memory of part of their wedding ceremony suddenly came alive to them: as the groom's father had begun to pray for them after their vows, he was moved to speak prophetically into their lives exactly the interest which had been brought to the forefront of their consciousness while speaking with Bruce Wilkinson.

Mention of that prophetic calling together with videotape of the incident exploded again that deep, deep yearning in my soul for a life-on-the-edge walk with God. From beyond the depths of my spirit I began to weep out my heart-cry to the Lord, words flowing in a language of the Spirit which seemed like an eloquent expression of the most basic, utter human need of God. The cry rose from the very depths of my being. The rest of the program no longer mattered to me.

I do not know just what my soul longs for; I do know that it is for something of God Himself. Whatever it is that blocks that—must go. It has been hard to write those last two words; there is a clear sense that it involves death to some part of my inner self which is hard to release. Nevertheless, I face Him, and open to Him that area of resistance, giving Him liberty to take it from me. The fires of this period of anguish will, no doubt, continue to work in me until He has removed this dross, whatever it is.

Through night hours there were periods of opening to the Lord, a flowing upward to Him from the depths of my soul. Emptying...

I do not like pain. I would far rather go through life without it. Yet it seems that pain is an integral part of this earthly existence. Sometimes it seems to be such a waste—as in a cancer death. At others, pain produces far more significant results than pleasure: take childbirth, for instance. Generally, some form of pain generates some kind of gain, as in acquiring an education, pursuing a career, raising a family. It is in the stretching times that we develop most.

Recently, the Scripture, *"God spared not His own Son, but freely delivered Him up for us all..."* brought new thought regarding this issue of suffering. Surely, no one has ever known suffering as did *"His own Son."* Yet God, Who is the very essence of Love, did not spare Him.

God freely delivered Him up; there was no hold-back. A God Who is Love itself, freely giving up His own Son? Where was the love in that? It flowed through His Son, beyond His Son, to an entire race of lost humanity who did not deserve it but was loved anyway.

But—His own Son! How could the love of a Father-God allow His own Son to suffer so totally? Where was the love in that, for the Son? Look beyond the cross! Jesus, *"for the joy that was set before Him endured the cross, despising the shame."* He knew that there was purpose in the pain, for through it *"He would bring many sons to glory."*

Jesus endured it. He *"set His face as a flint,"* amazing His disciples with His determination to go to Jerusalem in spite of the obvious danger awaiting Him there. He neither weakened nor wallowed in the course of His agony; He was not masochistic; He was real. The agony was real; a real means to a real end. It had purpose!

He despised the shame. He did not allow His true Self to be demeaned by it. He was still King all the way through Pilate's judgment hall, Calvary, the tomb, the descent into hell itself, the resurrection and ascension to the very throne of His Father. He will rule forever!

All other suffering pales compared to that of Jesus. I suppose that our human pain is large to us simply because we cannot see beyond our horizons. In the face of what He went through for us, how can we shrink at what we are asked to face? Let us look for God's purpose.

I would rather, much rather have been spared my suffering. How I have wanted a "hold-back" in my journey! I still struggle within to come to a place of willingness, let alone a "freely" state of willingness.

I do not know the purpose for my pain; but as surely as God is in His Heaven, there must be purpose as He plans it. May I find a way to give myself to that purpose, as He leads me!

35

BRUISED REEDS AND DIMLY BURNING WICKS

"A bruised reed He will not break and a dimly burning wick (smoking flax) He will not quench..." Isaiah 42:3; Matthew 12:20

I am glad for that. Those analogies are descriptive of my life over the last three years. The many-faceted trauma which followed Jim's death has been horrendous. Everything I built my life upon since I first trusted in Christ has been shaken. The grief of losing that precious person from my life was, in itself, enough to destroy me; what blew the trauma beyond comprehension was the fact that we had reached for the miracle held out by the many promises of God, and had come up empty.

Thus I stood not only bereft of my earthly love but also condemned, either for not having real faith, or for sheer unworthiness being rejected by the God I have loved. The most profound Love of my life seemed to have been ripped from me along with my husband. In light of the promises of God, the ministry of Jesus, and the very nature of God Himself as described in His Word, how could we have been denied that healing so dearly bought on Calvary—if it is all true?

"If"?

What hope can there be for one tormented by such questions?

"*If*"!

Should there be basis for that short but pivotal word there is no reality left in this life or the next. How can one bear that kind of inner tearing? Oh, the dreadful state of one caught in the vortex of that waterspout! The *fear* that accompanies it! The bruised reed feels that it deserves to be cut off and cast away; the dimly-burning wick dreads—anticipates—being snuffed out altogether.

Yet the reed, though bruised severely, still has tenuous connection with its root; some life still flows. The dimly burning wick or smoking flax has not altogether lost the flame; there is still some real, though struggling, remnant of the fire.

He has not let go of His hurting child.

Will the reed that is bruised mend in time, perhaps forever changed, yet living, even serving in some different capacity than it knew before? Will the fire, though burning low, burn deep—consuming dross, enlarging the base of the fire, perhaps to rise again in a different way, in a different place than it burned before?

He has not let go! There are still times when His touch assures...

Will the deep questions ever be answered? Will understanding come? Or will He so override the pain and confusion with His presence that, in some way, I may become rock-solid sure of *Him,* even without understanding His way with me?

He has not let go. He still draws near. I still love Him.

The journey is a long one, fraught with perils; yet He has not allowed the anguish to destroy me. His purpose: I reach for that. I do not yet see it, but I long for it!

He has tempered the testing. Though it has often seemed beyond endurance, He has not allowed it to destroy me altogether.

Where does this path lead?

There is still a sense of wooden numbness. Partly, this must be due to the rather hectic pressure of the days, but there is always that underlying heaviness, the profound sorrow, the lost-ness and uncertainty in so many areas of my inner life. I need help!

Time: 2:06 a.m. I had thought that I was weary enough to sleep tonight. The initial report from one newly returned from India stirred afresh the intense frustration, yearning, and perplexity regarding our current spiritual dearth.

There, where extreme poverty is rampant, there is richness toward God: deep reverence, heartfelt and exultant worship, and a profound sense of His presence. How can a heart which has known that state help but cry out from its deepest depths, longing to know that living reality again? What other answer is there to our desperate condition nationally, denominationally, personally?

How can church leaders—and their followers—go blithely on in their pretty ways, mouthing words without power, platitudes without peace, and theories without working, vital Reality?

Father, You Who see from Heaven, rouse us, lest we sleep the sleep of death from which there is no return. Stir us! Come upon Your Church with a sovereign outpouring of Your Spirit! Only You can open eyes grown spiritually dull and give hearing to ears that no longer hear your still, small voice. Only You can speak Light into hearts grown dark from distance from You. Only You can cleanse and give Life anew. We are in crucial need of Your quickening touch. Send the Fire!

36

"WHAT I DO. . ."

"What I do thou knowest not now, but you shall know hereafter."
John 13:7 KJV
"You do not understand now what I am doing, but you will understand later on." John 13:7 Amplified

Those words drifted into my mind in the early hours of the morning as I had begun to pray for those engraved on my heart. Such familiar words, spoken by the Lord Jesus as He stooped to wash Peter's feet, just before Calvary. I had read them, heard them often in that setting.

This time, they arose in a different context. Before retiring I had been editing some of my reflections regarding the painful confusion of my grief journey. *"You do not understand..."* There could be no clearer, more accurate, yet simple description of the last three years.

"You do not understand..." Those simple words obviously showed that He *did* understand. Now, that's encouraging! Not only did He understand Peter's confusion, He cared—enough to communicate that understanding. Love. That is what flowed through the issue.

He proceeded—even though Peter didn't understand.

He promised—that Peter would understand later on.

He purposed—to accomplish something life-changing by what He was doing.

He—was doing it!

What was He doing?

He was stooping to cleanse Peter's feet. They had become dusty from his journey. Feet. A rather inglorious part of Peter's body. It might have seemed strange enough to have Jesus wash his hands, or his face; it was downright humiliating to have Him focus on his dirty feet.

Jesus does that. He goes directly to that part of our lives that most needs His touch. Those are the areas we want to hide, even from ourselves. Especially from ourselves! It is not comfortable for us when He goes there. We squirm, we protest, we struggle...

Yet He proceeds. Gently. But thoroughly. Love motivates Him. In our confusion, our embarrassment, we pull away. We panic. We cry out in fear and despair. He is undeterred; He proceeds. He is in no hurry. He will work as long as necessary—until His work is finished.

And He promises: *"Though you do not understand now, you will."*

Painful as our confusion is, He sustains with recurring awareness that His love undergirds, overshadows—always, even when we cannot see.

He has a purpose. The assurance of future understanding clearly indicates purpose. The deep "Why?" of the soul in sorrow will be answered—not now, but when He has accomplished what He set out to do. Though anguish in our valley overwhelms, though bewilderment of that "Why?" would hide His face in shadow so deep the heart might question His very existence, still—He promised—and assures of purpose.

Purpose. What *was* Jesus doing for Peter?

Many things.

Physically, He was cleansing tired, dusty, uncomfortable feet. There would be rest, and a sense of well-being when that was done.

Mentally and emotionally, He was preparing him for restoration. He knew Peter would fail—fail so grievously that he would be driven to the brink of despair. He was saying ahead of time, "Peter, remember; I cleansed your feet from the dust of your walk; I will cleanse your soul, too, from the defilement of your ways."

Spiritually, He was commissioning him to touch with compassion those He would send across his path. He knew that, in so doing, Peter would share the exquisite joy of ministry that He, Himself knew—as He washed Peter's feet.

Jesus is at work. What He is doing we may not understand during the process. We do not need to. Deep in our hearts, we know of Him that He is Love personified, that He does all things well. Even the things that sear our souls with anguish are among those "all things" He assured us He will work together for good to those who love Him, "to those who are the called according to His purpose."

He is both Creator and Redeemer; He works according to His master-plan. He is the Designer; we are His workmanship, and all His works shall praise His Name when the plan is unfolded. We have his permission to rejoice, even as it is in progress!

He—is doing it!

Again I remember—one of His sent-ones said, early in my journey, that God might have a plan that could only be fulfilled in this way...

Currently, there is increasing awareness of a strong stirring within. Another phase? An approaching culmination of some kind? It is a sweet sense of God at work. Perhaps a strengthening. It is like "the Spirit of God brooding over the face of the waters."

One of those who corresponded with me when I was reaching out in all directions wrote:

> "It is not 'theological explanation' that is wanting in your heart, but a meeting of His Spirit that somehow transcends the very questions themselves."

Could that be what is happening? It does seem that as the inner stirring of the Spirit increases, the intensity of the questions lessens.

37

I CAN'T LET GO!

How many times have I felt I was coming out of the shadows, only to enter another pall of darkness? How many times have I felt a few hours or days of warm release, only to slip back into the prison of pain?

Is there some desperate measure to take which would once for all bring me into the sunlight? I begin to wonder if I will ever reach the exit from this valley by some one, final exercise; perhaps it is simply a journey which must be taken one step at a time, regardless of sun or shadow. Still, there is awareness that there is some recurring pattern to these ups and downs. If that could be identified, could a solution be found which would at least indicate a way out of this pain?

My friend senses something with which I tend to agree; I cannot seem to let go of Jim. I know that my "hanging on" will never bring him back again. I do realize that he is forever lost to me in this life—but my whole soul screams its protest. I fear life without him; "life" without *life* in it is nothing more than living death, a hollow existence, a shell of pain surrounding nothing.

I don't think I have been able to adequately portray why that is so. There is a saying that one cannot understand another's gait until one has walked a mile in his shoes. Unless someone could feel the rejection, the constriction, the deeply ingrained sense of fear, lost-ness and self-doubt which was an integral part of all of my life apart from those blessed years in Jim's love, it would be impossible to imagine what it was like. Or to grasp how deeply ingrained that sense of inadequacy remains, apart from him.

There were fifty-one and a half years with him. That is a long time.

The nearly twenty-three years before Jim's protecting love and the years since he was taken stand in pathetic contrast to the decades with him. Becoming permanently cast in that stark poverty is not anything to welcome with tremendous eagerness. Must I embrace that fate to go on?

What a sentence!

Could I even begin to write a "Good-bye" letter to Jim?

The thought brings the ship of my soul perilously close to an enormous iceberg. Immense cold washes over my heart in even considering the prospect. There is the sense of imminent peril; something in that huge coldness could crush me into total oblivion.

Something has to happen, though. This journey: from the joy I knew into painful darkness, through tremendous fear, into...?

At this moment, I cannot proceed.

I may leave the computer, but never the subject at hand. Since closing out of this writing last evening, there has been a lot of thinking. On different levels.

There is a part of me that would rather stay in the shadows regardless of the pain, heart clinging to the one I love, than emerge into sunlight, alone. I do not see how I could feel otherwise:

ONE
God made us one.
It must have been His hand, and His alone
That brought us gently, sweetly
To a oneness so profound
That every part of every essence of our lives
Was blended, interwoven in a union
Inextricable, inseparable—*one!*

The moment that we met
Ensuing timid, fleeting times we came
To know and understand
Each other's heart as friendship grew...
The golden day we recognized
That love was budding, though
As yet we dared not say it to ourselves...
The certainty that came, the vows we made,
The joys, the toil and tears of life together...
All knit us closer, ever closer;
One—oh, my darling, we were *one!*

One! Then how
In all God's earth can I endure
This tearing of my total inner self?
For you are gone!
Torn, ripped from my soul,
From all my life so rudely, cruelly snatched!

203

"An enemy hath done this!"
What, then, remains for one who's left behind?
Tears, agony so deep it swallows all...
They call *this*—LIFE ?

How can I live without my heart?
Father, show me!

– jbl

Words—can sometimes provide a charcoal sketch of reality, but never can they flesh out the actuality they try to describe. We were two very normal, flesh-and-blood people, each with our own package of faults and weaknesses; but somehow by the grace of God we were guided into a relationship in which each nurtured and supported the other, ignoring flaws in the simple delight of each other's strengths, and reveling in the deeply committed heart-love both given and received by the other. We treasured that. I still do.

That relationship became my identity. It was all I knew myself to be. I had never before become a *person.* Is it possible to describe that to anyone who *has* his own identity? That was my "personhood" for over five decades, too; it is just who I am. For a person in this situation, the prospect of cutting loose from that only identity is terrifying. It seems to be equivalent to choosing to become a non-entity—a step into self-destruction, oblivion.

And I am to go that route?

That is a frightening prospect!

In a more misty way, untried and at thought-level only, there is the speculation that all of those years in the shelter of Jim's love could have changed me...

When I think "without Jim," I think "pre-Jim"—a life of such constriction, self-doubt and inner imprisonment that it is too painful to contemplate. I cannot face that again! To force a crayfish back into a shell it has discarded would destroy it. Jim's love made a larger covering for me, one in which I could *live.* That covering has been torn away, leaving me very vulnerable—and afraid. I suppose those who understand these things would say that I have lost my identity. At my age, how in the world would I find a new one? Or, do I just face existence, without one?

"Stuck." But struggling. Like a swimmer lost at sea, who has no idea which way to swim. I see no landmarks. I have only a sense that there must be land somewhere, and a longing to reach it. That longing to find something solid under my feet may be the only strength I have; do I waste it, flailing around as I do? Yet, to stop may be to sink beneath the waves... There is a way to float, they say, if you know how to do it. If I could, where would the waves take me?

Struggling—in limbo.

Must I inwardly self-destruct by saying "Goodbye" to Jim? The road ahead, the right one—is it one of perpetual pain? Is there a different course, one which I do not yet see?

How am I to know what course to take?

Shepherd... !

Having spent myself in that last storm, there is, again, that numbness, the "washed-up-on-the-beach" part of the all-too-familiar pattern. The inner state has been put on hold by a rush of circumstances requiring time and attention; in other words, "time out." Maybe it was needed.

Looking again at the "Good-bye" thought: was the intent not to close Jim out of my past and my heart, but in some way to reconcile to this temporary separation? Could I do that?

If those years with Jim allowed some real changes to take place, what could they be? Full circle: Who am I, now? How does a person re-discover himself? I wish I had more understanding of these matters. I don't feel that I make much progress simply living day-to-day in the small round of activities which present themselves. I just do not know how to proceed.

LETTER:
"My Jim—

"Just that much, and tears form.

"I have not allowed myself to dream of you hovering near, for I know that you are no longer here. I have not permitted myself to play mind-games. It is important to me to try to keep reality ever-present, for that alone is true, and that alone, honest. It has been a long and painfully lonely path through shadows since you were taken from me. I see no escape from it.

"A good friend has suggested that I try to write you a letter. It is a make-believe exercise, for I cannot communicate with you now, and that breaks my heart! (Some have been deceived into trying to communicate with the dead and found themselves in the grip of evil.)

"Nevertheless, I suppose that going through the motions of writing to you might have merit if it were to clarify some of the issues that hold me in this darkness, and in so doing, perhaps point to a way of healing. If healing were possible it would be welcome, for the pain is intense; besides, if our Father has some purpose for my life which cannot be fulfilled without that healing or some measure of it, I must try.

"I am glad you didn't want to leave me. I didn't want you to leave! You were torn from me, and the gaping wound remains. I do not see how it can ever heal, for we were no longer separate entities, but *one,* and there is no part of me that is whole without you.

"Your love was so precious. I treasure it still. How I thank God for you! Perhaps God has let you know, now, just what your life and your love have meant to so many of us. The children rise up and call you blessed; they honor your God because of you. So many, many lives you touched for good; most particularly mine. You knew I was locked up when you reached out to me; you could never have guessed how desperately bound up I was. It was the sheer mercy of God that brought you into my life.

"From the first, I found your straight-forward ways reassuring, refreshing, attractive. Even at the age of seventeen you had a matter-of-fact maturity about you, which you had rightly earned. You loved God sincerely and with a full heart; that, too, made me know that you could be trusted, that one would be safe with you. Your sense of fun, your good humor and infectious laugh didn't hurt a thing, either. You worked thoroughly, honestly, and diligently at any task you undertook. Others saw these things, too, and appreciated every one of them; that is why you were voted President of the Student Body, 'way back then. Those traits only strengthened and grew throughout your life. And you always had a tender heart—toward God, and toward others.

"It seems so hollow, so dry, so devoid of living reality to try to portray your life with just—words. You were a living soul sent into this world from the hand of God; you were His gift. I am so thankful, far beyond anything paltry words could express, that His mercy brought me into the circle of your love for those years!

"I'm supposed to say "Good-bye" to you in this letter.

"In a very real sense, I cannot do that, for you are forever woven into every part of my heart. You have been a vital part of my life for more than two-thirds of it; the *good* part. I was at least partly alive in the shelter of your love. You were so out-going, so fun-loving, so involved with life that, in your shadow, I lived a little, too.

"Thank you for your tenderness, your faithfulness, your intercession. Thank you for opening your heart to me, and making me feel safe enough to open mine to you. Thank you for supporting me when I needed strength, and allowing me to support you in some of the storms we faced together. Thank you for sharing so wonderfully with me the joys (and stretching experiences) of raising the precious children that God sent into our lives. Thank you, my Love, for all that you have meant to me through all of our lives together. Thank you for—just being who God made you to be.

"Say "Good-bye" to you? How can I? Yet, you are no longer here...

"How can I go on, without you?

"But that is being required of me. It hurts!

"Why is "letting go" so very difficult? Maybe this hanging on is a form of self-preservation. After so many years of a wonderful marriage, how can I ever let go—of one so loved? Yet, you are gone, and somehow I must accept that, *must* let go.

"Let go! I remember, years ago, pressing a diamond into the wounded hands of my Lord... My Love, the only way I can begin to let go of you is to press you, and my pain, and myself, into those same nail-scarred hands. He understands. He cares. And He can absorb the pain, robbing it of the power to control and destroy. Precious Savior!

"I still feel that the enemy did this. Why was he allowed to? I have suffered from many painful questions, Jim. I still love you. I really, really miss you! "Good-bye"? I would rather contemplate seeing you again...

"I wonder if you had grown, matured as God had planned, and were ready for Home, while I still have a long way to go.

"I know that being in your life must have made changes in me, but I am unable to pin-point them; I guess assimilation does not leave particles on the surface for easy identification. My very personhood is subtly changed.

"How?

"For what?

"I return to that question often, though I know that God seldom reveals the entire journey at once. At the moment what seems uppermost in my mind is a desire for sensitivity to the "nudges" of the Spirit, a longing to sense His direction and simply follow.

"Is that what my friend meant by "living on the edge"?

"Experiencing that is precious; real living.

"Other than that I carry our children on my heart, always. Whether the concern lies somewhat in the background or surfaces with urgency, it is always there. That is one sense of purpose.

"Another is—what I am doing now. I spend a lot of time at the computer, trying to set down what stirs within. That has some purpose in that pressure is relieved, and some issues clarify upon reflection. (*Meditation;* you often spoke of that as being meaningful to you. Perhaps that is what I do when I write things down?) Is there some other reason I feel compelled to spend time this way? I wonder if it might eventually help another. I think that is not up to me, but to Him.

"Has God shown you anything of His purpose for me now? What must it be like to "*know as we are known*," having seen Him! It may be hard for you to remember now how life on this earth has so many unknowns. It seems that it would be a lot easier to move forward if one only knew what to move toward. I understand that, sometimes, God gives an overview, a main direction which enables a person to step confidently into a course of action leading to the work He has assigned. That would be wonderful! At my age can I anticipate any more than a day by day, step by step existence, with the odd tiny meaningful happening? How I long for meaning! Life has lost so much of that since you were taken.

"Yet I remember marveling at the sense of His presence when visiting that dear senior saint in Victoria and recognizing that, though she was much limited in things she could do, she was unlimited in what she could be—a dwelling-place for the Most High. May He enlarge my heart to give Him the room He looks for in me; out of that indwelling, He will do what He wants to do through me.

"Until my heart fills with joy in meeting you again, may I be pliable in those Hands.

"I miss you sorely, Jim. I still love you with all my heart!

"Au revoir... "

208

38

MOUNT MORIAH

There is a recurring, uncomfortable memory of Abraham's Mount Moriah experience. Does that dread mountain loom somewhere along this journey through Dark Valley? If so, have I the strength to climb those particular *"dangerous heights of testing and trouble"*? (Psalm 18:33)

I have recounted the anguished journey of my soul after my mother's death. My heart could not release the ring—until, in my spirit, I looked up into the face of my Savior and told Him I could release it—to Him.

There is a definite parallel between that incident and the turmoil of the moment. Jim is a most precious gem which I must release to the Lord I love. I cannot let go of him to Death—though Death has taken him. I cannot simply close him out of my life, though he is gone. I am becoming convinced that the only way I can let go of Jim, my dearest earthly love, is to once more make that trek to Moriah, and place him too, into hands that bear the prints of nails.

I do not think I can do it, unless the Bearer of those scars strengthens me. I love that One; I want to make the offering if that is what He asks of me.

Abraham could not accomplish his Moriah mission simply by accepting the thought; he had to take one step after another from where he had been when God made the request until he arrived at the exact place. I know that the idea does not suffice; I must wait, open before Him until every part of my heart arrives at the point where it can be done. It must be a full, irrevocable release. That will take a miraculous work of the Spirit.

There is a strong sense that, if He enables me to really give back to Him that most treasured gem—Jim's life—He will, at the same moment, receive all there is of me, for "God made us one."

39

"ONLY A TOUCH"

Only a touch of Thy hand, dear Lord,
Only a word from Thee
Will all my heart's wild anguish still,
Joyful my soul shall be.

Only a touch of Thy hand, dear Lord,
And o'er my soul shall sweep
Melody sweet from life's broken chords,
Awakened from silence deep.
— Ida L. Reid

"Will all my heart's wild anguish still." Tremendous picture, in so few words! Marvelous as they are, the thrilling wonder of experiencing what they portray is beyond the scope of mere words to describe.

Early this morning I thought of Paul's words in 1 Corinthians 14:15:

"I will pray with the Spirit, and I will pray with the understanding also."

A choice. So, I chose. A bit later, the old hymn "Have Thy Way, Lord" came to mind. I found it and began to play it on the organ. It is a beautiful outpouring of the soul to the Master. I seldom ever sing any more, but did start following the alto, with all my heart:

"Jesus, see me at Thy feet,
With my sacrifice complete;
I am bringing all to Thee,
Thine alone I'd be.

Have Thy way, Lord, have Thy way;
This with all my heart I say;
I'll obey Thee, come what may,
Dear Lord, have Thy way.

O How patient Thou hast been
With my pride and inbred sin!
O what mercy Thou hast shown,
Grace and love unknown!
　　　　　　　　– G. Brennard

As I was about to start the third verse, there came a beautiful, quickening lift of the Spirit from the absolute depths of my being, His touch to my lips, and He gave other words which I did not understand but which I knew carried to the Father the fullness of my heart. Precious!

There is such life, such awesome reality in one simple touch from the Master. In one swift second, there came such a quality of knowing—a soaring, overwhelming fullness of the reality of His presence—through my entire being. Beautiful. Wonderful. Alive!

Yes, "smoking mirrors" notwithstanding, He has been there, all the time.

Yes, He is real!

Yes, He still lives within!

Allelujah!

Even when we feel utterly abandoned, we do not travel alone. When we cannot see His face, cannot even sense His presence, He is there. He will *never* leave us alone. He will not allow the testing to destroy, only to refine. His love will never fail, however we doubt or stumble.

He has a purpose!

> *"What I do you do not understand now... but you shall know later..."*
> John 13:7

The test will be seen to have wrought something good, when His purpose is shown, in His time.

Yes, it is a matter of "for love's sake yielding to Love."

Mount Moriah.

Making Him Lord.

But enveloping all of that and going infinitely beyond, the answer to the "heart's wild anguish" is that miracle touch of God. As one correspondent wrote:

> "It is not theological explanation that you need, but a meeting of His Spirit that somehow transcends the very questions themselves."

He has touched the depths of my spirit!

Final breakthrough? I don't count on it; I have become very familiar with the cycles—the ups and downs of this path through the Valley. And issues have surfaced which have yet to be worked through. I trust that, having caused them to be raised, He will guide in their solution.

I do know that this Touch has done much to clear the major agony of the journey, the fear that He had abandoned me.

Slow learner as I am, I begin to understand that whatever I face, I face with Him, whether His presence is clear, or hidden.

40

GOD—IN LITTLE THINGS

Bruce Wilkinson's teaching is so absolutely on-target. He mentioned again that when God begins to enlarge our borders we discover that the boundaries are—fear. As he said, it takes some preliminary ventures to begin to realize that God calls us beyond our comfort zone, but never beyond His. Whatever He nudges us to do He will bless and prosper in His plan, astounding us, leaving us in no doubt whatever that it was His doing, not ours. That, in itself, is release from fear—of either failure or a swelled head.

Sometimes the living touch of God bursts upon us in tiny jewel-like moments. Some of us had a spur-of-the-moment birthday party for a friend last evening after watching a video together. One of our friends, Jim, was seventy-five. I poured his tea in a mug that had been my husband's, with "Jim" fired on the side. He liked that, and on a nudge, I gave it to him. What joy to see his happiness!

In the early hours of this morning I began to feel that I had failed last night; perhaps we should have gathered around Jim and prayed for God's blessing. That is sort of a Christian tradition; nothing wrong with it. Then I remembered the very clear, distinct nudge to give him the mug. How beautiful, how life-filled are those unexpected prompts which come to our hearts from His Spirit! Tradition: all well and good perhaps, but there is such fresh *life* in those special times when He gives specific direction.

One of my sons called yesterday morning, his heart so full of the glory of dawning awareness of the calling of God. Yes, Lord! Yes! Watch over him and perfect that which concerns him. Members of a cult are hot on his trail; he appreciates the attention, for he has known so much abuse and neglect. He says that they are the only religious group that has shown interest in him. I put him in Your hands, Father. Bring others of your servants into His life. You are the One Who created that unique person, for Your own unique purpose; watch over him, shield him, protect him; and, most especially, draw Him into a one-ness with Yourself which he has not even imagined. Do Your skilled work within him, then pour Your love through Him to fulfill that purpose for which You gave Him life.

At a recent early service a man who has a ministry at the maximum security prison told of the last time he gave his testimony there. Rather than the two hundred or so that usually attend, there were only about sixty. Although eight people responded to the invitation to accept Christ, he was perplexed, and asked the Lord why the crowd had been so small. He felt the Lord saying, "I am doing more behind the scenes than you can imagine."

Later in the week, a sixty-five-year-old native man met him, and told him that during the testimony he had realized that he wasn't junk. Further, he had committed himself to the Lord, and when he got out he planned to go from one reservation to another to spread the message. The following Wednesday at a "smoke circle" of natives, where anyone can pray, that man stepped into the circle and told them how he had discovered that he wasn't junk, that they were not junk either, and that God had a purpose for each of them. There was good response.

Again, confirmation that even when we cannot understand, God, though unseen, is always at work. Regardless of our weakness, questions, and doubts He is patiently, constantly at work—in us, and everywhere, in far more ways than we can know.

When I began to pray for my mentor this morning, I found myself praying, "Lord, release the eagle in his soul." From that, with thought, I set down these words:

> May He release the eagle in your soul
> To soar, to ride the winds of God—
> To rise, to reach the very heights of Heav'n
> So to see His face, to hear His heart,
> And revel in the knowledge of His love.
> Rich with His presence, insight keen be giv'n
> To see the hidden pain in lives
> That come; to be His instrument, to watch
> With joy incomprehensible
> The growing wonder of His work through you.
>
> – jbl

> "...He enables you to soar the exalted corridors of heaven and brush your wings against the face of God."
>
> — Jamie Buckingham, *Where Eagles Soar*

So be it, Father; increase his joy, multiply his effectiveness in You.

41

WHERE DOES IT LEAD?

The precious assurance remains, sweet in my soul; I am still His; I am still "in Him." That is the main thing. Perhaps the Valley will open out from here, offering release and purpose. Again it surfaces, this need to know why I am here. I am definitely not content to pass my remaining days drifting, following meaningless pursuits, accomplishing nothing.

Lead me, Shepherd.

You have really stretched my heart over these last three years. When you did that long ago with the anguish of childlessness, you made room for those precious children. This has been an even greater stretching; I long to see it, too, lead into some purpose You have had in mind.

I have mentioned that the Shepherd recently brought to mind the phrase,

"Why are you so far from helping me?"

...together with the nudge to look it up. As I wrote earlier, it was with considerable shock that I read what came just before those words—

"My God, my God, why have You forsaken me?" Psalm 22:1

I realized that Jesus, too, had questions—profound ones! And a sense of abandonment—which He expressed. It helped so much to realize that questions are not wrong, even questions toward our God Himself. He wants us to be honest, to be real.

In the last while the Shepherd has seen to it that I found different writings which confirmed His own whispering to my heart in this, and thereby freed me from a great deal of the self-condemnation which has haunted me. The first was a book by Ronald Dunn, *When Heaven is Silent;* and the second, *A Sacred Sorrow* by Michael Card.

Both of these men wrote powerfully of the Biblical validation of those times of sorrow when the Master hides His face, those periods of darkness, fear, lost-ness, and sense of abandonment which draw out the lament of the soul. As I had glimpsed earlier, it was clearly pointed out in these writings that questions, even those directed to God, have definite Scriptural validation; they are evidenced many times in the Old Testament and, as noted, even in the life of our Lord. It is even stated that turning those doubts to the Lord is an act of trust, that pouring our very worst at His feet is a move of profound worship.

When you think of it, doing so is not only acknowledgement that He is supreme, but also that He loves, and that He can be trusted with the very depths of our hearts.

"To whom shall we go...?" How else can we dispose of our doubts, our fears, our failures?

Who else can deliver?

Perhaps in our natural human reluctance to experience hard things we have rather persuaded ourselves that only joy, victory, laughter and rejoicing are acceptable in the life of a Christian, even in the sight of God. *We have not got that perspective from His inspired Word!*

A loving parent does not spurn a child when he falls in the mud or skins his knees, but wants nothing more than that the child come to him for the help it needs. Our God is our Father! He just wants us to be real, and to press close to Him. Is that not the reason He allows hard things— to more profoundly turn our hearts to Him? It is good to watch for that wide-open coming to God in Bible characters as we re-read His Word; there is a lot of it recorded there—as good examples for us to follow.

My heart melts as I read and reflect on this.

All of this time while I wept, questioned, wrestled—then beat myself up for the struggle—was He really treasuring my openness and honesty of heart before Him? Beautiful Lord! Father, if that is so, please take it all, and all of me, and use me. Please show me what You want from me, and give me strength to carry out Your will for me.

What do You want me to do?

I know that there are still unresolved issues in my own journey. However, since that fleeting, vibrant touch of His Spirit upon my soul a while ago, I no longer wonder if He has forsaken me. That has stilled the most severe aspect of the tempest within. For now, I rest in this "cleft of the Rock," perhaps evading other issues—those of faith, and the bewilderment of unanswered prayer.

I still feel that God wants the children of His love to benefit from all He provided at Calvary. It will take a miracle of His precious Spirit to break down the obstacles to the glorious fulfillment of those promises that came from His heart, which He chose to bind Himself to fulfill. Yet, He remains faithful, and powerful. He has a Plan, one which He fully intends to carry out to its completion, for His own glory.

I will wait patiently for Him. I will hold His Word close in my heart and wait quietly in His presence until He causes His life to flow from it through my spirit with the touch He promised.

Father, pour upon us Your precious Spirit; give sight to our spiritual eyes and strength to our weak knees and dangling hands. We need You!

42

WEEPING WITH OTHERS

This has been a difficult day for a treasured friend: the funeral of a precious life-companion. *Father, hold the family close to you in these shock-filled days, and especially later, when shock lifts and reality sets in. They will need you!*

My friend and mentor himself suffered the sudden death of his precious wife, leaving him alone with five grieving children. The shock alone must have been most traumatic, to say nothing of grief at his loss and concern for his motherless young people. The sensitive, caring heart he carries for others in pain of all kinds makes him very vulnerable to the full impact of the tragedy. May God, Himself, minister to that servant of His!

When in touch with him briefly, he signed off with the words, "Standing still. Silently." Such eloquence! I urged him to complete the poem. When he sent me a draft of it, my heart broke and I wept—with him, for him, and for his children.

Now I begin to understand what it means to weep with those that weep. It is impossible to really empathize with another's pain without having personally experienced the same thing. Empathy, that compassionate lending of one's understanding to another, cannot come from the mind, but must flow from a heart which has drunk from the same cup. Those who have not trod this pathway not only fail to understand, but instinctively shrink from such pain.

My own journey through Dark Valley has shaped my soul to tears; I no longer shrink from those shadows. If that inner experiencing of the "Valley of Baca (weeping)" has been preparation in my own soul to understand the anguish in others, and, weeping with them, to support and strengthen them on their way to wholeness, then let it be so. That would lend purpose to my pain. I do know that, without the understanding and caring which was ministered to me, it is highly unlikely that I could have survived my own traumatic grief. Such caring is rare indeed. And hard-won!

My mentor's closing words kept stirring in my own mind, so I began to work with them, too:

> Standing still.
> Silently.
> Life in shattered fragments at his feet.
> Head bowed. Heart wrung.
> His dearest love no longer by his side.
> Tears flow. Soul cries,
> Calling out to One Who knows his pain.
> Standing still.
> Silently.
> Alone.
>
> Standing still.
> Silently.
> The storm of grief breaks full upon his soul.
> Raised eyes. Broken heart.
> All that is within poured at His feet.
> Tears flow. Soul cries,
> Laying all he is before the throne.
> Standing still.
> Silently.
> With God.
>
> Standing still.
> Silently.
> Thunder rolls with lightning flash and rain.
> Open soul. Listening heart.
> Then in God-breathed stillness, deep within
> God speaks. Peace comes.
> Strength beyond his own flows, full and free.
> Standing, still.
> Going on.
> In God.
>
>   –   jbl

In my own journey there came a time when I wrote,

> "I will wait patiently for Him. I will hold His Word close in my heart and wait quietly in His presence until He causes His life to flow from it through my spirit with the touch He promised."

With greater eloquence, that friend in pain wrote,

> "Standing still. Silently."

What a beautiful thing it is when the Shepherd whispers something precious to your heart, then later shows you that it is truly from Him, for it is in His written Word! This "Standing still. Silently" is a Biblical concept:

"For God alone my soul waits in silence: from Him comes my salvation." Psalm 62:1

"Be still and know that I am God." Psalm 46:10

"In quietness and confidence shall be your strength." Isaiah 30:15

"It is good that a man should hope and quietly wait for the salvation of the Lord." Lamentations 3:26

I forwarded two wonderful, very old songs to that one in grief. One of the songs was "Jesus Whispers Peace." The second verse of that one is particularly beautiful:

"When grief seems more than I can bear,
My soul weighed down with heavy care,
And I am sorely tempted to despair,
Jesus whispers peace."
— Della McChain Warren

Part of the other, "Under His Wings," reads,

"Under His wings—what a refuge in sorrow
How the heart yearningly turns to His rest.
Often when earth has no balm for my healing,
There I find comfort and there I am blessed."
— Wm. J. Cushing

Father, shield him from the attack of the Destroyer. Infuse Your strength into his spirit in such measure and fullness that his heart will know that You are holding him, close! Help him to reach out to his children in ways that will mutually strengthen every one of them. Heal the deep wounding; minister to him.

Later the friend mentioned that he had given his daughter a task which she might find difficult and confusing, leaving with her his words, "Remember, I love you!" What a beautiful Father-picture! The incident made a lasting impression in my heart, and as I meditated on it, I wrote these words:

I LOVE YOU!

I love you, Child.
Do not troubled be
When all around you chaos reigns
And in the dark you cannot see.
I love you!

I love you, Child.
Cease your anxious care,
For when you feel the most alone,
Afraid, and lost—lo, I Am there.
I love you!

I love you, Child.
When your heart is torn
With anguish most profound and deep
Know this, while lonely and forlorn,
I love you!

I love you, Child.
Trust your heart to Me.
You do not weep alone, for I,
The Man of Sorrows, also weep!
I love you!

I love you, Child.
There is joy to come.
The path that leads through pain, though steep,
Leads to my arms and to my heart.
I love you!

– jbl

43

WHOLENESS

Wholeness: I really never expected to think of my life again in terms of wholeness. Even now, remembering the immeasurable depth of the trauma, it is beyond my comprehension how any semblance of wholeness could follow. Perhaps I am just getting a glimpse of the greatness, the delightful fullness of what an Almighty God can do.

In speaking of emotional healing, my mentor often uses the analogy of healing after amputation, pointing out that though the limb would always be missing and there would be some on-going discomfort, adjustment and healing over the stump would come in time.

There is a definite parallel. I am still much aware of my loss; there is an aching emptiness where once a beautiful relationship enriched my life. Time brings some adjustment. Reason and counsel help to address some painful issues. A measure of acceptance comes from the simple, unrelenting evidence of what now *is*. That might be construed to be a measure of healing. But our God is One Who deals in the over-abundant, the *"beyond all we could ask or think."*

Wholeness: how has it come?

It has been necessary to fully enter the Valley, and to walk through it, step by step. Wholeness could not come by evading the pain; it must be faced full on and dealt with. How I thank God for sending someone to help me in this! Issues had to be worked through. The process could not be rushed. It was helpful to understand that cycles of darkness and light are normal in the process. That certainly was the case for me; from darkness to hope to the utmost last notch of utter despair, to another gasp of hope—these were part of the recurring pattern of my journey. But God never let the overwhelming darkness quite overwhelm me, or the clawing agony quite destroy.

Perhaps the first gradual, yet definite change came as I realized I was able to take my pain more directly to my Lord Himself. Pouring out all that was in my heart, just "as is," was so very necessary. Jeremiah recommended it:

"Pour out your heart like water before the Lord." Lamentations 2:19

Deliberately giving that pain to Him proved, later, to be a most important step.

It was necessary to face certain life issues—wounds from the past—which, still being raw, prevented healing in this new, most devastating, all-encompassing agony. Such a difficult process! Again, dealing with painful episodes of life, squarely, with the help of someone of understanding and wisdom—total honesty in hard places—helped a lot.

The darkest shadow that hovered low and heavy over my pathway throughout my journey was the testing of my faith. The God I love, the Almighty One, my Savior, Who bore every sin and every sickness on behalf of mankind, Who healed all that came to Him in His earthly manifestation of the will of the Father, whose many immutable promises remain firm and vibrantly alive—this One could so easily have touched and delivered the one I loved so dearly.

I still do not understand what prevented that touch, though I strongly suspect that it must have been the current blanket of unbelief pervading His Body, the Church (including me). How that must grieve Him! He will meet that need, too; He has promised an out-pouring of His Spirit in these last days.

After crying out to my Shepherd to find this lost and confused sheep, He dropped into my heart those Words from Romans 8:28:

"All things work together for good to them that love God, to those who are called according to His purpose."

"All things" would have to include even my failure to touch God on my husband's behalf. That realization was a ray of light through still dark and turbulent shadows. How real are His Words! They do not shake and vary as we do; they remain firm, everlasting. The storm raged on, but there was an Anchor.

After some time of unremitting darkness, eventually there came a sweet, familiar lift of my spirit toward the One I have loved so long—a gentle, tender touch from Him. Shadows closed in once more, but throughout the remainder of the journey, those moments came again, refreshing, reassuring, precious.

I learned so slowly; yet He led on. He never gives up, for He intends to win. Who knows what He has been working in those unknown depths of my spirit through this time? I am grateful for His faithfulness. He has never allowed the overwhelming agony to overcome, the raging fires to consume, or the darkness of despair to swallow up; He has remained in control. He sent help alongside. Thank God for one who placed himself in the hands of God as His instrument, and so patiently ministered as his Lord enabled him.

As I have said, the darkest shadow in my darkest hour was the attack on my faith. I felt I deserved abandonment, and feared it. How my heart cried out to my God in this! A real turning-point came when He touched me—the touch of Life, when He had gently brought me to the point of laying my whole heart wide open at His feet; a Touch which filled my whole being with vibrant, unassailable assurance. Peace!

It was deep confirmation of a less spectacular but unfathomably precious reality: the growth of a quiet, solid understanding that has stabilized through this time—the *fact* of His faithfulness, the unshakeable reality that, always, He is there. Regardless of what I *feel*, the *fact* of His presence is unshakeable. He never lets go! There is still much I do not understand; however, "*I know Whom I have believed...*"

But our God is a God of more than enough! He began to *use* what I had put into His nail-pierced hand at the beginning, that pain which was more than I could bear:

"I bring to You my pain; poor offering!" – from "Broken," jbl

I had no way of knowing that He would actually accept that offering, take it into those wounded hands as given, then begin to *use* it. How like Him! To see God use one's brokenness to steady another is a humbling, wondrous experience. Truly,

"*beauty for ashes, the oil of joy for mourning."* Isaiah 61:3

Literally, sorrow itself turned into *joy!* Today He has been breaking my heart—with joy. Even pain, when God uses it, can become beautiful. What a God! Not content with "just" healing, He actually *turns* sorrow into *joy.* There was no wine like water He turned into wine. There is no joy like sorrow which He has turned into joy!

A few days ago, as I read Peter's quotation from Isaiah,

"*By His stripes you were healed...."* 1 Peter 2:24,

...the "you" seemed to break into layers. I had always taken such verses to refer to physical healing; but it says *you* are healed. You, on every level! That includes deep wounds of soul and spirit, and distress of mind. Though research would yield many more, here are another two which have come directly to my attention in the last few days:

> *"Behold, I will bring it health and cure, and I will cure them, and will reveal unto them the abundance of peace and truth..."* Jeremiah 33:6

> *"For I will restore health unto thee, and I will heal thee of thy wounds, saith the Lord."* Jeremiah 30:17

This morning, just after I sat down in the meeting-place of some senior saints, He did it again. Into my mind drifted the quote:

> *"...that the bones which Thou hast broken may rejoice."* Psalm 51: 8

With the words came the thought that the bones that were broken (that *He* had broken) were not simply healed, they were made to rejoice! Others followed: Jesus told His disciples that they would sorrow, but that their...

> *"...sorrow would be turned into joy."* John 16:20

The Psalmist said that the Lord had...

> *"...turned for him his sorrow into dancing..."* Psalm 30:11

The prophet wrote of God giving the...

> *"...oil of joy—for mourning..."* Isaiah 61:3

Who but our God could go so beyond as to not only comfort and heal, but to actually turn the sorrow itself into joy? He is the God of far more than enough!

What does He want of me? My love. My sensitivity to the nuances of His Spirit. My obedience. He wants—me! Let me be truly His, to follow closely. There could be no greater fulfillment. Could there be greater joy?

Wholeness. Yes. The one I loved is still missing from my life; I feel it. But in the last while there has been a most unbelievably wonderful sense of God using that very vacuum, that pain of loss, to help steady one of His choicest servants. That being so in even the smallest measure, there is function in my loss; *wholeness.* Almost like a prosthesis—of light.

When God begins to *use* the pain—that is when true wholeness comes.

****

1 Peter 1:8 (Amplified) has long been a treasure to me:

> *"Without having seen Him, you love Him: though you do not even now see Him, you believe in Him and exult and thrill with inexpressible, glorious, triumphant, heavenly joy."*

Just today I realized the setting of that verse. Now, at the end of this journal, it throbs with such a depth of meaning:

> *"...now for a little while you may be distressed by trials and suffer temptations so that the genuineness of your faith may be tested, (your faith) which is infinitely more precious than the perishable gold which is tested and purified by fire. (This proving of your faith is intended) to redound to (your) praise and glory and honor when Jesus Christ, the Messiah, the Anointed One, is revealed.*
> *"Without having seen Him you love Him; though you do not (even) now see Him, you believe in Him, and exult and thrill with inexpressible and glorious (triumphant, heavenly) joy."* 1 Peter 1:6b-8

Much earlier in this Journal I longed for a brief, concise summary of what I was going through. All the while, it was already in The Book!

"The trial of your faith..."

I have quoted those very words several times in this writing, but now, in a way that is hard to explain, they open wide and come alive—and alight—with such *meaning*. What a simple, yet profoundly accurate summary of this entire journey! And there is the analogy of gold again...

> *"Without having seen Him, you love Him..."* *"...though you do not even now see Him..."*

A most severe part of the testing has been just that: not seeing Him as I longed to see Him. God allowed that fiery storm of "ifs" and "whys," but held me through it. It is that very testing which, leading into renewed relationship in believing anyway, opens into that...

> *"...inexpressible, glorious, triumphant, heavenly joy!"*

What a God!

44

STEPS BEYOND

The disciples called Him "Teacher." Jesus knew just how to impart Truth in such a way that it went to their understanding—via their *hearts*. There has never been His equal.

Part of Paul's prayer for the Ephesian believers was:

"(That you may really come) to know, practically, through experience for yourselves, the love of Christ, which far surpasses mere knowledge (without experience); that you may be filled (through all your being) unto all the fullness of God, (that is) may have the richest measure of the divine presence, and become a body wholly filled and flooded with God Himself." (3:19)

How incredibly beautiful! What a prospect!

"...really come to know... through experience for yourselves..."

To really know the love of Christ through personal experience, until filled to all the fullness of God—a body wholly filled and flooded with God Himself—what *life!* (See John 17:3)

We don't really know until we experience. Theory is one thing; knowledge by experience is something else again. Theory, theology, doctrine: all well and good, but alone they are lifeless—until the truth is experienced.

Mind-truth (intellectual understanding) is tremendously enriched when it comes through the heart. It is the intellect-only level of understanding from which may spring those dread clichés so often tossed at the grief-torn heart. When the heart hears, facts become vital, living reality.

Experience. A most excellent—and costly—teacher.

I have been amazed at the timing of the Lord. He intended that needed truth be implanted in my life—at heart level. With hindsight, the pattern has become clearer: experience first, then understanding. In whatever manner Truth comes, it is only really learned where the rubber meets the road.

Before I had gone through my own dark night of the soul, the teaching in Ronald Dunn's *When Heaven Is Silent* or Michael Card's *A Sacred Sorrow* might (hopefully) have lodged in my mind and been interpreted intellectually; it is unlikely that I could have begun to really grasp what they had to say. Coming just when they did, their teaching built upon truth which He had already broken open to me in my Dark Valley; the books brought confirmation and further understanding to my mind of what He had been teaching me in my heart.

Thank you, Lord!

I wish every Christian who draws breath could read Michael Card's book, *A Sacred Sorrow*. In it, the author points out that the place of the *lament* is overlooked in the church today. He cites Scriptural examples of those who recorded their laments: Job, David, Jeremiah—and Jesus!

Although I had been aware that some of the Psalms were cries of a desperate heart (I'd prayed a few of them!), I hadn't realized that almost half of them are—laments; true, unvarnished, rubber-meets-the-road outpourings of the depths of the heart, just "as is": deep, genuine, *raw*. Part-way through, most of them have the Hebrew letter *"vav,"* indicating a change of tone or turning of thought: "...*then I cried to the Lord in my distress*," "... *but to You, O Lord, do I lift up my soul...*" but some do not even have that. Psalm eighty-eight, he points out, is just a record of David's outpouring of—anger. (How wise to pour it *out—to God!*) All of them have been kept as part of Sacred Scripture.

I remember again how I was impacted when I realized that Jesus, Himself, had felt abandoned by His Father while He hung on the cross— *and expressed it!*

It is not only right, but *necessary* to engage in lament when that is in our hearts. "*To Whom shall we go...?*" In fact, as Michael points out, our turning to God in those times of extremity and brokenness is most precious to the heart of God.

We understand this on a human level. Parents rejoice in their children's triumphs; but isn't it true that we appreciate most the deep trust that is evidenced when children confide in us during their times of difficulty and defeat?

What astounding Love! When those things I subconsciously kept hidden—from Him (?), but especially from myself—are flung at His feet, barriers between my soul and my God fall away. That is just what He longs for—as does my soul.

Jeremiah wrote, "*Pour out your heart like water before the Lord.*" Ronald Dunn, in *When Heaven is Silent,* reminds us that inner pain *must* be expressed for any healing to begin to take place. Yet, the church generally is uncomfortable with any such expression. There is a prevailing mind-set which insists that the Christian must always manifest joy and victory—at least, outwardly: "*Thanks be to God Who always causes us to triumph...*" True, but there would be no triumph without a preceding battle! Jesus said that if anyone would be His disciple (taught of Him) he must "*take up his cross and follow...*" There is no happy-dance in that! Jesus went through Calvary, the tomb, and a trip to hell itself before resurrection Sunday. His followers may walk through a few shadows, too, on their way to victory. We need to be honest before God—to be *real.*

****

BROKEN...
It's broken, Lord—
This little alabaster heart of mine.
Hot tears that rush from depths within
I never knew existed
Now flood my world with sorrows
Overwhelming—so profound, immeasurable—
That I am lost within their dark
And heaving tides.

I kneel before You, Lord,
And only ask that as they flow, my tears
Shall fall upon Your feet
Nail-pierced for me.
I bring to You my pain. Poor offering!
Yet, may the simple coming to Your heart
Be something 'kin to spikenard,
Which You accept—and bless.
  – jbl

"I bring to You my pain..." We never know what Jesus will do with broken things that are given to Him. Remember the little boy's lunch— five loaves, two small fish?

Bread: made from grain, something natural and good—which had been thrown into the ground to die. Yet life had sprung from it, grown, and borne fruit. But then it had been cut right off from its roots, threshed, beaten and ground to powder, had water thrown on it and strange ingredients mixed in. And if that were not enough, it then made its acquaintance with fire...

Fish: creations of God which had grown up swimming in pleasant waters—but had been caught by net or hook, drawn out of their natural environment so that they died; then they, too, had been held to the flames, perhaps salted...

Bread and fish, in a boy's lunch-basket.

Andrew found the boy with his lunch and brought him to Jesus. Thank God for the Andrews! When the boy put those beaten loaves and dead fish, both "tried as by fire," into the hands of Jesus, He accepted them, just as they were given. He blessed them. Then He broke them—again—opening them up to make them available, first to the disciples, then to the crowd. And with them He fed a multitude!

All they had been through had prepared them to nourish life in others, once placed in the Master's hands.

What can we *do* with things that break our hearts? Press them into hands that bear the prints of nails! He died to carry our griefs and our sorrows as well as our sicknesses and our sins. Only He can take our pain, releasing the weight of it, and rescue us from its power to destroy. We can give the pain to Jesus; He will actually *accept* it, as given. Who knows how He will use it? He will draw us close in the process; then He may use what we give Him to bless someone else. Our Lord has a way of not only *taking* our sorrows, ("poor offering!") but turning them—into *joy!*

How amazing to realize that all of my life has fit into the planning of God—that the life-long loneliness, rejection, even the consuming sorrow, were allowed knowing that they would turn my heart so desperately to Himself—for there was nowhere else to go.

To Him: what a destination!

I have lived for a while. Physically, it would be lovely to lose some of this aging, but not at the cost of the life-learning that has grown in my soul. No. That is too valuable, too hard-won.

Surprisingly, in a similar way somewhere in the deep recesses of my heart, there is the beginning of a sense that through this stretch of time in which all areas of heart, soul and mind have been shaken, tested, and tried as by fire, His nail-pierced hands have been shaping, sculpting, bringing together something of His own design—something He had planned before the world began. I have often mentioned the treasured remark of the mentor He sent into my life: "Maybe He has a purpose which could never be accomplished any other way." As time goes on, that statement becomes more and more meaningful. His purpose. I want that! More and more, as inner hindrances are jettisoned at His feet, I want that purpose. I don't know what it is, but I sense that there is eternal value in it. And because I love Him, my heart longs to become truly one with His heart, His will, His plan.

Oh-h-h. Is He showing me, bringing me to *"Not my will, but Thine..."*? Let me wash His feet with tears...

The Lover of my soul longs for me to know Him in the deepest depths of my heart, not just to know about Him. Since this deep, full knowledge of Him is eternal, He works within me from the profound, eternal perspective of the soul and spirit. It is a costly, painful process, requiring fires that burn deep to purify the gold He put there. He watches over each detail of it, for it is precious to Him. He permits pain. He allows tears (which mingle with his own) but He works with a wondrous end in view when He shall bring many sons—to glory!

> *"... if we are His children, then we are His heirs also: heirs of God and fellow heirs with Christ, sharing His inheritance with him; only we must share His suffering if we are to share His glory. But what of that? For I consider that the sufferings of this present time (this present life) are not worthy to be compared with the glory that is about to be revealed to us and in us and for us and conferred on us!"* Romans 8:17,18

> *"For our light, momentary affliction (this slight distress of the passing hour) is ever more and more abundantly preparing and producing and achieving for us an everlasting weight of glory—beyond all measure, excessively surpassing all comparisons and all calculations, a vast and transcendent glory and blessedness never to cease!*
> *"Since we consider and look not to the things that are seen but to the things that are unseen; for the things that are visible are temporal (brief and fleeting), but the things that are invisible are deathless and everlasting."* 2 Corinthians 4:17,18

"Light affliction..." You could have fooled me! *"Light"*? But light *"compared to..." "compared with..."* Then even Paul found that words failed him. The best he could do to capture the other part of the comparison is itself beyond my ability to absorb it: a *"weight of glory"*— glory so great that it overwhelms, *"an eternal weight of glory."* Permanent. Immeasurable: *"beyond comparisons and calculations."* No, *"excessively beyond,"* even *"excessively beyond all"* of them; *"a vast—and transcendent—glory,"* plus *"blessedness, never to cease!"* Glory that is *"deathless and everlasting...."*

Burden of grief / growing weight of glory. No comparison!

Even if I can't take it in.

What is He shaping in my spirit?

There is growing awareness of His own hands at work. Through anguish stripped of all but God, I sense this; I find rest in my "Yes" to His purpose. It has been costly; yet He has wept with me...

Not 'till I see Him, "not 'till the loom is silent and the shuttles cease to fly" and I stand with Him in His likeness, will I be able to understand what those nail-scarred hands have wrought within by His own Spirit—a work which will be to His glory, displayed to all creation for all time! In that sacred moment I will see in His heart the transcendent joy and overwhelming Love that shaped His purpose. I will really need to be made new in His image to survive the healing tsunami of Joy!

I must not wish to escape too soon; let Him complete His project!

****

I suppose that whatever measure of healing from deep trauma one experiences, there will always be on-going changes and difficult things in the pathway. Perhaps growth, stretching, and a measure of pain are to be expected for a very long time. For the rest of one's life? Only by traveling on will I know.

There are twists and turns found only as one progresses, and many of them seem to exceed in painfulness all preceding steps. After God brought me to the point of being able to finally release my precious husband into the nail-scarred hands of Jesus, there followed a lengthy period of feeling "in limbo," perhaps like a sea anemone plucked loose of its moorings. It was a feeling of insecurity, of floating free when one longed for an anchor, a base.

Following that there came a dreadful deadness. In releasing my dear one to the claims of death, all of my heart which had been one with him (which left little out!) seemed also to die with him.

These things are processes, not events. They cannot be hurried. What can one do but look for the Shepherd in the shadows, wait for Him when one cannot sense His presence, and call out to Him when one cannot hear His voice? He is faithful! Even when we feel most lost and alone, He holds us; He will bring us through.

I feel a deep need now to know His purpose for my life. Purpose: a reason, a drive to find and fulfill His plan in my being here, a breaking free of the prison I have been in. May I be fully open to Him so that He can prepare me, then enable me to be faithful to His plan.

Purpose: how often the need for that arises! Our Father has told us that He will work all things together for good, not only for His kingdom, but for *us, "who love him, and are the called according to His purpose."*

Perhaps His most wonderful purpose is the skilled work of His Spirit within the traveler, that precious shaping of the human spirit into a likeness of His Son.

I am learning, all too slowly, that it is not so much what I do for Him as what I let Him do in me that is valuable to Him.

****

Many times I have referred to words of my mentor which raised the possibility that God had some purpose of His own that could be fulfilled in no other way.

Perhaps you are holding in your hands a small part of that purpose; this writing could have been birthed "in no other way." There is no more wonderful purpose than that of helping a fellow-traveler. If this record of pain, struggle, and healing has helped you in any way, then He has given meaning—purpose—to my Dark Valley.

May He continue to bless your heart with His presence!

45

LETTER TO ANOTHER COUPLE...

Sunday morning I met another couple embarking upon the same journey; the husband was diagnosed in May. As I have been thinking about them, feeling for them, there is such a desire to help them if I can. How I pray that they will not fall as I have done! I printed off a copy of the Ephesians prayer poem I wrote long ago, and have worked on an accompanying letter. Should I? In trying to help, this is what I would like to say:

"May I encourage you?
"Be confident in your God!

* **"Take His Word**—*just as He gave it.* Do not let it slip. Let it say what it wants to say!

"The Sower plants good seed: seed that has in it inherent Life—Life intended to grow to abundant harvest. "Birds of the air" come from every direction to devour it, to take it from you not only for your own hurt, but also to rob the Sower of the harvest that is His due. Refuse them, for your sake—and for His!

"Close out any inference, from any source, that would dilute God's Truth from his Word to your spirit. Let what He says stand.

"Bow only to His Word.

"Recognize the thief by his intent! Whatever thought, from whatever source, that would take from His Living Word in any way or in any measure, comes from the evil one, the thief, to rob you of blessing both promised and provided—and thus rob Him of the glory that is His due.

234

"God has given Strong Words:

> *"God is not a man, that he should lie; neither the son of man, that he should repent: hath He said, and shall He not do it? Or hath He spoken, and shall He not make it good?"* Numbers 23:19
>
> *"For as the rain and snow come down from the heavens, and return not there again, but water the earth and make it bring forth and sprout that it may give seed to the sower and bread to the eater, so shall My word be that goes forth out of My mouth; it shall not return to me void [without producing any effect, useless] but it shall accomplish that which I please and purpose, and it shall prosper in the thing to which I sent it."* Isaiah 55:10,11

"What effect did Jesus' miracles have? They brought restoration to those who received them, and great joy. Their God became more real to them. And people gave glory to the God Who wrought them.

"How many times, in His last words to His disciples, did He bid them to *ask*—and *receive?*

"Jesus did not suffer those stripes on His back for the fun of it! In taking them, He took suffering *in our place;* with them He purchased our healing.

> *"By His stripes we are healed"* Isaiah 53:5
> *"By His stripes we were healed."* 1 Peter 2:24

"What parent would sacrifice to buy a treasure for his child—then withhold it? Would our Father (and His Son) pay such an enormous price and not earnestly want His children to have the benefit?

> *"And therefore the Lord (earnestly) waits [expectant, looking and longing] to be gracious to you, and therefore He lifts Himself up that He may have mercy on you and show loving-kindness to you; for the Lord is a God of justice. Blessed—happy, fortunate (to be envied) are all those who (earnestly) wait for Him, who expect and look and long for Him (for His victory, His favor, His peace, His joy, and His matchless, unbroken companionship)."* Isaiah 30:18

"Inspired by the Spirit, David wrote:

> *"Bless—affectionately, gratefully praise—the Lord, O my soul, and forget (not one) of all His benefits, Who forgives (every one) of all your iniquities,* **Who heals (each of) all your diseases,** *Who redeems... beautifies... dignifies... crowns... satisfies your mouth (your necessity and desire at your personal age) with good; so that your youth, renewed, is like the eagle's (strong, overcoming, soaring)."* Psalm 103:2-5

"God's Word is a treasure-house of His precious promises, every one of them *"'Yes' and 'Amen' in Christ Jesus.''* 2 Corinthians 1:20

"Others:

> *"Let him that glories glory in this, that he understands and knows Me (personally and practically, directly discerning and recognizing My character) that I am the Lord Who practices loving-kindness, judgment and righteousness in the earth; for in these things I delight, says the Lord.''* Jeremiah 9:24

> *"Seek out the book of the Lord and read: no one of these (details of prophecy) shall fail, none shall want her mate (in fulfillment) for the mouth of the Lord has commanded, and His Spirit has gathered them.''* Isaiah 34:16

> *Fear not, (there is nothing to fear) for I am with you; do not look around you in terror and be dismayed, for I am your God. I will strengthen and harden you (to difficulties): yes, I will help you; yes, I will hold you up and retain you with My victorious right hand of rightness and justice.*
> *"Behold, all they who are enraged and inflamed against you shall be put to shame and confounded; they who strive against you shall be as nothing and shall perish. You shall seek those who contend with you and shall not find them; they who war against you shall be as nothing, as nothing at all. For I, the Lord your God, hold your right hand; I, Who say to you, Fear not, I will help you!''* Isaiah 41:10-13

> *"I have not spoken in secret, in a corner of the land of darkness. I did not call the descendants of Jacob [to a fruitless service] saying, Seek Me for nothing [but promised them a just reward]. **I the Lord speak righteousness—the truth [trustworthy, straight-forward correspondence between deeds and words].** I declare the things that are right.''* Isaiah 45: 19

"Paul wrote,

> *"... do not be vague and thoughtless and foolish, but understanding and firmly grasping what the will of the Lord is.''* Ephesians 5:17

"His Word is His will!

"God will quicken His Word to your hearts; search it, treasure it—hold it close; never let go of it! He is in His Word to fulfill it.

"For on-going encouragement, you can sign on for a daily healing promise at <u>www.terrylawonline.com</u>."

His Word is the ultimate authority.

In the beginning, His bare Word called worlds into being, and step by step brought about what was in His mind as He created all things.

When the enemy sought to wreak havoc in God's world he, too, used—*words*. With audacity beyond belief, he used his words cast doubt upon the Words of the living God! The venom of that serpent's *"Yea, hath God said..."* did a deadly work. And, once injected, it has continued to manifest its treachery through countless generations. Its essence infiltrates human thinking at every level, both secular and sacred. Always, it works to undermine, to destroy the good thing that God wants to do by *His* Word. It subtly issues even from pulpit and from pew, invariably bringing death and destruction wherever it is allowed to remain.

May the Spirit of God quicken our hearts to discern quickly when that insidious *"Yea, hath God said..."* presents itself, and instantly reject it!

There is only one anti-venom—the same that Jesus used during His time of temptation: the living Word of Almighty God! It is that very same two-edged Sword that He has put into the hands of His children, which makes them mighty to do battle. Nothing can withstand it; nothing can overcome it, for it is *alive*. It is that same Word of ultimate Authority which called worlds into being, a powerful Word still vibrant today, for the I Am is in His Word to perform it. What He has said—He is still saying!

Let my heart leap up to receive that Word, to rejoice in it, to revel in the God Who gave it. Let me exalt His Name with others who love Him. Let me magnify His Name. Let me honor that Word which our Lord Himself exalts above even His own Name. Let the victory of my God be manifest, for the joy of both Heaven and Earth. Let me enter into the triumph of the King of kings!

Precious Spirit of the living One, open the eyes of my heart to see my Lord *as He is*. Confirm to my innermost being the transcendent power and authority of His Words. Let my soul leap within me in true and utmost worship. Burst forth in my life in true manifestation of His power, His goodness, His loving-kindness. Let the glory of His majesty be seen in all His earth!

Let God be *God.* Let my soul exult in Him!

EPILOGUE
Walking With Grievers

I am so grateful for the gentle wisdom of that one whom my Father sent to guide me through the shadows. He allowed my grief, though, as he said, my pain was subjective—mine only, in my deepest heart. Though at first he could not actually feel what I felt, he recognized it, and my right and deep need to grieve. I think the anguish would have destroyed me if he had not been there to offer that understanding.

If others should read this Journal who have not walked the path, please take note of this: grief must be allowed to flow, to be expressed, to be walked *through.* It is crucial! Repression, either by the one grieving, or by those who "pass by" wreaks havoc in the soul and heaps anguish upon agony. Grief is a natural process, as is birth. To disallow either invites disaster.

May I share with you, as one who has walked Dark Valley, some things to remember when meeting someone else leaving footprints in those shadows?

Remember the priest and Levite who "passed by on the other side" of the man who fell among thieves in Jesus' story? They were among the "spiritual elite" of the day. Unfortunately, their "elite-ness" made it beneath their dignity to become involved with that fallen, broken one. Some of their ilk in this day even feel it necessary to deliver a good kick or two to the wounded one before journeying on. Rare, and exceedingly precious, is the *Samaritan* who stoops to administer understanding, genuine care and healing touch or words to one sore wounded on his journey.

Be that one—if you can be genuine. Those dealing with the most profound realities of life and death can sense a phony a mile away. And that is probably a good distance to keep, unless your heart makes you real.

Paul was inspired to write that believers should rejoice with those who rejoice and weep with those who weep...

"...and so fulfill the law of Christ." Galatians 6:2

That law of Christ can be fulfilled in no other way than by entering into the joys—and sorrows—of fellow travelers.

It is instinctive to avoid pain—physical, emotional or spiritual. A grieving person makes people on a regular track feel uncomfortable. King David commented that when he was in deep trouble, people passed by on the other side of the street to avoid meeting him. That was part of his pain. All too often those who have not experienced heartache do not know what else to do. They don't want to bring it up for fear of making it worse. Besides, they almost fear that it might be "catching"; the pain of another is a pointed reminder that trouble can come to anyone at any time! Yet, if one's heart really cares, there are simple, genuine ways to gently touch the pain in an effort to promote healing.

Don't take a "get happy" approach; that is shallow mockery to one working his way through Dark Valley! If you don't know what to say, the simple touch of a hand on the shoulder can mean a great deal, can indicate that you care.

It is not wrong to grieve; Jesus did. Don't despise a person for grieving. There are those among the religious elite who consider grieving to be only a lack of submission to the will of God. There is a lot more to it than that—a very great deal more. Don't kick the bruises! Nearly half of the Psalms are laments, and in Scripture, kings, priests, and prophets freely and openly expressed their confusion, doubts and questions directly to their God. As Ronald Dunn points out in *When Heaven is Silent,* it is not only right to do so, but absolutely necessary! Inner pain must be expressed if healing is to occur.

Don't necessarily bring up the subject of grief every time you meet a griever. Be natural.

Do allow the griever to speak if there is a desire to confide in you; it can be healing to remember the lost one. Listen, if that one feels like talking. Perhaps, at the right time, you can help by encouraging the person to express what he is going through.

Don't be too free to offer advice, even if you have drunk from a cup similar to theirs; each person is unique, each relationship is different. No two people will walk the exact same pathway on their journey through Dark Valley. Respect the griever's right to his own, individual way of dealing with heartache.

Grievers are still people; don't treat them as outcasts or social misfits.

Grief lasts long after floral tributes have withered and died. Be a friend, through the "official mourning period"—and beyond.

Timing is important. There will be a period while grief is new when the griever may feel emotionally unstable and not ready to mingle with people. That does not mean that the person will never want to do so; be understanding, and ready to include the wounded one again when the need for fellowship returns.

Encourage writing; that exercise can be a great help in sorting through the tangle of shredded emotions, regrets, memories and thanksgivings. Understanding can come and order return to scattered thoughts through doing that.

Encourage a grieving heart to open up to someone skilled in helping those in that situation. It is well worth the effort—can be a tremendous blessing. God cares about those who grieve; He has placed His servants here and there at the right times and in the right places to be His hands and heart in the healing process. Take advantage of that provision!

Recommend some good books. Two of the best are: *A Sacred Sorrow* by Michael Card, and Ronald Dunn's *When Heaven is Silent.* (That one is not available in bookstores, but can be ordered from Lifestyle Ministries, P.O. Box 153087, Irving, TX 75015; Tel. 972 570-1570.) *Up from Grief* by Kreiss and Patti is also excellent.

Pray. The strength to go on, to make progress in the journey, is greatly enhanced by prayerful concern of one alongside who is not afraid to be God's heart to that one "fallen among thieves."

If God places you in a position to "lift up the fallen one," listen for His voice; you may become His hands and heart to that one.

Be gentle. Be faithful. You minister—to Jesus!

"Whatever you do to the least of these My brethren
you have done it unto me."
Matthew 25:40

Dark Valley ...and Beyond

Printed in the United States
81335LV00004B/130-138

9 781600 349577